SECOND CHANCES

ALSO BY CRAIG GROSSI

Craig & Fred

SECOND CHANCES

A MARINE, HIS DOG, AND FINDING REDEMPTION

CRAIG GROSSI

wm

WILLIAM MORROW
An Imprint of HarperCollins*Publishers*

SECOND CHANCES. Copyright © 2021 by Fred the Afghan Inc. All rights reserved. Printed in the United States of America. No part of this book may be used or reproduced in any manner whatsoever without written permission except in the case of brief quotations embodied in critical articles and reviews. For information, address HarperCollins Publishers, 195 Broadway, New York, NY 10007.

HarperCollins books may be purchased for educational, business, or sales promotional use. For information, please email the Special Markets Department at SPsales@harpercollins.com.

FIRST EDITION

Designed by Kyle O'Brien

Library of Congress Cataloging-in-Publication Data has been applied for.

ISBN 978-0-06-300952-3

21 22 23 24 25   LSC   10 9 8 7 6 5 4 3 2 1

For the men of Maine State Prison

SECOND CHANCES

Shawshank

April 11, 2019

It's a sunny, warm, spring day in Maine, and I'm going to prison. Thankfully, I'm not alone. I've got my dog, Fred, with me, and unless something goes terribly wrong, we'll be walking out again in a few hours. For now I'm in my faithful 1988 Land Cruiser, making the two-hour drive from our home to the state prison. It's not our first visit, but today we're heading up with a new purpose. I've volunteered to teach a writing class to a group of incarcerated men, many of them veterans. Over the next year, I'll be meeting with the guys on a weekly basis to share writings and stories.

We take Route 1 up the coast, watching the sun dance on the water as we pass through quaint coastal towns awaiting the summer tourist season. Fred's in the back, alternating between napping and surveying the passing scenery. On the seat next to me is the syllabus I've written with each of the different topics I'm planning to cover in class in the coming weeks. We continue on Route 1 for a little over fifty miles before making a right turn just after reaching the small town of Warren. The peaceful coastal scenery quickly transitions to rolling hills and farmland. In a field on the side of the road, a few men in white T-shirts and jeans spread hay with pitchforks. Our next turn is up a hill and into another world.

You may have heard of Maine State Prison. This maximum-security prison was the inspiration for the Stephen King novella *Rita Hayworth and Shawshank Redemption,* which was made into an iconic film in 1994. Although the original Maine State Prison was built in 1824, it relocated to the town of Warren, and into a modern building, in 2002. Since then, under the guidance of prison warden Randy Liberty—his real name—it's grown to become one of the most unique prison environments in the country, known for its progressive programs that help prisoners prepare for life on the outside, if that's what's ahead of them, or help them deal with life on the inside, if that's where they'll remain.

I crest the hill, and there it is, rising up out of the hard Maine earth, a complex of bright white concrete buildings that could be mistaken for a large high school if it weren't for the rows of razor-wire fencing encircling the perimeter. It's a familiar sight to me by now: I've been a regular visitor to Maine State Prison for about a year, invited either as a guest speaker or to attend volunteer events. But this is my first time in any kind of official capacity. Part of me is excited about this new opportunity. And part of me is on edge. How will the guys who signed up for the course react to the syllabus I've put together for them? Will they engage with the topics I've suggested, or do they simply see this as a convenient way to spend time outside their cells?

I quickly find a spot in the parking lot; here, unlike at other prisons I've visited, there's no gate or entry-control point for vehicles. Fred hops out of the truck, and we walk together toward giant glass doors. I see the words MAINE STATE PRISON over the entrance and the state's coat of arms with its familiar pine tree and moose above.

Inside, I sign into the logbook, and a prison guard escorts me into the facility. We step outside, walking down "The Mile," a stretch of concrete that serves as the main thoroughfare for foot traffic around the prison. Looking across to the other side of the open yard, I see men wearing white T-shirts and jeans, kneeling beside beds of freshly tilled soil, working with their hands, growing vegetables for the prison kitchen.

Soon enough we approach the housing unit where the writing classes will be taking place. My middle-aged chaperone looks tired and seems a little annoyed about his role as my escort. After my attempts at small talk fail, I realize that my nerves are starting to get the better of me. Inmates walk past me and look me up and down. Another guard gives a friendly hello to my escort but ignores my attempt to say good morning. The thought goes through my head, *What the hell are you doing here, Craig? This is a terrible idea.*

The men I'm coming to see here are serving lengthy sentences for some serious crimes. Is this really where I'm meant to spend my time? Or am I being lured into some kind of trap, drawn by my desire to help? Luckily, trotting happily at my heel is Fred, his joy and positivity impervious to my jitters or our gloomy surroundings. I focus on him, pressing on toward our destination.

Finally we arrive at the cellblock where former U.S. military members are held—known as the Veterans' Pod. Randy Liberty, the prison warden, is a veteran himself, and as many of the guys locked up here have served in the military, he decided to create a special area where the vets could be housed. As a veteran I feel a connection to what Randy's doing here, and it's a big part of the reason I volunteered to spend my time in his prison.

We walk down the freshly mopped hallway that leads to the pod. Suddenly it occurs to me that although eight guys have signed up for my sessions, there's no guarantee any of them will show up. What will I do if I get there and the class is empty? I can only imagine the smug look on the face of the reluctant guard escorting me if *that* happens.

To my relief, as I walk into the Veterans' Pod, I can see through the large rectangular window of the classroom directly in front of us that inside there are four guys waiting for me, seated at the table.

My chaperone makes sure the guard at the supervisor's desk knows I've arrived before leaving me on my own.

All around me the dayroom buzzes with other inmates coming and going from their rooms on their way to different jobs and activities within the prison. But even though it's a beautiful spring day outside, one of Maine's first of the season, four men are seated in a classroom, ready to talk about our first subject.

Okay, I think. *Let's do this.*

I've never taught a writing class before, but I know that it's important to at least act as if I have. Before walking into the classroom, I put a mask on my face. It's a mask that says, *I know what I'm doing, I'm in control.*

As I walk in, I'm trying my best to convey confidence and expertise to the four men in jeans and white T-shirts staring up at me, the tattoos on their arms and necks seeming brighter and more menacing than on my past visits. I realize I will need to lead while creating a constructive and peaceful space for them.

I sit down at the table and take a deep breath, ready to get started. Thankfully, I recognize everyone from my prior visits. I even know their names: Michael Kidd, Michael Callahan, Nate Nightingale, and Robert Craig, otherwise known as Mr. Craig.

What I don't know is that over the next twelve months I will learn more from the men seated in front of me than they will ever learn from me.

As with most good things in my life, I ended up at Maine State Prison thanks to my dog, Fred.

I met Fred almost nine years earlier, on a battlefield in Afghanistan. I was a marine sergeant at the time, serving in the Sangin district of Helmand province as an intelligence collector assigned to support RECON marines, the Corps's most elite fighters. Sangin was a remote and dangerous post. If the heat and dust didn't get to you, the constant threat of a violent death certainly did. The Taliban were relentless. We were on their turf, and they let us know it. Each day started with coordinated attacks on our exposed and isolated position. We'd defend ourselves during the day and then infiltrate enemy territory at night on covert patrols, meeting with villagers caught in the middle and helping them escape the Taliban-controlled territory to safer ground.

One day, between Taliban attacks, I spotted a skinny pup with a big head and little legs, the kind of dog who immediately puts a smile on your face. Unlike most of the strays I'd encountered while in Sangin—vicious mutts who had more in common with coyotes than dogs —this one seemed friendly. I approached the goofy yet still-handsome pup, just to get a better look at him. As I got closer, I could see he was covered in bugs and his ribs were protruding through his matted coat. I almost turned around, assuming he wouldn't want anything to do with me. A wag of his tail said otherwise, and I offered him a piece of beef jerky. We spent a few peaceful moments together, and as I stood to walk away, he began to follow me.

"Looks like you made a friend," one of my fellow marines called out.

What I thought I'd heard him say was, "Looks like a Fred." The name stuck.

In the coming days, I learned that Fred wanted nothing more

than to hang out with us—and to eat. He quickly became a part of our unit, following us around wherever we went. In the days and weeks to come, Fred stole my heart, winning over the entire company of RECON marines along the way. Life in Sangin meant constantly facing death. At times we were surrounded by Taliban fighters who often outnumbered us and used the civilian population as human shields to launch their attacks. We never knew when the next mortar, RPG (rocket-propelled grenade), or machine-gun round would find its target or if we would survive it. But when I was with Fred, the stress of combat melted away. I wasn't on a battlefield thousands of miles from home—I was just a guy with a dog.

When it came time to leave Sangin, the thought of Fred staying behind to fend for himself broke my heart. He deserved better, and I had to find a way to give him the peace he'd given to my fellow marines and me. So we came up with a plan that involved stuffing Fred into a duffel bag and smuggling him out of the country. It was a crazy thing to do, one that could have cost me my military career and possibly my freedom, but with the help of my fellow marines, my family back home, and a crew of DHL workers who took care of Fred while I worked on the logistics and paperwork, Fred eventually made it from Sangin all the way to my family in northern Virginia, where I'd join him four months later.

Back in the States, Fred helped me to adjust. Like so many vets, I was caught off guard by the challenges that came with returning to civilian life. I'd suffered a traumatic brain injury in Sangin from a 107-millimeter rocket blast, an injury that awarded me a Purple Heart and the survivor's guilt that comes with it. A visit to the VA a few years after returning home gained me a posttraumatic stress disorder (PTSD) diagnosis, a condition I ignored for a long time. Close friends had been killed, and I constantly questioned whether I was worthy of outliving them. But even as my frustrations grew and I struggled to find my place after the military, I never felt lost. Fred was my compass. One look at him and I knew that I had a lot to be grateful for, and as long as I started my days in that spirit, I'd find my way. Fred connected me to the people around me in the neighborhood of Washington, D.C., where we were living. Strangers at the dog park and on the street would often stop and ask me about the distinguished-looking dog by my side.

"What kind of dog is that?"

"Is he part corgi?"

At first I didn't engage. I made up breeds for Fred.

"He's a pocket wolf," I'd answer dismissively, or "He's an Afghani foxhound."

But eventually I started to tell our story, and the more I shared, the more I saw it as an opportunity. Talking about their experiences is a challenge for many veterans. We're often told to come home and move on. Like the generations before us, we're expected to process our trauma in silence—or at the end of a bar. Fred's story showed me another path. It gave me an easy way to talk about what had happened to me in Afghanistan, casting it in a positive light. It lent purpose to what often felt like a senseless and victory-less war. The story I told people was about how I'd rescued Fred from the battlefields of Afghanistan. But the truth of the matter was, I'd only rescued him once. With his constant love, attention, and stubborn positivity, Fred has rescued me countless times.

After leaving my job as a government contractor to pursue a degree in liberal studies and international affairs at Georgetown University, I fell in love with writing. Expressing myself and defending arguments in papers and essays, I discovered that I enjoyed the task of putting words down on the page. But at the same time, I realized that making "author" my full-time profession was a long shot. After college I drifted from job to job, wrestling with my ambition to become an author and the practical choices that offered stability in exchange for those dreams. It was my girlfriend, Nora, who was the first person to really encourage me in my writing. We'd met at an event in Boston during my second year at Georgetown and bonded over our dogs, as she had just adopted a scrappy little terrier she named Ruby. Nora is equal parts beauty and badass, with deep green eyes and unflinching loyalty to her family and friends. She came into my life right when I needed her most. A lifelong musician, she'd spent her twenties touring the world with her four sisters in their band, the Parkington Sisters. I instantly felt comfortable and confident around her, two things I'd had difficulty experiencing in relationships after leaving the military and starting over. Her creative background made it easy for me to share my writing with her, and her feedback and encouragement made me feel like I actually had a voice. After a month of long-distance dating, with her in Boston and me in D.C., Nora boldly chose to pack up her things and relocate to D.C. We both realized that we'd found in each other the person we'd been searching for.

In December 2016, about a year after Nora and I had started seeing each other, I submitted an article about my journey with Fred to The Dodo, an online media outlet devoted to animal stories. When the story was published, it went viral, and before I knew it, I had a publisher who wanted to help me turn our story into a book. By now, Nora and I had both grown weary of city life, and I was craving someplace quiet to live where I could focus on writing. The book became the perfect reason to pack up and start a new adventure beyond D.C. We were both dreaming of the ocean and mountains.

On paper, Maine was the least likely place that we'd end up

calling home. The most I'd seen of the state was the inside of the airport terminal at Bangor International when the troop greeters were the last American faces we'd seen as we headed to Afghanistan and the first to welcome us home. Nora had been there only a couple of times to perform concerts with her sisters. Neither of us knew anyone there or had any relatives that we knew of. Yet somehow when I began looking for a place to write, my search led me north. The Blue Ridge Mountains in Virginia and West Virginia were too familiar from when I was growing up, and everything I saw as I expanded my search into the mountains of Pennsylvania and New York didn't fit the bill. I wanted something remote but inspiring. I wanted it to really feel like a place where there was nothing else to do except write. Just for kicks I searched around in Maine, scrolling through the pictures of a small cottage on the ocean overlooking Cadillac Mountain and Acadia National Park. I knew I'd found them: our ocean and mountains. Without even looking at the map, I contacted the owner and excitedly shared the listing with Nora.

When the book deal came through, the money was enough for her to quit her tech job in D.C., a position she'd taken to keep us financially afloat while I figured out what to do with my life. And so we packed up and moved to Maine. We were starting a new chapter in more ways than one.

The cottage was idyllic. Ordinarily it was rented during the summer, but the owners were more than happy to open it up for us when I told them what I needed it for. The home had been built by their grandfather, who'd served in WWII, and they loved the idea of a veteran writing and living in their family retreat. Maine was just supposed to be a place where we could get away and I could devote myself to writing. But after a few weeks, we realized that the state had a lot more to offer. It felt like home to us, and we began to look around for a permanent place to live. The cottage was too far north for us to realistically live there on a longer-term basis with the busy travel schedule of the book tour coming up, but we soon found another place, not far from Portland, also on the water's edge. Driving along a dirt road that opened up into a rolling field leading to one of the most beautiful pieces of coastline we'd ever seen, we fell immediately in love with the small cottage and its spectacular views. The dogs felt the same way. As we made our way inside to meet the owners, Fred stayed in the yard, happily sniffing the ocean breeze and watching the seagulls dip and dive around the bold coastline. We signed the lease on the spot but wouldn't be moving in until September 1.

The summer went by quickly, and before we knew it, we were getting settled into our little seaside home, excitedly waiting for our first copies of *Craig & Fred* to arrive in the mail at the end of October. The moment I held my first book in my hands and flipped through the pages was the realization of a dream I'd often thought out of reach. Trying to become an author had always been a gamble, and the day *Craig & Fred* hit the shelves, I knew I'd made the right choice. I'd done more than written a book—I'd created a career for myself.

In the months after publication, Nora, Fred, Ruby, and I embarked on a book tour that took us from Maine to Florida. Fred was a hit everywhere we went, from small independent bookstores to appearing on *Rachael Ray* and the *Today* show. It was a dream come true. We spoke in high schools and at local libraries, at community centers and colleges, and to veterans' groups. Everywhere we went, we were greeted by people who told us that our story mattered to them, that Fred's stubborn positivity had inspired them as much as it had inspired me.

It was our book tour that brought us to Maine State Prison. The connection came a few months later, through a radio interview I was invited to do with Jennifer Rooks, the host of a show titled *Maine Calling* on Maine Public Radio. In true Mainer fashion, Jennifer made me feel right at home in her studio, and the hour-long interview felt more like a conversation with an old friend than an official press appearance. She put me at ease and asked questions that inspired me to share more about my journey from marine to author. She asked about my friends who hadn't made it back and how I was handling their loss. It gave me a chance to talk about PTSD and my ongoing struggle with it.

After the interview was over, Jennifer mentioned that she wanted to introduce me to the warden of Maine State Prison, Randy Liberty.

"He's a veteran, and he's doing really great things since taking over up there," she'd said enthusiastically.

When she mentioned a dog-training program at the prison run by a nonprofit, America's VetDogs, I was immediately intrigued. However, years of having people pay me lip service and make empty promises in D.C. left me skeptical that she'd actually follow up. So I was happily surprised when I checked my email a few hours after our interview to find a message connecting me with Randy Liberty.

In his email Randy told me more about the America's VetDogs program at his prison. The idea was to teach inmates who are former members of the military to train purebred Labradors over a period of eighteen months. Under the guidance of the inmates, the puppies are transformed into service dogs that can be paired with veterans outside the prison who are suffering from physical and mental challenges. These incredible dogs go on to give struggling vets a newfound sense of freedom, freedom that they lost as a result of trauma incurred defending ours.

Randy went on to write that seven dogs from the prison were scheduled to be fully trained and certified within the next year.

"The dogs' impact is felt long before they are ever paired with a veteran on the outside," he explained. "The inmates who train the dogs at Maine State Prison are given a purpose, they're given experience, and most importantly they're given a sense of self-worth."

Randy invited me to visit the prison as a guest speaker. The guys had read my book as part of their book club and wanted to meet me. From there I started volunteering at the prison, spending time in the Veterans' Pod with the guys. I developed a connection with Randy and the men that led to me suggesting and developing the writing program. I hoped I could give the guys what writing had given me, an opportunity to express myself and connect with others.

At the same time, I could see how unlikely all this was. For anyone who'd known me early in my military career, it'd probably be a major shock to learn that I would volunteer to go anywhere near a prison. Before I went into military intelligence, I served as a 5831, military police correctional specialist. I was a brig or prison guard, which meant that I spent the first four years of my military career in and around correctional institutions, including Camp Delta located aboard the U.S. Naval Station in Guantánamo Bay, Cuba. While I loved being a marine, the work was not for me, and eventually I was able to retrain into the field of human and counterintelligence. Before long I was sent to Afghanistan, and that's where I met Fred.

And now, in a bizarre and poetic twist, thanks to Fred I was back inside a prison, willingly spending my time with incarcerated veterans, helping them share their stories through writing and storytelling.

I didn't realize it at the time, but despite my success in publishing my first book and the national attention that came with it, I was still searching for my purpose. I had accomplished my goal of getting Fred's story out into the world, but I wasn't done. I still had the same demons on my back that I'd had before, demons that didn't care how many books I sold or what TV shows I appeared on. On my first visit to Maine State Prison, those demons were waiting for me.

CHAPTER 2

Fish

My first visit to Maine State Prison was in January 2018, a whole year before I would give any thought to starting a writing group there. Nonetheless, visiting the prison that day was an unforgettable experience, one that triggered a whole bunch of feelings—about my past, about the chances I'd been given, and about what my future might hold.

The first thing that hit me walking into the prison was the smell: lemon disinfectant on a freshly mopped floor and the unmistakable aroma of humans in captivity. Then there were the sounds: the heavy clunks and pops of automated doors echoing off the concrete in some distant corridor and murmurs on radios worn by the staff at the front desk. Right away I was thrown back to my time as a military police officer working in prisons in South Carolina and Guantánamo Bay, Cuba. Being on the inside was a daily reality for me back then. The sounds, smells, and sights of prison were a big part of my life, but they weren't something I had spent much time thinking about since I'd transferred from the military police into intelligence. Ultimately I had chalked up my four years as an MP as a bit of a blip, a learning experience where I had learned that I did *not* want to work in corrections.

Stepping inside Maine State Prison, I suddenly felt a little uneasy. Not because of the prison environment per se but because I immediately started wondering how the guards would react to my visiting with Fred. I remember when I was a prison guard how closed-minded and judgmental I felt toward anyone or anything that brought comfort to inmates. I remember scowling at prisoners during their holiday dinners, when they'd get extra helpings of turkey and mashed potatoes. I hated seeing them laughing and smiling with one another as they stuffed their faces. They were criminals, and I felt they needed to be reminded of this at all times. How would these guards at Maine State react to me and my message of stubborn positivity with my happy little dog at my heels?

Fred was completely unfazed, of course, acting as if he'd been here a hundred times before. That's the amazing thing about a dog like Fred. He finds joy everywhere he goes, treating every moment as a gift, even in unfamiliar or hostile environments.

As we approached the front desk, we were intercepted by a tall man with a big smile.

"Craig and Fred, I presume," the man said, enthusiastically thrusting out his hand for a shake.

He was about six foot two, with a short haircut, a clean shave, and lines around his eyes from years in the sun. His suit hung on him as if it were tailored for a less athletically built man.

"I'm Randy Liberty, the warden here," he explained, giving me a firm pat on the back before kneeling down to rub Fred's ears.

After receiving Fred's approval, Randy stood up, grinning at me with his eyes. I noticed that Fred's hair had coated his trousers, and I apologized, joking about filling pillows with all the hair I find around the house.

"I've got a bunch of folks from my staff in a conference room, and they can't wait to hear you share your story," Randy told me. "I figure you can talk with them for about an hour or so before we go and meet the men."

I noticed right away that he used the word "men"—not "inmates" or "prisoners."

Randy led me into a space that looked like a cross between an office and a conference room.

"Have a seat wherever," he said, holding the door for me.

I sat down in a firm but comfy desk chair at the conference table as Randy shut the door, signaling to a couple of his staff that he'd need just a few minutes. I wasn't expecting to have any one-on-one time with the warden, but I was intrigued and grateful for the attention.

Randy sat in the chair to my left at the head of the conference table and let out a big sigh. Meanwhile Fred was wandering around the big room, sniffing the bookcases by Randy's desk and inspecting an empty cooler that had once contained someone's lunch, before finally settling down in a sunny spot on the carpeted floor.

"I really liked your interview with Jennifer the other day," Randy told me. "It was honest. We need more of that, especially within the veteran community."

"Thank you," I responded. "It took me a while to work up the courage to talk about the more challenging parts of my story, but having Fred really helped. It gave me a way to talk about PTSD and my service without making others feel too uncomfortable. I've been really lucky in that respect."

"I don't think we're ever prepared for the challenges we face when we come home," Randy said contemplatively. "I know I wasn't, and I've seen a lot of guys in here that would've been much better off if they'd had a constructive outlet to express themselves."

I could sense that Randy was someone who was going to level with me. He was easy to talk to but firm and direct.

"I have a great deal of sympathy for the guys in here," Randy went on. "The first time I came to Maine State Prison, I was a little boy. I was here with my mother and my older brother and we'd come to visit my dad. He was a prisoner."

I was stunned, a hundred questions already stacking up in my mind. I couldn't imagine how Randy had gotten from being a little kid with a father on the inside to running the entire prison.

"Really?" I managed to respond.

"Yeah, he was in and out my entire life. Drinking, burglary, and assault stuff mostly."

"Was that what made you want to go into law enforcement?" I asked, somewhat sheepishly, not wanting to assume too much.

"Yeah, partially. But mostly I just wanted to be sure I never made the same mistakes as my dad. I wanted to break the cycle of poverty and crime within our family, and the best way to do that was to throw myself into a life of service, instead of being a burden on others. People are always a little shocked when they learn about where I came from, and sometimes almost a little embarrassed for me. But I'm proud of it, and I never miss a chance to talk about it."

Randy went on to tell me about his time serving as sheriff of Kennebec County, where he'd made implementing addiction treatment and educational programs his first priority.

"Even then I saw that locking people up for crimes related to addiction, especially opioids, was a one-dimensional approach that deserved more attention and creativity," he explained.

Randy had started a Veterans' Pod in Kennebec County Jail, the first and only one in the state, and he'd also assisted in creating a veterans' court for Maine that takes into account the unique challenges veterans face when they reenter society.

Randy's interest in veterans' issues grew even more important to him after his own service. In 2004 he became a combat veteran, serving with the Army Reserve as a leader of a military transition team in Fallujah, Iraq, alongside American marines and Iraqi troops in one of the war's most contested and brutal battlefields. During his tour in Iraq, Randy was promoted to command sergeant major. Returning home to Maine to his job as the chief deputy of the sheriff's office was more difficult than he could have imagined.

"My PTSD from Iraq gave me firsthand knowledge of what veterans face when they come home," he told me, shaking his head. "I wanted to provide a different solution for any of them that found themselves on the wrong side of the law. Their crimes aren't always attributable to their service, but they often are, and that is where we want to make sure it's taken into consideration."

Instead of keeping his issues a secret, he chose to discuss them in public, knowing that honest conversations about mental health were needed in the veteran community and in society at large. Randy emphasized to me how important it is to be open about our backstories, sharing both the bad and the good, and I agreed with him.

During this time I completely forgot that I was in the office of a warden, about to speak to the staff and inmates of a state penitentiary. I had been there for less than an hour, and it already felt like a familiar place to me, and not because of my time working in various military prisons. It was the sense of comfort that came from Randy and the environment he'd created.

Randy filled me in about the prison's many programs he'd started since taking over as warden. I learned about the Veterans' Pod, a specialized housing unit within the prison for inmates who have served in the military. He'd also started an agricultural program providing fresh vegetables to the prison's kitchen, with enough left over to donate to local food banks and shelters.

"Anywhere I could till the earth, we're growing something,"

he said proudly. Thanks to Randy the prisoners were also main-taining beehives. "The bees buzz around, in and out of the grounds, and pollinate our crops," he explained. When it came to waste, he hadn't missed any opportunities either. The prison had three gigantic plastic bins that hold all the food waste from the kitchen, turning it into compost that helps the garden grow, saving the state thousands in waste-disposal costs. In Thomaston, the next town down Route 1 from the prison, a retail store sold products made in the prison: intricate wood carvings, beautiful furniture, hand-drawn greeting cards, and other artisan keepsakes created by the inmates. The proceeds generated from the popular store went right back to the prison, funding more programs and providing more opportunities for the men.

And then there were the dogs. Randy told me more about the four Labrador puppies currently living with veteran inmates who were responsible for training them for the first twelve to eighteen months of their lives.

"It's a lot of extra work for these guys," Randy pointed out. "It sounds great for them to have a dog, but it's not all fun and games. These dogs are expected to perform complicated tasks and address critical needs."

Randy looked at his watch. I could tell we needed to wrap up our conversation so we could go and meet the others. But before we did, he had one last message for me.

"All these programs have one thing in common," he said. "They help the men. The fact that they look good on a budget is just a happy accident. I don't have any money for new programs, but I've found ways to create them while actually saving the state money."

He smiled and looked down at Fred, then stood up.

"We can probably head in now. Everyone is going to love you."

Fred stretched his little legs, preparing to meet his newest fans.

For about an hour, I shared the story of Fred and answered questions from Randy's staff, many of them veterans themselves.

"Okay, folks, we've gotta get back to work," Randy told them. "And these two are gonna go back and spend some time with the men."

Randy and a small entourage led us through security. The guard running the metal detector stopped me and asked if he should search Fred for contraband treats.

"I don't want him corrupting our dogs in training back there!" he joked.

"I can see why you'd be concerned with that," I said, "given how he made it into the country. But I assure you, if he had any treats, he would've eaten them on the ride up."

The guard laughed and hit a button on his desk. There was a loud pop, and the electric lock on the big metal door released. We made our way forward and all piled into a small space about the size of an average elevator, called a sally port. Moving around a correctional facility requires a lot of patience. Most of the internal doors are controlled by keys or fobs, but anytime there's movement from secured areas, it's done via a passageway, like the one ahead of us. Fred and I stood waiting for everyone to shuffle in. While standing there we got a chance to meet the rest of Randy's staff who were joining us on the tour.

Randy introduced us to Mike Fournier, a well-built man in his early forties, a little taller than me with a salt-and-pepper beard and a self-assured look in his eye. In fact, Fournier was the recreational therapist and liaison to the Veterans' Pod, in charge of implementing and overseeing many of the programs that Randy came up with. As such he worked behind the wall with the inmates on a daily basis.

"Fournier's my eyes and ears in the Veterans' Pod," Randy explained. "He communicates with the men and is a big part of making the VetDogs program a reality. He's also former army, so looks like you're outnumbered, marine."

"Sounds like a fair fight to me," I said playfully before asking Fournier how long he'd been in the army.

"I did eight years back in the mid-nineties and early two thousands," he replied, with the characteristic quiet confidence that I was beginning to recognize in Mainers when I saw it. "I got deployed three times, twice to Bosnia and once to Kosovo during the conflicts there."

"Right on," I told him, thinking about how easy it is for the rest of us to forget about the wars in the Balkans of the 1990s. I bet it wasn't as easy for Fournier.

"How long have you worked here?" I asked as we passed through the first sally port.

"I came on several years ago," he said. "It was very different then. I almost quit after my first year."

"Wow, what changed to make you stay?" I pressed.

"Well, for one thing, when I came here, I was working in our solitary-confinement wing," Fournier explained. "Back then we had dozens of guys in solitary, one of the largest populations in the country at the time. It was bad for everyone."

In my experience solitary was used for extremely high-risk inmates or for those who were a danger to themselves through self-harm. Excessive numbers of men in solitary was not a good sign for any prison. It meant that things were out of control.

Fournier continued, "What we realized was that when we gave the men something to work toward—something that meant something—they were less likely to act out."

We passed through a second sally port and were back outside, walking through the long breezeway known as The Mile.

"Something that meant something . . . like the dog program?" I asked.

"Exactly," Fournier replied. "There are lots of programs and classes in here centered on different types of adult education, but for a lot of these guys it's difficult to see the point in acting right and participating in a class when the length of their sentence means they're never going to be able to use the lessons they've learned. When you try to push a class or program on people who've given up on bettering themselves, they don't always see the value in it because they can't see the value in their own existence. The dog program was different. The men realized they were contributing to something that went beyond the walls of the prison, and that gave them a new sense of purpose."

I wondered if the inmates here were living vicariously through the dogs they fostered that went on to be adopted outside the prison. If they knew it was unlikely they would get out anytime soon, were they preparing the dogs for the life and freedom they wished they had?

We'd reached the entrance to the building that held the Veterans' Pod. As Randy opened the door for Fred and me, he elaborated on Mike's point.

"A lot of these guys have been in and out of the correctional system their entire lives," he told me. "They might have started out with minor offenses, but once they got into the system, their self-worth was one of the first things to go."

As we approached the Veterans' Pod, I could see Fred's tail wagging like crazy—he could sense that the other dogs were close.

"Nobody likes to feel like they're worthless," Randy continued. "One of our most important jobs in here is to show these guys that they don't have to be defined by the mistakes they've made. It's never too late to have a positive impact on the world."

We entered the Veterans' Pod, and the first thing I noticed was how quiet it was. Men were sitting around tables with their faces in books, playing chess, or quietly talking with one another. It could've almost passed for a social club if they weren't all wearing the same prison-issue faded denim clothing and the walls weren't so high.

Sunshine poured in from floor-to-ceiling windows, and at each window's base, a collection of vibrant green plants grew in planters. The walls were decorated with murals. I almost did a one-eighty in order to fully take stock: a painting of a big POW/MIA symbol on the second level, an Abrams tank cruising through a desert scene, a pair of boots with a rifle propped up behind it, and a set of dog tags hanging off a buttstock. There was no other way to say it—I was astonished.

"Wow, did the men paint all these?" I asked Randy.

"They sure did. We've got every branch represented in here." He pointed to a big army seal on one wall.

"Where is the most important one, though?" I laughed, referring to the Marine Corps seal.

Just then a middle-aged man in a wheelchair, wearing glasses and a smile, made his way toward us.

"Right over here," he said, pointing to a four-foot-tall rendition of the seal of the Corps.

"Ah, there it is," I said, doing my best to restrain Fred from jumping on the man's lap.

"Oh, that's okay," the man in the wheelchair said. "He smells the dogs we've got in here, I'm sure."

He let Fred sniff his hand before rubbing him behind the ears.

"Craig, this is Mike Callahan," Randy told me. "He's one of our trainers."

"Right now I'm just helping out with some of the dogs where

I can," Callahan said. "Sometimes the guys need an extra hand, but I've got some mobility issues, as you can see, so I can't take on a dog full-time."

"I understand, and glad to hear you're helping where and when you can," I replied.

I looked around, wondering where all the dogs were hiding. A group of men were starting to pick up chairs, assembling them in a row in an open area of the pod. I had to look twice before I even noticed the sixty-pound black Lab on one of their heels. He was clearly a young dog, maybe only twelve months, but very attentive and mild-mannered, which might have been part of the reason I didn't notice him in the first place. It seemed that he hadn't even noticed Fred. Instead this obedient pup looked up calmly at his trainer, a man in his late twenties with a fresh, closely cropped haircut, a cleanly shaven face, and a confident posture. The man was dressed like the other inmates but wearing a little treat pouch on the hip of his prison-issue jeans. The dog was completely connected to the man—and vice versa.

As the trainer finished setting up a row of chairs, he noticed Fred and me watching him.

"Can we say hi?" he asked politely as he approached. By now Fred had also noticed the dog and was predictably pulling at his leash with a look on his face that was a mixture of frustration and excitement, desperate to make a new friend, demonstrating the complete lack of discipline he regularly enjoys getting away with.

"I don't think we've got a choice," I said with a laugh as Fred dragged me forward. With a wave of his hand, the trainer signaled to his dog that he was no longer on the clock. The Lab lumbered toward Fred with a goofy gracefulness that made me smile. While Fred and his new friend got acquainted, I dropped his leash so he wouldn't be restricted from getting a good whiff of this new buddy. I stood next to the Lab's trainer as we both admired our dogs, as I'd done countless times at dog parks with fellow dog owners.

"Michael Kidd," the trainer said, extending his hand, "but most people just call me Kidd."

"Hey, man, very nice to meet you. I've never seen a dog respond to a nonverbal command like that. What's his name?"

"Ah, thank you," Kidd replied. "His name is Chess. He's a good boy. He's really taught me more than I've taught him."

"Oh, I know how that goes," I said, looking down at Fred. "Seems like you've taught him an awful lot, though. You should be very proud of that."

I wanted to ask Kidd more questions about his relationship with Chess, but the other men were sitting down in the chairs, getting ready for my talk, many of them sipping paper cups of coffee. A man in the front row had a copy of my book, and I could see that it had been dog-eared in several places, the dust cover taped in a few spots where it had torn.

"The book club is all here, and they loved your book," Randy said, smiling at me proudly before turning to address the members of the club. "Okay, men, I got him here as promised, so you can stop bugging me about it."

I noticed that Kidd had taken command of Chess without even saying a word, and I did my best to settle Fred down as his new friend walked away at his trainer's heel.

"Craig and Fred are here to spend some time with you, and we should be very grateful for that," Randy continued. "Fred is a very popular dog with a busy schedule, and Craig is his full-time driver."

Already I liked this introduction better than the formal one he'd given to his staff. Randy finished and then said, "They're all yours," patting me on my shoulder as he made his way out of the pod.

I found myself standing in front of a group of inmates who were looking back at Fred and me with an intense curiosity that took the air right out of my lungs. I'd become used to presenting our story in front of diverse groups of people in a variety of situations and locations, but the concentrated attention these men gave me was intimidating and flattering at the same time. And there was something else that had been gnawing at me all day, a feeling that I wrote off as hunger at first but in this moment knew to be something more. It felt as if everything I'd done in my life—the marines, Afghanistan, writing a book, and everything in between—had led me to Maine State Prison. I felt my face get hot and tears well up behind my eyes. I shook them off and managed to regain my focus. I had work to do.

I shared a shortened version of our story, for those who might not have had a chance to read the book and to give me some time to collect myself. When I was done, I opened things up to questions from the group. In the corner Fred was already snoozing on the freshly mopped tile floor, no doubt dreaming of his new friend, Chess.

After some hesitation, a couple inmates raised their hands. Initially it was just two, and then almost everyone in the group had a hand in the air. I picked a middle-aged man in the back, with a scruffy white beard and tattoos running down his arms.

"How long did it take you to write the book?" he asked.

"It took me about three years," I said. "At first I just wanted it to be a children's book, something cute from Fred's perspective, but the more I wrote, the more I realized that I had a bigger story to tell and that I loved writing. I probably started over from the beginning five or six times until I really felt confident with the story."

I was ready to move on to the next question, but the man politely followed up, happy to be heard.

"Wasn't it hard to start over again from the beginning?"

The question threw me off. Though it was one I'd answered before at book events, in this room I could feel the group waiting for the answer with a sense of urgency. I wasn't sure why.

"I can see how you'd think that," I explained. "But for me it didn't really feel that I was starting over. It felt like I was continuing on, with a better understanding of my abilities as a writer and the strengths of the story. Each time I wrote it, I remembered a little more, and the more I felt it was my responsibility to share this story in the best way I could."

The man seemed satisfied enough with the answer and gave a subtle nod and said a quiet thank you.

I looked around for the next hand in the air, picking my friend from earlier, Mike Callahan, in the wheelchair, who had shown me the USMC mural.

"Hey, Mike, what's your question?" I said, making sure he knew I'd remembered his name.

"Did you get in any trouble for sneaking Fred out like you did?" he asked.

The reality was that I could have gotten into a lot of trouble. Smuggling Fred out of Sangin was against many very official rules. But I didn't say that to the guys.

"I got away with it," I told this room full of convicted criminals. After a momentary pause that made me almost question the destiny that had brought me there, the group let out a collective chuckle.

"We'll save a bunk for you just in case!" one guy even shouted.

We laughed together, and the questions continued. After I wrapped up my presentation, several of the men approached me to thank me for coming in, giving Fred a quick pet. One of them was about my age, a tall man with long black hair and a kind but cautious nature. His name was Chester Birmingham, but he went by Chet, and he'd been in the navy for several years. We chatted for a few minutes and I told him I hoped to see him again, never imagining that I would start a writing group and he would end up being one of its most loyal members, along with the other guys I'd met that day, Callahan and Kidd.

The session was over, but Randy had offered to give me a tour of the rest of the prison, so I stayed for the afternoon. For the rest of the day, as I walked the corridors of Maine State, I kept thinking about the men and their opening questions:

- *How long did it take?*
- *How did you start over?*
- *And did you get in trouble?*

Several hours later I found myself standing in the yard, the wide-open outdoor space where the men grow vegetables and flowers. Mike Fournier had helped finish the tour, since Randy needed to go back to his desk. The interior walls of Maine State are made from white concrete, and on this cloudless day it was blinding to look at their bright, reflective surfaces.

Mike squinted as he pointed to a building on the opposite side of the yard.

"Remember what I said earlier about nearly quitting?" he asked. "Well, I spent my first two years in that building. That's our segregation wing, and it was a nightmare just a few years ago. One of the guys you met today, Kidd, the one who's training Chess, he was in there for a while. The first time I met him was when he'd cut himself with a razor. There was blood all over his cell, and it was starting to pool out from under his door. The extraction team went in and got him, but he didn't put up a fight. He was just out of his mind from being in isolation."

Fournier looked at me, and despite the grim story he was smiling.

"Now look at him," he said with what can only be described as pride mixed with a little disbelief. "He's come such a long way."

I nodded, not entirely sure what to say. I thought about Kidd and Chess and how obedient Chess was to Kidd's commands. In less than a year, Kidd had forged an unbreakable bond with that dog. It seemed the process had mended whatever parts of Kidd that had been broken.

I could feel Fred against my leg. It had been a long and emotional day, and soon I needed to get him home.

"I'm really glad I came here today," I said. "You all are doing some incredible work, and the feeling is contagious."

"Come back anytime," Fournier replied, and like every Mainer I've met so far, I could tell that when he said it, he meant it.

In the lobby I met up with Randy and more of his staff who were waiting to say good-bye to us. I thanked them for their time and for the opportunity to share our story. They, too, invited us to visit again.

Fred and I headed out into the parking lot toward the Land Cruiser. I'd managed to choke back my tears in the Veterans' Pod, but now that I was safely in the truck, I let them work their way up from my heart to my throat to my eyes, stinging my face. Fred sat next to me, grinning from ear to ear, and for a moment we just looked at each other.

"Good boy," I said to my best friend. He immediately leaned forward to lick the salty tears off my cheeks as I turned the key in the ignition and the engine roared to life.

CHAPTER 3

Not Okay

— How long did it take?
— How did you start over?
— And did you get in trouble?

Leaving that day, I passed by the big brick sign at the entrance that read MAINE STATE PRISON 1824–2002, overwhelmed by the memories swirling in my head. Yes, I'd told the men about Afghanistan and about Fred's rescue, but that in many ways was the easy tale to tell. As I pulled the Land Cruiser onto Route 1 heading south, that wasn't the only story crashing around in my head like ball bearings in a tin can.

What I didn't confess to the men was that instead of giving speeches and taking questions about my dog and my book, I could just as easily have ended up on the other side of the room with *them*. I could have been the one asking the questions, reading books, and playing chess, counting the days and months.

In many ways my life had been one long series of lucky breaks, especially since I'd joined the marines. In fact, I'd been given so many second chances I began to think I was invincible. The first happened soon after I signed up, when I was a twenty-year-old marine, on an air force base in San Antonio, Texas. It was 2003, and for some reason I'd decided it was a good idea to get behind the wheel of a car after a night of underage drinking at the bars that lined the city's famous River Walk. Once I was on base,

I was stopped by air force cops, who immediately determined that I was over the limit. I should have been thrown in jail and charged with disorderly conduct, driving under the influence, and underage consumption of alcohol. If that had happened, my military career would have been over before it started—and I would have deserved it. Instead the officers left it up to my command. Thankfully, the training staff at the military-police corrections school I was attending were concerned only with getting marines in and out of the course. They let me off with a warning and allowed me to graduate on time. The sooner I was out of their hands and to my first duty station, the better.

The fact that I was able to continue with my military career led to my next, and perhaps luckiest, break. At age twenty-eight I smuggled Fred aboard a military aircraft inside a duffel bag, during a combat extract in one of the most heavily contested areas of Afghanistan. As I'd hinted at to the guys at Maine State Prison, the defining moment of my life was also one of the riskiest. I knew as I was zipping Fred into that bag and sneaking him out of the country that if I were caught, the consequences would be career-ending. I could even spend time in the brig or in military prison, not to mention that Fred would be euthanized. The odds were against me, and I knew it, but I also knew I wouldn't be able to live with myself if I left Fred behind. Again, through inexplicable good fortune, I managed to escape without the powers-that-be discovering so much as a single Fred hair on my uniform.

Then there'd been a much more recent event. Only a month before my visit to Maine State Prison, at the age of thirty-five, I found myself in a situation that could easily have escalated into a serious crime. Thinking back on it sent my mind into a state of shock, gratitude, and confusion that I was saved from getting into some very real trouble.

My girlfriend, Nora, and I were on the road, promoting my book, *Craig & Fred,* with Fred and our other dog, Ruby, of course along for the ride. That day we were scheduled to speak at a high school in northern Virginia. I was all set to tell my story, to speak about Fred's stubborn positivity and its impact on my life. As we drove, Nora gave me a rundown of the school assemblies and what I needed to focus on during my talks—there would be three of them, each with several hundred kids—and then we'd hang out and sign books and chat with students and staff.

I was at a sweet spot in my life. Nora had taken on the role of managing my book appearances and social media as well as designing and managing our online store. An incredible photographer, she filled our feed with pictures of Fred and our road trips, finding new ways to share Fred's message with the world. With her at my side, I had grown and developed, not just as a writer and a speaker but as a human being. While Nora was one of the first people to support and encourage my writing, she was also the first to call me out on my drinking. For a long time after I came back from Afghanistan, I used alcohol as a crutch. It was a way of blocking out any anxiety or negative emotion that I felt, as if drinking to excess somehow proved that I was "living life to the fullest" when many of my friends had gotten their lives cut short. When I drank too much, my frustrations and anger came to the front of my mind, and all the pain I'd packed away spilled out. The smallest thing would set me off. I turned into someone else; I became loud and mean, and there wasn't anything anyone could do to calm me down. The first months of our relationship, the time when most couples are getting to know each other and creating new memories, Nora was weathering a storm that had been gathering inside me for years. She was a beacon for me, leading me through the fog I'd created. One night, after I'd again taken it too far, she sat me down and said simply, "I want you but I don't need you." It was clear to me that she loved me but that she wasn't going to tolerate my behavior. Eventually, I started to cut back on my drinking, and it was then that I realized how long I'd made excuses for my reliance on alcohol. I saw that I was able to make more of myself when I wasn't constantly between hangovers. I was a better partner to Nora and a happier, more positive version of myself.

To anyone on the outside looking in, my life since then had been pretty perfect. I was in a great relationship, I had a new career as an author and a public speaker, and I had an Instagram feed full of photos to prove it. I had my drinking under control, and as a result my self-confidence was at an all-time high. But the outward success and emotional growth I'd achieved in recent years still wasn't enough to protect me from myself.

That morning, on our way to the school in Virginia, we were merging onto Route 66 in rush-hour traffic, the kind of gridlock that was one of the motivating factors behind our move to Maine. Everyone was going about fifteen miles per hour through a construction zone as we merged onto the highway. I put my blinker on, glanced in my sideview mirror, and saw that the work truck behind me was giving me a little space. The flow of traffic had picked up a bit, and we were now moving at about thirty miles per hour through the construction zone. Just as I began to ease into the lane, the driver of the work truck gunned it, coming within inches of my mirror, intentionally closing the gap that he'd left for me, running me off the road. I swerved between cones into the construction zone. Fortunately, no workers were around.

It was a malicious maneuver made by an inconsiderate and hostile driver. My reaction, however, was nuclear. Something in my brain clicked into a place where it hadn't been since Afghanistan. The man in the truck might as well have been a Taliban fighter taking potshots at me and my family. Everything I cared about was in this vehicle, and he had just tried to kill us.

The pace of traffic picked up as we headed out of the construction zone. I saw an opening and swerved into the neighboring lane so we could come up alongside the enemy, my headlights flashing. I didn't want to flip him the bird or call him any names. I wanted him to pull over so I could kill him. Nora's voice faded into the distance. I couldn't hear that she was crying, pleading with me to stop, that our exit was coming up. She was terrified, but I was focused on defending myself and my family. We blew right past our exit as I maneuvered in front of the enemy, slamming on my breaks and turning on my hazard lights. *If he has any balls, he'll pull over and go toe-to-toe with me. He doesn't know who he's messing with, but he's gonna find out,* I told myself. Lucky for me, he swerved onto an off-ramp and off the highway, escaping my wrath.

With the threat gone, I took a look around. Fred and Ruby were staring at me with big, terror-stricken eyes. Nora's head was in her hands, and she was leaning as far away from me as she could. At that moment I realized that there *had* been an enemy on the road that day, and it was me.

My rage was replaced with deep regret and shame. How could I lose control like that? I was a published author, on my way to speak to an entire school full of children about the power of positivity and kindness. But my morning had been hijacked by demons that I thought I'd dealt with long ago. In a 7-Eleven parking lot near the school, I did my best to apologize to Nora and the dogs.

I tried to explain myself, but there was no excuse or justification for my reaction. In the past I might have been able to blame it on alcohol, but I hadn't had a drink in weeks. Nora was confused, angry, and worried. I'd transformed before her eyes, endangered her and the dogs, and there hadn't been anything she could do to bring me back. Gently she took my hand, looking me in the eye.

"I love you, and I'm worried about you," she said. "You've got to talk to a professional. We need to understand what just happened."

I didn't resist. The evidence was too strong. She was right. We agreed to talk more about it later as a couple, but it was clear to me that despite getting my drinking under control and my life on track, I had more work to do if I really wanted to be the best version of myself. I'd already been given countless second chances in my life. Was I really going to throw this one away? If I didn't learn from them, I might run out of them.

Our event at the school went off without a hitch. The kids in the assemblies lifted me up and shook me out of the rage I'd been consumed by less than a few hours before. Even so, I felt like a fraud. If I couldn't even handle such a simple situation, an asshole driver who didn't warrant my attention let alone the full weight of my fury, then what did that say about the message I was sending with my story?

I knew I needed help, and I vowed to get it. I made the call to the VA in Maine before we left Virginia. I told them about what had happened and that I wanted to see some kind of counselor. Up until now I'd always been skeptical about therapy. I'd had some counseling after I came back from Afghanistan, just a few sessions with someone as a part of my coming-home screening. But my training as an interrogator and a human-intelligence collector made me hypercritical of anyone attempting to use a casual conversation to elicit information from me. The idea of sitting down in a small room with someone I didn't know and having that person poke around my head tripped my mental alarms. The difference was, now I knew it wasn't just about me anymore. This was about Nora, Fred, and Ruby, too. And about all the people reading my book. The coordinator at the VA explained they could set up a session with a therapist the week after we got home.

When my appointment came, I showed up early. The Portland VA clinic felt different from the VA in Washington, D.C., which I'd visited in the past. The D.C. VA was always overrun and hectic, but here in Portland I got a spot in the parking lot with ease, the waiting room was relatively calm, and I was checked in quickly. No veteran enjoys going to the VA, but the more relaxed vibe of the Maine office immediately reduced my anxiety levels and made me feel less as if I were being reduced to the last four digits of my Social Security number.

My therapist was Greg, a middle-aged guy, very approachable and professional. Right away he put me at ease. We laughed about the similarities between our names, how he was often called Craig and I was often called Greg. Our session began with some basic questions about my background. I did my best to silence the alarms going off in my head telling me to stop offering too much information about myself. Instead I found myself giving short answers that didn't encourage any follow-up questions.

Greg's office was windowless and small. It immediately reminded me of an interrogation booth. During my human-intelligence training, I'd spent months inside cramped rooms and hot shipping containers with role-players whose job it was to resist my questioning. We'd been trained to focus on the fundamentals, identifying people's body language and the inflections in their voices. We were learning how to control conversations and manipulate minds. In a mock village on the base, we'd patrol through a marketplace packed with role-players. We'd have to identify suspicious people and elicit information about insurgents in the area through casual conversation. By the time training was over, I'd learned how to weaponize communication. It was a skill that kept my fellow marines and me alive in Sangin but made it difficult to open up back home. Especially sitting in a cramped room with a stranger. Greg was nice enough, but my mental walls were up.

That is until he asked me why I suddenly felt like I needed therapy.

"You've been out for a while now, and you haven't needed much from the VA," Greg pointed out, pushing his chair away from his desk and squaring his shoulders with mine for the first time since I'd sat down in his office. "What's changed?"

I explained what had happened on my way to the school event the week before and how it scared me.

"The only time I'd ever get that mad I could usually blame it on alcohol," I explained, letting my guard down a little. "But this time it happened at eight-thirty in the morning—and I haven't been drinking much in the last year or so."

"Well, if it helps, I'm not surprised," Greg said bluntly. "You're a combat veteran. You routinely used a part of your brain that most people go their entire life without triggering. Once you open up those pathways, you react differently than most people. I have Vietnam combat veterans that are still dealing with the same anger-response issues they've been struggling to manage since the 1970s."

"Somehow that doesn't make me feel much better," I said, trying to find the bright side to the realization that I might be a ticking time bomb for the rest of my life.

"Well, it's not meant to make you feel better," Greg pointed out, "but it's certainly not meant to discourage you. You just need to understand how your brain works and why. That there isn't anything wrong with you—you're just wired differently."

What I learned in that single session with Greg served me

far beyond the one hour it lasted. It gave me the perspective to understand my triggers. In the same way I downplayed the traumatic brain injury I suffered in Sangin from a 107-millimeter rocket blast, I tried to minimize the anger associated with my PTSD. It took the risk of losing everything for me to take it seriously. I should have known better.

I had a strong, supportive family. I had Fred. I had Nora's unwavering love. The fact that I was able to find ways to thrive after coming back from serving overseas was thanks to all these factors. And even with so much support, I had come close to throwing everything away. The incident on the road in Virginia had led me to a therapist's office, but it could just as soon have led me to prison. The experience gave me a vivid understanding of how easy it can be for veterans to fall through the cracks and find themselves on the wrong side of the law.

Back in Maine I found myself thinking about Kidd and the other men, wondering when I would have another chance to spend time with them.

It's a common experience for vets to feel stripped of a sense of purpose after they leave the military. In large part Fred had helped me to regain that sense of service, of doing something useful with my life, by telling our story. But I was still looking for ways to play my part, to contribute, as I had been ever since leaving the marines. Sharing my story with the guys at Maine State, I had a strong sense that rather than stumbling here by accident, I was being called to a kind of duty. I knew I wanted to take advantage of my connection with Randy and his staff to help out however I could.

In April I took Nora to visit the prison for an orientation event being held for volunteers. We learned that Randy was always looking for ways to get the men exposure to the outside world. He felt it was important for when they were released, helping them feel more connected to society before returning. It was great to take Nora on the same tour I'd received during my first visit.

The others touring the prison that day consisted mostly of weekend puppy raisers, a network of people living in the surrounding communities of Maine State Prison, who take time out of their weekends to expose the puppies there to the outside world: crowded markets, playgrounds, cars, and other things they couldn't experience during the week at the prison. Had it not been for our constant travel and two dogs that took up most of our attention already, Nora and I would gladly have stepped in to fill one of the spots in the program.

While in the Veterans' Pod, Nora and I took the opportunity to chat with some of the guys. She ended up connecting with Chet, the incarcerated navy veteran with long dark hair whom I'd met on my first visit. I introduced her to Michael Kidd, the army veteran I'd met the first time around. He introduced us to Nate Nightingale, another army vet and dog trainer in the VetDogs program.

At first Nate was slightly more awkward in his manner than Kidd. He had thin-rimmed glasses and a muted posture that might have made him easy to miss, but once we started talking to him, he came to life, especially when he told us about his dog, Bergie, another black Lab like Chess, and about how training the dog had given him the skills and confidence he'd lost since being locked up.

"It's really great to talk to you guys a little bit. Thank you for coming here," Nate told us as we said our good-byes. "You're the first people from the outside, besides my family, that I've talked to in over eight years."

His words plunged straight into our hearts like fishhooks.

I tried to imagine not talking to anyone besides inmates and family members for that long. Most of these men in the program would be getting out of prison at some point, but how could we expect them to properly reintegrate into society if they weren't exposed to people other than those in their family and the prison system?

In the truck on the way home, I asked Nora what she thought of Randy and the prison.

"It's pretty incredible," she said. "Randy treats everyone the same. You wouldn't know if he was talking to a staff member or an inmate. But my heart aches for those guys anyway." She agreed with me; something special was going on at Maine State.

The summer of 2018 was a whirlwind. In June, Nora and I moved out of our house in Maine. The owners had rented it for the summer, and it wouldn't be available again until the end of August. We spent the next three months exploring the country and promoting the book, all the way to California and back again. We camped and we couch-surfed. We caught up with a bunch of the guys from Sangin, including my good friends Mark, Dave, and Joe. It was great to be on the road again—especially since biting the bullet on a gently used, bright white 2017 Toyota Tacoma with plenty of room and ice-cold air-conditioning. It was quite a change from my 1988 Land Cruiser, the same one I'd used to cross the country with my buddy Josh in 2015, a journey I described in *Craig & Fred*. With the Land Cruiser, you never knew if the engine would start, if the windows were going to work, or if you would actually make it to your destination. It added a degree of adventure and unpredictability to my life, but I could no longer travel that way. We had places to go and people expecting us. Our work and life on the road demanded a vehicle that could get us there and back. As we drove west, I'd look around the truck and smile thinking of how far Fred and I had come from our early days in the big blue beauty, whom we still have to this day. She'll always be a part of our family, enjoying truck retirement.

Toward the end of September, we circled back to Maine, happy to get settled again in our little house on the water. It felt great to have a home base after roughing it all summer. As soon as we returned, I got in contact with Randy at Maine State. Even though our travels had taken us far from the East Coast, the prison had been on my mind. Something was calling me back there.

CHAPTER 4

Playing Chess

When I emailed Randy, he responded right away, letting me know that Chess, one of the first dogs in the America's VetDogs program at Maine State Prison, was graduating at the end of the month. The dog had been trained by Michael Kidd, the army veteran I'd spent time with during my previous visits. Randy invited me to come up for graduation and reconnect with Kidd and the other guys involved in the dog program. I immediately accepted.

The day of the graduation I left Fred at home. He would only be a distraction to the other dogs on their special day, and I didn't want him drawing any attention from them. When I arrived at the prison, Fournier, the prison recreational therapist, met me in the lobby, taking me to the visitation room, a big, wide-open space with tall ceilings and a carpeted floor. As I walked in, I noticed Kidd and the other trainers sitting in a little row of chairs in front of the room, their black Labradors at their feet. Two others would be leaving the program today. Baxter needed some follow-up training before he could graduate, and Bergie had some medical issues that had to be addressed; his fate in the program was uncertain. Chess was the only dog so far to have fulfilled the requirements to graduate. Callahan, the leader of the book club, was there in his wheelchair, chatting with the guys. The rest of the audience was made up of the weekend puppy-raiser volunteers.

It was almost showtime, but before he started the proceedings,

Fournier introduced me to Jason Palmer, another key Maine State Prison staff member.

"Craig, I'd like you to meet Jason, a fellow marine and Iraq war veteran, currently serving as the lead Correctional Care and Treatment worker in the Veterans' Pod."

"Pleased to meet you," responded Palmer, a shorter guy with a stocky build and a well-groomed beard. We shook hands, and as Fournier walked up to the front to begin his introductions, I asked Palmer about his job. It turned out he was in charge of day-to-day issues and implementation of programs within the pod. Yet another veteran serving other vets—Randy clearly saw the virtue in hiring former military.

The small crowd gathered on the folding chairs and settled down to listen, and I took a seat next to Palmer as Fournier began. Fournier started by thanking the men and the weekend volunteers for doing such an amazing job training and taking care of the puppies, and then he introduced Randy Liberty, the warden.

Randy kept it brief: His primary focus was the men and their achievement.

"What a gift you've given to the world," he said, turning to address the men directly. "To be able to change the life of someone in need, someone who has served their country and needs help. For those of you graduating a dog today, saying good-bye will be difficult, but I hope that you all see the value in your work. If you need to talk to someone, please know that you can. It's okay to be upset, but never forget the purpose you serve in this program."

Next Randy introduced Paula Giardinella, the prison program director from America's VetDogs. A middle-aged woman with an olive complexion and shoulder-length chestnut hair stood up and walked to the front of the room.

"I'm extremely proud of these dogs," she said. "They've come a long way in the time they've spent here. Their growth is a reflection of the hard work you've put into them. It is not an easy task, and we ask a lot of you, but you've really risen to the challenge, and you should feel very good about that. All of these dogs, one way or another, will go on to change the lives of veterans and their families. On behalf of everyone at America's VetDogs, thank you."

Then Paula called Kidd up to the stage, with his dog, Chess, right at his heel.

"You have successfully trained the first America's VetDog from the program at Maine State Prison," Paula explained. "When Chess came here, he was just a puppy. Over the course of fifteen months, you have molded him into a highly trained companion through exhaustive training techniques that would test the patience of the most experienced trainer."

The black Lab sat patiently beside his handler, listening to Paula with a curious look on his face. He was calm but in tune with what was going on around him, ready to respond to whatever his person needed. Paula knelt and slipped the official yellow vest over the dog's head. Along the side was the America's VetDogs logo and the words SERVICE DOG in bright red stitching. Chess had just been given the equivalent of a doggie diploma. He was officially a graduate, and everyone stood to give him and Kidd a much-deserved round of applause.

After the ceremony was over, we all stood around in the visitation room while the men spent their final moments with the dogs they'd lived with for the last year-plus. Dogs they'd taken from goofy puppies and molded into disciplined, highly trained companions for people in need. It was Michael Fournier who introduced me to Paula. Even though I didn't have Fred with me, I told her a bit about my story, how I'd rescued him from

Afghanistan and how I'd grown to understand the importance of the bond we share with our dogs. I explained that my experience with Fred made me appreciate the work of America's VetDogs and everything they were doing to help veterans who were struggling. As we finished up talking, Paula asked me if I could give her a hand walking the dogs out of the facility, helping to load them into the van that was waiting to take them to the America's VetDogs campus on Long Island. There they'd await the next class of veterans to be paired with service dogs.

"If you could take Chess, Michael Kidd's dog, I'll take Baxter, and, Fournier, you can grab Bergie," she said.

I told her I'd be honored.

"It's going to be tough for these guys to say good-bye to their dogs," Fournier observed. "Their bond really goes deep."

Paula agreed. "It's necessary for the training process. We're actually engineering the bond to be incredibly close—the dogs' instincts are integrated into the men's lives at every level. It helps them connect and identify certain behaviors in us that we might not even realize are warning signs for anxiety or even seizures. It all starts with the bond between man and dog, and we build it out from there. This way when the dog goes on and is paired with a veteran, the two of them are able to connect in similarly deep ways. This is the hard part for the guys, but I hope they know how important the work they've done is. They're changing lives."

I tried to imagine what it would feel like to say good-bye to a dog you'd trained and loved, even if that dog was going on to a good home, to help another veteran in need. The thought of being separated from Fred when I was leaving Afghanistan had been so painful and intense that I'd literally defied orders and broken every rule to avoid it.

I went over to Kidd. He was sitting on the floor with Chess

between his legs, rubbing the dog's big black ears. Nate and Bergie were in another corner also saying their farewells.

"What will you miss most?" I asked Kidd.

After a brief pause, he looked up at me and then looked down at Chess.

"The authenticity," he said. "Having somebody that doesn't judge you or care about your mistakes or failures. You feel like you can be yourself. Our relationships and interactions here are often only skin-deep. They can be superficial. Chess just wants love and to give love. I never have to wonder about his intentions."

This was exactly what I loved about my relationship with Fred. From our first moments together between gunfights in Sangin, he had stripped away all the stress and uncertainty of life in a combat zone. And he continued to do that for me back home. Chess and the other dogs in the program offered the same level of authenticity to the men who were their partners.

There were so many questions I wanted to ask Kidd, but I didn't want to press him too much or take any more time away from their final moments together. Instead I watched as he gave Chess one last hug and a rub behind those big ears.

Then Kidd handed me the leash and immediately turned away. I could tell he was trying to get the good-bye over with. He didn't want to drag it out, fearing that if he stayed too long, he might break down in front of a room full of other inmates and strangers. I got the impression he was trying to make it easy on Chess, too. If he left quickly, that wouldn't give Chess a chance to turn around and see Kidd as he headed out the door.

Uniformed guards walked Kidd, Nate, and their fellow inmates back into the bowels of the facility. I watched them go. I didn't want to dwell on the pain of separation they must be feeling at that moment. As Kidd had just expressed, this was a world where the dog was the only thing that was authentic, true, and loving—and they were saying good-bye to that. The dogs were their light in an otherwise dark place. The coming days were going to bring challenges I didn't envy as the men relearned how to navigate prison life without their dogs.

Next the volunteers who'd taken care of the dogs on the weekends also had a chance to say good-bye and good luck. Then, together with Paula, Michael Fournier, and Jason Palmer, I helped escort Chess, Bergie, and Baxter from the prison for the last time. As we stepped outside, the cool, clear September air hit me. Chess was at my side. I noticed immediately the difference between walking Fred and walking a fully trained service dog like Chess. Fred is okay on the leash, but if he sees something he wants to sniff or chase, he's quick to pull or hit the brakes. At times it's clear that it's *his* walk and I'm just lucky to come along. He's very much his own dog, a characteristic I love about him, and I wouldn't have it any other way. With Chess, however, it was obvious that he was walking *with* me. His instincts had been fine-tuned to focus on the needs of his person. He could ignore the kinds of distractions that capture a typical dog's attention. It made it easy for me to appreciate the support he was going to provide the veteran he was about to be paired with.

Though the dogs had regularly left the prison for their week-end families, this time was different: Their bags were packed, and the same van they'd been delivered in more than a year earlier waited in the parking lot—they weren't coming back. As I walked Chess around the parking lot so he could stretch his legs and relieve himself before the long ride, I noticed he turned to look over his shoulder at the front door. Was he hoping to catch a glimpse of Kidd looking back at him? Or was he saying good-bye to his first home?

Now that his bladder was empty and his legs were thoroughly

stretched, I walked Chess toward the waiting van. Without hesitation he hopped up into his kennel and made himself comfortable. As I watched him settle in, it occurred to me that this exceptionally well-trained dog would have closed the heavy van door behind him if he could. His work here at Maine State Prison was over. Although part of his heart would always be with Kidd and the men who were his first family behind the concrete and barbed wire, it was time for his next mission in life, to help a veteran and a family that needed him.

The following week I asked Randy's permission to go back to the prison. I offered to spend a couple of hours with any of the guys who were interested, to chat and get them accustomed to someone from the outside world. The crisp fall air had begun to mix with the warm, lingering sun of summer. Fred and I arrived and made our way back to the Veterans' Pod.

Kidd, Nate, and Calli—as Mike Callahan is known to the guys—were waiting for us in the small classroom. Right away I thought it was interesting that the guys who had just said good-bye to their dogs the week before had all taken time out of their day to meet with me. As we walked by the classroom, I noticed Kidd sit up a little in his chair, craning his neck to see if Fred was with me. I held up my end of the leash to reassure him that I'd brought him along. Even in a prison, people were more excited to see Fred than me. I couldn't blame them. These guys were likely missing their dogs, and Fred was a much-needed dose of fur. Fred can always sense when he's needed and happily bounded into the classroom, making his way around the table to spend a few seconds with each guy, wagging his tail, looking up at them with his big Fred grin. All the guys greeted him using their best puppy talk while scratching him in all his favorite spots.

I found my seat next to Kidd and let Fred settle in, laying his head on my foot after getting his fill of attention from the guys.

We spent the next hour talking about the dogs and what the men's lives were like now that they'd said good-bye.

"Well, I'm getting to the gym a lot more," Kidd said.

"Ya, and I was so used to getting up early with Bergie that I volunteered to work in the kitchen to stay on the same sleep schedule," Nate explained, going on to say that he planned on training another dog and he didn't want to get used to sleeping in just to have to train himself to wake up early again when a new puppy arrived.

"You guys seem like you're doing great. I'm glad to see smiles on your faces," I said, looking around the room.

"You should have seen us a few days ago," Kidd confessed. "I was fine until I found an old picture of Chess when he was a pup in my notebook, along with some of my initial training notes. I cried like a baby for ten minutes."

"Ya, I found a sock Bergie had torn up in my laundry, and that got me going," said Nate.

"It's funny how you think you have it under control and then something reminds you of them and it all comes crashing back," I said, trying to ease any embarrassment the men might be feeling.

"It helps that we all were going through it together," Kidd pointed out.

"We all miss them, they were great dogs, and we put a lot of hard work into them," Calli echoed.

"But I think what helps the most is hearing that we've already got new dogs coming our way. They'll be here within a week, if not sooner," Nate added.

"Well, I'm glad you guys have a little support group here," I said.

Listening to them talk about their shared pain reminded me

of the camaraderie I'd felt with my fellow marines. There's something special about relationships forged in adverse conditions. When you share misery, you become closer, you learn a lot about yourself, and you see the virtues of the people around you.

I told the guys I planned to make more visits as soon I was back in Maine but that I had a few speaking events coming up, so it might be a while before I saw them again.

After we came back from our latest round of appearances, I kept going up to Maine State—sitting with the guys, drinking coffee, catching up, finding out about their lives. I wasn't the only volunteer paying regular visits to the prison. In the lobby each week, I'd regularly see two others. The first was the nun from a church in Bangor who came in to pray with the men in hospice care, men who would take their last breaths on this earth behind the walls of Maine State. The other was a yoga teacher who drove up from Portland every week to donate his time and energy, teaching the men peaceful and practical forms of meditation. After meeting them on a few occasions, Fred began to expect to see them. He'd trot over to them with his full-body wiggle, dancing and howling with joy. After a short while, it felt like we were coworkers, walking into the office for another day on the job. It was an unexpected bond that lifted my spirits. The only difference was that they had defined roles within the prison, and I was just coming for a chat.

I began thinking about what else I could offer the guys besides sitting around swapping stories. They had access to college courses and lots of different programs to occupy their time. What could I give them besides my attention and an affinity for prison coffee?

One afternoon I was sitting with Kidd at a table in the common area of the Veterans' Pod. We were waiting for the rest of the guys to get back from their various duties around the prison so we could hang out in the classroom. He had a new dog now, Emma, and the training was going well. America's VetDogs had brought her up from Connecticut in the middle of her training program there, as she'd had some bad habits that the first trainer couldn't get around. Paula thought Kidd was the only one who could give Emma her best shot at graduating, because she needed to work through a lot of the same behavioral stuff he'd dealt with in Chess. Emma was smaller than the other Labs I'd seen before, with a tan coat and attentive brown eyes. I could tell that Kidd was working his magic on her by the way she leaned against his chair as she napped on the floor, making sure she'd know if he moved or got up.

Kidd explained that Emma would be ready to be paired with a veteran soon, and it wouldn't be long before he would have to say good-bye again, his wounds from parting with Chess still fresh.

"When Chess left, I swore I'd never take on another dog," he told me. "One and done for me, I said. After a few weeks, though, I realized that it was okay to miss Chess, but that I wasn't doing anyone any favors by holding on to something that was never mine. I became grateful for the experience of training him. I realized that I owed it to myself to open up again to another dog. It's kind of like a breakup in a relationship. The first few months, you swear you're never gonna get involved with another person again, but then you come around and you start to realize that if you want the highs, you gotta be prepared for the lows. They go hand in hand.

"Problem is, I don't think I can handle another dog after this one," he went on, shaking his head. "It was bad enough saying good-bye to Chess, but at least I didn't know how painful it would be. This time I know exactly how much it hurts, and that makes it even worse."

Despite how much Kidd had gotten from the program, he was going to tell Paula and Fournier that he'd be happy to help out other trainers but he couldn't take on another dog.

I thought about what Kidd was going through and about the impact my bond with Fred has had on my life. It was something I hadn't been fully able to understand or appreciate until I started writing our story. The process of writing the book had been a way to make sense of my experiences, but—more important for me—it helped me find purpose in them.

Perhaps writing could do the same for Kidd.

"If you ever have time, maybe you could put down in words what Chess means to you," I told Kidd before the rest of the guys showed up.

"Ya, maybe," he said somewhat reluctantly.

Early in February, to my surprise, I got an email from Mike Fournier at the prison. Kidd had written something, and he wanted to share it with me.

Sitting in our makeshift office, in our house on the edge of the water, I clicked open the attachment.

What The Dog Means To Me

1/28/2019

In 2005, my father passed away from Malignant Melanoma; at fourteen, I knew not much else about how this would define my youth aside from my deep desire to make him proud of me. As I sat by his bedside for the last time, holding his hand, I told him that I had decided to join the Army as soon as I was old enough. His face lit up, and he seemed so happy to hear that. Who knows what was going through his mind; joy for the knowledge that I would do something so meaningful, happiness to know that I would have such discipline and structure in my life? Probably these things, and so much more. But the memory of seeing that lit up face made that decision mean so much more to me.

During my junior year of High School, I told my girlfriend that I was going to the recruiter's office, and we went together. I signed up for the Delayed Entry Program (DEP), and began to build my life around the fulfillment of this vision. During our senior year, my girlfriend became pregnant. After graduation, and a summer that cruised by, I left for basic training in October of 2009, anxious, apprehensive, optimistic, enthusiastic. I knew that my life was in my hands; that as long as I was willing to do my absolute best, and never quit, I would achieve the promise to my father that had been the only lasting light in my young life of darkness after losing him.

I was a good soldier, well-rounded at survival skills, great at shooting, athletic, and able to push past the feeling that I had nothing left. And above all, I was so proud. I felt like I had done the biggest thing anyone could do; a decision that exceeded self, and served the greater good for the greatest number of people. Also, I felt like I could be a husband and a father by providing for my family. I was young (18), so I felt like this decision would automatically make everything fall into place in my life.

Toward the end of basic training, I had a conversation with my girlfriend about our lives beginning together, and about how we needed to really push beyond our past and make things work for our son, but I learned she had developed feelings for someone else while I was away. This should have been an automatic deal breaker for me, but I was an idiot and listened to her crying "I'm sorry," thinking it would be best for my son to forgive and try to move forward. Don't ask me why now, because I couldn't tell you why.

I came home to Maine briefly after graduating before flying to Fort Bliss, Texas. I prepared my paperwork at Fort Bliss, and on Christmas block leave I married my girlfriend in Maine, and began the drive back to Texas with my nine month pregnant wife to begin the new life I had put everything into. Five days after arriving, my son Dayton Tyler Kidd was born, in January 2010; this seemed like a final peg in my board of achievements and at 19, I felt a sense of fulfillment. Although I had done the things I had set out to do, I still struggled processing my father's passing, and drank often after work. My wife was not content in our marriage, and inviting them over to our home when I was training. It was not long before I found this out, and I shut down completely. I had no idea what I should do in the moment, because my false hopes and dreams made me too passionate to decide what would be best for myself, as well as my son.

As my marriage crumbled, I just fell into a phase of not really being present at home, and not really caring about work. I got in trouble for drinking while on staff duty, and had my first bout of extra duty. While at extra duty, I was surrounded by men who did not care anymore about their military service for their own reasons, and this caused further cloudiness in my decision making. My wife and I had a pretty big argument about our future together, and after returning from a week of training in New Mexico I found an empty home. My wife had taken my son and returned to Maine, and at nineteen, I felt like I had every hope ripped from me. Despite having every opportunity on my plate to still be successful and do the things I desired to do, I lacked the perception to see any of it. Shortly after this event, I approached my platoon sergeant and told him that I needed to process out. With my drinking and lifestyle continuing to spiral, I was in no condition to serve myself or others.

In 2011, I returned to Maine, and life became the complete

opposite of when I had left for Basic Training. I now lived fully in my failures, and surrounded myself with others who lived with a lack of caring and empathy. I began using prescription pills, cocaine, MDMA, and anything else I could get my hands on. I also began robbing houses, and random people on the streets, to finance these habits and lifestyle. One of my bigger regrets is using skills the Army had taught me in order to cause trauma and commit crimes. After nine months of living like this—if you could call it living at all—I committed an armed home invasion with two other men. Worst of all, the individual we robbed was an elderly Vietnam veteran suffering from PTSD and night terrors. I think about this fact every day, and feel so horrible for allowing myself to ever commit such an atrocious act against another human, let alone a Veteran.

After coming to prison, I went through an acclimation phase. I continued using to mask my life's mistakes, and pretended to have no inclination of remorse. I fought, trafficked in drugs, got caught with weapons, syringes, tattoos, alcohol; but I could not continue to allow myself to be defined by my worst decisions. Now, at the age of 22, I could not concede that fifteen years in prison was a death sentence to any redeeming qualities I possessed. I experienced a change one day that can only be defined as super-natural. On father's day 2014 I gave my life to Christ, and completely changed my pursuits, presentation, and character. I know that often seems like such a cliché to people in society; admittedly I would have such similar thoughts if I had continued to make "good" choices in life. But my change was undeniable by all who were in contact or communication with me.

When the idea of training service dogs was first proposed, I thought about what that would mean to me. I considered how much potential this would hold to give back to an area of my life that was currently filled with thoughts of failure. Although this feeling of a counterbalance to my shortcomings in my own decisions in the past is a large part of my motivation to train the dogs, it is not my only motivating factor. I thought about individuals who have come home, and could not find that camaraderie that they had found in service, and about my ability to play a part in offering that service.

When I first was offered to be the handler for Chess, I was apprehensive. Not because I didn't want Chess, but because I immediately understood the implication of failure, and what that would mean to me. When I accepted, Chess was nothing short of a blessing to me. He has a personality unrivaled by any other dog, and was eager to simply work for my love and affection. Chess also KNEW much more about human consciousness than he should as a dog. The first day I had Chess in my cell, I was eating a bowl of food leaning against the sink. Chess sat, intently looking at me; I knew that begging was not something I would want him to get in the habit of doing, so I looked at him and opened the door to his kennel. I said out loud to him, "If you don't cut it out, I'll put you in there till I'm done eating." I could tell that Chess knew what I had said, and no dog analyst could tell me otherwise, because Chess looked at the kennel door, walked over, nosed the door closed while wagging his tail, and sat back down under the full knowledge that I didn't want to put him in there anymore than he wanted to be in there. He had my heart right then and there.

It could be easy for some to forget what purpose these dogs are serving, but I could not place that thought aside, even for an instant. I grew attached to Chess based on what he had done for my own character, in the time I was afforded with him; and I knew that his purpose was one of immeasurable value. Sometimes while incarcerated, it is easy to think of society as another planet; that you are not impacting it any longer, and that whatever you are doing behind the steel fencing and cement is irrelevant to those in society. Providing Chess to the Veteran in need broke every falsehood of that thinking in my mind. The fence and cement no longer existed, and I realized that every thought, word, and action I produce in this environment has the potential to transcend every physical barrier. Also, the barriers I placed in my own life were broken down piece by piece; barriers of failure, inadequacy, desolation, invaluableness. These feelings were replaced by the knowledge that I was serving a purpose for a soldier that I may never meet, or even know their name; an unsung hero, who may not even realize his own worth to someone he has never met, someone struggling with feelings of isolation or lack of camaraderie as well. Someone like me.

Doing this service has an ability to foster growth in both lives, the soldier, and the inmate handler. While Chess is moving on to assist the Veteran to live a fuller life after leaving here, while he is here he is doing those things in my life. His purpose for the Veteran is more fully realized as I see what he is doing in my own life here. I think back to the person who committed the crime all those years ago; that young man who saw no redeeming characteristics or inherent worth in himself. Training Chess has made me not only realize that I am capable of living a productive life, but has grown the characteristics in myself that will make this prison sentence not a waste of time. I have developed characteristics that are selfless in nature, and thought about implications for my actions and choices; these attributes have created a man who can be a member of society, a son, a neighbor, a father, a husband.

No one would ever need to thank me for training Chess. There is no thanks deserved aside from my own gratitude for the opportunity to change my perspective on life, and realize I can still be valuable to those outside of this environment. My capacity to serve

will never be defined by my environment, and my environment will never define me.
    Michael E. Kidd, MDOC#100766

I was blown away by what Kidd had written. As I read, I could feel the pain in his story—and the frustration. He'd had such a bright beginning, but things had gotten out of control quickly. Comparing the trajectory of his early twenties to mine, I was filled with sympathy for him. If life had gone differently for me, I knew I could have ended up in the same downward spiral.

I wanted to help Kidd. Just reading his writing, I knew he had a lot to say and offer. I saw what Randy Liberty saw in all these guys, their overwhelming potential and a belief that their loss of direction didn't have to be permanent.

I realized I wanted to give the guys at Maine State what Fred had given me—a chance to express themselves. I knew they had stories and memories and that they had plenty of time to reflect on them. When they finally got out, I didn't want them to feel as I had in my early days after coming back from Afghanistan. I wanted them to be able to understand their own stories, so that they were better prepared to share them with the world.

My mind spun with ideas and methods for what I was now convinced should be some kind of writing program. I suggested it to Randy in an email.

"How about I start a writing group at Maine State Prison?" I proposed, getting straight to the point.

"YES," he wrote back within a few minutes. "We love when you come up and it means a lot to the men. We'll make sure to support whatever you have in mind as best we can."

Soon after I went up to the prison to talk to the guys to see if they would be receptive to my idea.

"I want to start a weekly writing group with you guys and whoever else wants to join up," I told them. "I've gained a lot of perspective on my own life through the writing process, and I want to create a way for all of you to experience that."

Without taking a breath, I continued, trying to stay ahead of any questions or concerns they might have.

"It will be very informal. I'm not an English teacher, I'm not interested in punctuation or spelling. I just love a good story, and I know you guys have a lot to share."

"We sure do," Kidd said with a smile.

"Ya, I could write a book about what *not* to do in life," Nate said, drawing a collective chuckle from Kidd and Callahan.

"The bottom line is, I like coming up here and spending time with you guys, and I think this is a way I can do that. If all goes well, I could see maybe writing a little about my time here and the dog program, too."

I was trying to lay all my cards on the table.

"That is great, man," Kidd told me, looking under the table at the sleepy Afghan dog. "We'd love to see more of you, but only if you bring Fred as often as you can."

I told him that I would definitely bring Fred whenever possible. I knew that would be a condition of the group for sure.

With the guys and Randy's approval, I started drafting a syllabus. At the top of the page, I wrote the name I'd come up with—the Purposeful Tails Writing Group. The name summed up what I wanted the group to be about, while also being a playful dog pun.

"The purpose of this group is to enhance our ability to communicate our experiences with the world," I wrote in the syllabus. "We will do this by reading, writing, studying, and sharing stories from our lives or from our minds. At the end of our time together, you'll have a better understanding of the importance of storytelling and the importance of your own life story. Because so much of what happens in our lives, either to us or around us, is lost in our mind until we take the time to reflect and share. I've learned a lot about myself in the last couple of years through writing. Working on my first book, *Craig & Fred,* revealed details about my life that I had either forgotten or failed to see the relevance of. By sharing my story both verbally and in written form, I've been able to communicate with myself and others more effectively. It started by having conversations with the people around me about Fred and how we'd found each other. The more I opened up, the more details I remembered and the more I was able to see how my life had taken shape. The little and big moments, some of them perceived as victories and others as failures, are all important when we take the time to see their role in our own stories."

The syllabus included writing topics, prompts, and readings. I was trying to strike a balance between a formal class and a casual meeting. I stayed away from words that killed fun, like "work" and "assignment." I didn't like the weight they carried with them. My idea was to offer five sessions to the group with the promise of more if they wished. I didn't want to have an end date or a specific arc of the class, because I didn't know how the men would respond. If they wanted to continue meeting beyond five weeks, they could come up with topics and readings based on what they wanted to share.

I also made some important disclaimers:

- This is NOT a punctuation or English class.
- Reading aloud and sharing is OPTIONAL.
- Everything we share in our group will stay within the group. If you wish to share with others, please do so only with your own story.

I sent a copy of the syllabus to Jason Palmer and Mike Fournier, the programs director and recreational therapist for the Veterans' Pod, and they posted a sign-up sheet on the guard desk, a common gathering place for the men to receive mail and other information. The next day I got a quick email from Fournier.

"There were eight guys that signed up right away! They're all looking forward to it. See you next week!"

I was starting to feel some pressure now, but it was the good kind, the kind that meant I was doing something challenging and worthwhile.

Then, on April 11, I climbed into the truck, Fred at my side, and swung the car out of the driveway, heading for Maine State Prison.

A few hours later, I found myself sitting around a table with four guys in the little classroom in the Veterans' Pod, about to begin our first writing session.

CHAPTER 5

Car Crashes

Around the table that day were Michael Kidd, Michael Callahan, Robert Craig (Mr. Craig), and Nate Nightingale. Michael Kidd, the star dog trainer, was seated at the head of the table closest to the door. He had a clean shave and a fresh haircut and sat upright in his chair, ready for the session with his laptop in front of him, playing some country music from it as the rest of the men chatted.

Callahan was the small, unassuming-looking middle-aged guy with glasses who sat in a wheelchair, the leader of the book club. He was also very involved in the dog program, and I knew from past meetings that he somehow managed to be soft-spoken and extremely social at the same time.

Then there was Mr. Craig, in his eighties, his round frame stuffed into a wheelchair, a wave of ice-white hair resting perfectly upon his pumpkin-shaped head. He's an army veteran from the mid-1950s, and although he never saw any overseas time, he'd once pointed out to me that being in prison reminded him of his military days. "It always amazes me how many nice people there are in here, just like when I was in the army," he told me. "I met some of the best people I'd ever known in the army. It's the same in here, lots of nice people."

Nate was on the quieter side. He usually hung back from group discussions, but if he was asked a question directly, he'd always have a thoughtful and articulate answer. We'd gotten to know each other sitting around the pod talking about dogs and his life, in prison and before. He wore thin-rimmed glasses, the kind you barely notice the first time you look at him, because you're too distracted by the full-length sleeve tattoos on both his arms, mosaics of skillfully drawn demons and skulls woven within a backdrop of smoke and flames. Today he was seated at the opposite end of the table from Kidd, chatting quietly with Calli.

I noticed that Kidd and Nate had pieces of paper and notebooks with them. Fournier had already warned me that not everyone had access to a computer, although Kidd did because he was enrolled in college courses. His writing was printed out and stapled in front of him. Nate's notes were handwritten on paper he'd ripped from his notebook, similar to Calli's. The only one who hadn't written anything down was Mr. Craig.

I sat next to Kidd, facing the door with my back to the wall. Fred did the rounds, saying hello to each of the guys before settling between my feet under the table. Nate filled a cup of coffee from a large cafeteria-style coffee dispenser on his end of the table and handed it to me. I thanked him and took a sip.

I realized that this visit felt very different from the other times I'd come to the prison. Until now, visiting here had always been a casual thing, a chance to hang out with the guys in the Veterans' Pod. Now I was putting a name on something that we'd already started through our conversations. We were going to apply techniques and procedures to our weekly interactions. What would happen now that we had an obligation to a syllabus? Would it kill the tentative connection we'd made or give our group a boost of the legitimacy we were lacking? Would there even be enough to talk about to fill the three-hour time slot allocated for the class?

And how were the guys going to react to the weekly questions? Although I'd met everyone around the table before and

CRAIG GROSSI

felt reasonably comfortable with them, these were still inmates in a maximum-security prison. Would they be quick to anger when the discussions took a personal turn? What about their motives for participating in the writing class? What if they were just here to cut up with one another, taking any opportunity they could to get out of their cells and goof off? Was it possible they were all simply putting on a mask, feigning interest in the program as some kind of ruse?

My training as a military police officer had taken place a long time ago, but the cynicism I'd learned from that experience was still lodged somewhere deep within me. *Don't let the guys take advantage of you*, we were told. *They're career criminals. They're never going to change. Give them an inch and they'll take a mile. Establish who's in control, don't let them get one up on you.* The lessons I'd picked up during that time buzzed around in my head like a confused housefly. At the same time, as I sat at the table that day waiting for our session to begin, my heart was saying something else. It really wanted to believe that the guys were capable of change and worthy of redemption. I just didn't know yet whether my worst assumptions would be confirmed or if the guys would defy the stereotypes rearing up in my mind.

I'd sent the syllabus around to the men, and they had all brought a copy with them. Kidd kicked off the conversation that afternoon by pointing out that there were grammatical errors in the document.

"Shall I presume your work is grammatically pure, then?" I asked with a smile.

"Not even close, but you're the pro," he responded.

"Ya, but Fred is my editor, so . . ."

As we were chatting, waiting to begin, I was wondering what had happened to the other four guys who'd signed up for class. Fournier had said there were eight altogether.

At that moment a guy about the same age as Kidd bounded into the room. I recognized him from my prior visits to the prison. Maine State Prison's population, like the rest of the state, is majority white, and all the members of the writing group thus far were Caucasian, while this man was Black. I hoped he was here for the class, thinking he would have a valuable perspective to share. Instead he said hi but was gone before I could invite him to join us.

After he'd left the room, Kidd turned to me and said, "That's Marcus. He's my buddy. I'm working on getting him in here, but he's not ready yet."

Calli must have noticed me glancing toward the door to see if anyone else might be filtering in, because he answered my question before I could ask it.

"It's a visitation day today, so some of the guys can't make it," he explained.

"Is every Thursday visitation day?" I responded, curious as to why we'd decided on Thursdays.

"Ya, it is," Calli replied.

"Well, let's move the group, then. Wednesdays okay? I don't want you guys to have to choose between seeing visitors and being in this group."

"Whoa, bud, we like you, but not *that* much," Nate said with a smile.

"Oh, okay, okay. But let's move it to Wednesday afternoons? If that works for you guys, it'll work for me," I replied.

"We're not going anywhere," Calli replied with a shrug.

"I'll clear it with Palmer and Fournier," I said

Then I opened my notebook and titled a new page:

April 11, 2019: First Meeting of Purposeful Tails Writing Group

I'd picked the topic "car crashes" for our first session, thinking this subject would be a great way to kick off our official meetings. I figured everyone has a story of a car crash, either one they've witnessed or one they've been involved in.

"When you begin writing your story about a car crash, try to begin in the hours or days leading up to your involvement in the crash," I wrote in the syllabus. "Think about what you had for breakfast and/or the things that held you up or went your way during the course of the day, that ultimately led you to either witnessing or being involved in the wreck."

This felt like an opportunity for the men to tell a story without necessarily diving too deeply into a subject. I was hoping it would give me a constructive way to talk about the importance of using concrete details in a story—how things looked, sounded, and smelled—to bring a scene to life. And then, after that, perhaps we might be able to talk about the emotional significance of storytelling, if they were open to it.

I also wanted the guys to think about the concept of close calls.

"We've all had times when a step in another direction could have changed our lives forever," I wrote in my instructions to them. "Think about the people on 9/11 who missed their flights, were late for work at the World Trade Center, or got called in to a meeting on the other side of the Pentagon. To them their day started out with something annoying and frustrating, but it could have been much worse. This is an extreme example, of course, but we've all had moments where the fragility of life becomes very clear."

When I wrote those words in the syllabus, I was still shaken by the incident in Virginia where an aggressive truck driver had run us off the road and I'd come closer than I cared to admit to doing something I might have regretted forever. It was a real close call. Since then I hadn't told anyone except for the VA counselor about how I'd lost control. It was a topic I probably should have been exploring myself, but instead I was pushing it out to the guys in the hope that it might feel relevant to them as well.

"Take your time and write however much or little you see fit," I told them in my description of the assignment. "We can either share them verbally or you can hand yours in to me and I'll read it and give you feedback. If you can't remember details or are a little foggy about things like dates, times, or locations, don't worry about it. We're not writing a history book, we're sharing experiences, and those are always subjective."

Sitting at the classroom table, I was just about to ask who wanted to start off by sharing his story when we were interrupted by a familiar face. Randy Liberty popped into the room, drawing a smile from all of us. It was clear that the men appreciated the work he was doing as warden and even clearer that Randy had an ability to genuinely connect with them.

We all regarded him as he stood in the doorway, like doe-eyed boys watching their father cut the grass.

Randy looked right at me.

"You engaged to Nora yet?" he asked.

It was the kind of bluntness that I was beginning to love about Mainers. I attempted to explain the logistical reasons for Nora's lack of a ring.

"I'm planning on it," I told him. "I just need some of the cards to fall in the right places."

"You better marry her quick. She's one of the good ones, I can tell," he insisted.

"Just gotta sell my D.C. house first. Shouldn't be too hard," I replied.

"So Maine is home now? Well, we're glad to have you. Let me

know if you need help looking for a place when the time comes, but first things first—you better put a ring on Nora's finger!"

After one last fatherly jab at my romantic life, Randy spent another few minutes chatting with the guys about some administrative stuff that went right over my head. Behind him, outside the classroom, a line of men was forming, each respectfully waiting his turn to have the ear of the warden.

Randy thanked me for coming up and politely excused himself. I got the feeling that he would gladly have joined our group if his duties hadn't pulled him in another direction.

With the door closed to the chatter of the dayroom, our first official meeting finally began.

"Who wants to kick us off?" I asked.

There was a brief pause as they all looked at one another. Then Kidd responded.

"I'll go first. I wrote it out, so I'll just read what I got," he said confidently.

He started to read aloud.

It's noontime on Sunday, and I'm staring out the window of Tyler's truck at a flock of ten to twelve turkeys in a field on our way home from town.

"Too bad we didn't keep the twelve-gauge behind the seat from the other day, huh?"

Tyler can tell how bad I wanna snatch a fresh turkey and feeds my desire by reminding me that we don't have the shotgun. I snap the tin of Copenhagen, pinch about a quarter of it into my lip, and hand him the tin. I wait until I see him about to open his mouth before I pop the clutch of the little Ford Ranger, spilling tobacco all over the front of his KVCC sweatshirt and flinging rooster tails thirty feet behind the truck, whipping the steering wheel back and forth as fast as I can to fishtail and laughing at Tyler.

"You spilled something on your shirt there, buddy."

We laugh and each grab another Twisted Tea from under the seat. I've been living with Tyler and his Uncle Bub for a few months now. We lived in a double-wide trailer together, us three boys and Uncle Bub's girlfriend, Janette. Country music, Twisted Tea, chewing tobacco, work and play. We were still in school, but you wouldn't know it from the life we lived. At sixteen we've grown up drinking with the best of 'em, and know all the back roads to tear down. We think our entire lives will be this exact way, with each other; we'll die old and gray doing the same things we were doing at sixteen, side by side on these same dirt country roads, the same way our fathers had done and same way we hope our future sons would do.

I was impressed by how confident Kidd was. If you closed your eyes, you wouldn't even know he was reading words he'd written down. It was as if there was a direct connection between his thoughts, what ended up on the page, and what came out of his mouth.

Uncle Bub was at the kitchen table when we came in the house, waiting for us to hang out. The radio was already blasting, and you could tell he was ready for a good night.

"Matt is takin' a piss, then we're driving up the mountain real quick in the truck to find a spot for the deer camera. You boys ready to go?"

I guessed we wouldn't make it down the mountain till we were low on gas or out of teas, so I figured I would be wise to call my girlfriend before I got in the truck. There was no way I would hear her over the radio and truck exhaust.

"Yeah, I'm gonna call Paige real quick before we leave, Uncle Bub."

"Don't be on the phone with her all night, dickhead, or I'll flush that friggin' thing before we leave!"

Uncle Bub laughs, routinely taking advantage to pick on me with my many girlfriends.

Matt is our other friend. He's just like us, though not as close as Tyler and me, if not only because he can't move out of his mom's house yet to stay with us. He comes out of the bathroom, and our night begins. By the end of the night, Paige has come up, all four guys are dancing in blue jeans and ball caps with no shirts and long-necks in hand, and laughing until we can't stand anymore. Typical Sunday night before school on Monday.

As we ride to school together the next morning in my truck, we take the dirt road we had been down yesterday and see the same turkeys.

"We gotta get one of 'em this week," I tell Tyler, and we start plotting our hunt, figuring out when we can get it cleaned and taken care of before Uncle Bub gets home from work and finds out we got a turkey without him. Paige hears me talking about Wednesday and kicks the back of the seat. I remember I told her and her mom I would go to the movies with them Wednesday after school, but I don't wanna listen to Tyler give me the guilt trip about ditching the boys for her, so I don't say anything.

School passes by quickly for the next two days. Tuesday night I break the news to Tyler and Matt that I can't go with 'em after school. I already know what's coming next: The rest of the night is filled with puns about bros being before hos and Mikey being pussy-whipped. I know at heart that they just want us all together, because that is when we have the greatest time. But I also know that I'll lose my girl if I keep blowing her off for a shotgun and a fishing pole.

At school Wednesday I am bombarded with puns from Tyler and Matt as I stand outside his truck window spitting chew on the side of his ranger when he isn't looking.

"Fuck you guys. You better save me some turkey for to-night when I get home, or I'll take the distributor cap off your truck again."

"If you want some turkey that bad, you'd be coming with us!"

I realize I'm feeling super on the fence, trying to figure some excuse I can possibly muster to tell Paige I can't go, but I know it's futile. I'm going to have to keep impressions up with her mom if I plan to make it last with her. Her mom thinks the world of me, and I learned early on that is the key to a successful relationship.

At two o'clock school gets out, and I wave to Tyler and Matt as they get in Matt's F-150 and burn out, leaving the parking lot. Paige has an all-wheel-drive Jeep, so I can only manage a quick squawk of the tires in return.

We meet Paige's mom, Wanda, at the movie theater, and I give her a big hug and smile, joking that she looks beautiful and that we should ditch Paige and see the movie together. Wanda laughs and punches my arm. We buy tickets, and I become lost in the sight of how beautiful my girlfriend is and how picturesque our young life has been so far. Living all summer in a camp together, with no one else around, brought us so close that we often felt as if we had been mar-ried fifty years. I'm not even watching the movie as I feel her hand in mine and see her mom smile looking at us. I don't ever want these feelings to end. I ignore my phone vibrating in my pocket, not wanting anything to get in the way of my euphoria. Finally, on the third call, I check to see the ID on the screen. Patrick. My stepdad never calls me unless I have done something wrong. I just ignore it again.

But of course if it's not one thing, it's another, because that's simply the order of life. I have to piss and might as well grab a chew out of the Jeep and check my voice mail. When I tell Paige what I am doing, she comes with me, and we tell Wanda that we will be right back. I think about how much her mom trusts me already, that she knows we are not sneaking off, doesn't even question us.

As I put a pinch of dip in my lip, I listen to Patrick on my voice mail and hear a tone in his voice that I have never heard prior nor since this day: panic.

"Mikey, *please* call me, please!"

I dial his number and hear the exact opposite in his tone when we connect: relief.

"Phew, I'm glad you're all right. Where are you? In New Vineyard?"

"No, I'm at the movies with Paige and Wanda. Why? What's up?"

"Well, the scanner came on that two juveniles flipped their truck out on Ramsdell Road, and I wanted to make sure you were all right."

"Yeah, I'm good. I'll call Mom when I get out and let her know."

As soon as I hang up the phone, my heart sinks. I feel a sense of dread as I remember that the Ramsdell Road is where our turkeys have been in the field on the way home from school. Paige asks me what's going on. She can read my face. I don't answer, I just call Tyler's mother on her cell phone. When Trixie answers the phone, I can't make much else out besides, "Tyler and Matt . . . oh, my God . . . Life-Flight . . . Central Maine Medical Center."

I don't remember seeing Wanda come out of the theater or if Paige went in and got her, but she is standing next to us when I get off the phone. I don't need to explain anything. I simply ask Paige if she is getting in the car with me or not. She gets in the Jeep. Wanda's only words are not to drive too fast, and we leave. I make the hour drive to Lewiston in just over half the time.

When I get to the hospital, I go straight into the emergency room. When the female nurse asks me if I am immediate family, I say yes. For me this is absolutely true. Tyler and Matt are my brothers in every sense of the word. I remember going down a hallway and there are beds lined up on my left. In the distance I can hear someone crying and trying to articulate something in a half scream. When I reach the noise, it's Matt. He's hooked up to an IV, and he doesn't even look like himself. He is strapped to the bed, and his leg is in some sort of contraption. He's fighting the braces, trying to get out of the bed. When he sees me, I realize what he is saying:

"I didn't mean to! I'm sorry, I didn't mean to. . . ."

I grab his hand and ask him what happened, but I can't even come close to understanding him. The nurse tells me that Tyler is down the hall further, but to keep in mind that he is being prepared for a CT scan and that he looks very bad.

When I get to Tyler, his family's all around the bed, and Tyler's face is wrapped up with countless bandages. I can't even see his eyes. His head is swollen so big, I've never seen anything like that. I can't even approach him. I turn around and walk out into the hallway and just drop. Moments later the nurses rush his bed out and into the bowels of this place where I'm wishing I never came. After talking to Uncle Bub, trying to establish what happened, what is happening now, and anything else, I learn that we don't know much of anything yet—other than that Matt had rolled his truck and they were found lying in the road by another driver.

When I leave the hospital, I go to my mother's house instead of Uncle Bub's and find that my grandfather has towed Matt's truck to our house and put it in his garage. I don't even go in there. I have no desire to see it and want above everything else to just distance myself from this situation as a whole. I don't sleep that night at all, even after drinking half a bottle of vodka. And the next day, deciding I am not going to school, I go into the garage and see the Ford. Both windows are broken out, and the windshield is spiderwebbed with a distinct hole in the top passenger side, where I later find out Tyler was ejected. That is when everything *really* hits me, and I realize that I was supposed to be there with them. I didn't know if I was thankful for not, or guilty or not. Would it have been the same? Worse? Not at all?

Tyler ended up pulling a great deal of the skin and muscle from his face in the crash and broke every bone other than his jaw: both orbital bones, his nose, both cheekbones, even fracturing his forehead. Much later the doctor would joke that Tyler should have been a boxer. When he got ejected through the windshield, he hit the road face-first and slid into the ditch facedown.

Matt stayed inside the truck until the second roll, when his left leg came out the driver's window, the truck's weight came down on it, breaking his femur in half and knocking him out. When he awoke, he was lying in the road and could hear Tyler gurgling for air in the ditch. When he tried to stand to walk to him, his femur slid down on itself inside his leg, knocking him back out. A teacher from our high school, Mr. Tierney, was driving home when he found the truck, and them, and called 911. It was a very sparsely driven road, and if Mr. Tierney hadn't shown up, Tyler would have most likely choked to death in the ditch.

Tyler received extensive facial-reconstructive surgery, and Matt had a rod and a ton of screws and pins that went from his hip to just above his knee.

Matt and Tyler's friendship faltered after the accident, but Tyler and I grew even closer after he came home and spent every single day together until I left for the army. I ended up naming my son Dayton Tyler Kidd.

As Kidd read, I could tell by the emotion in his voice as he got to the difficult parts—the memories of seeing his friends bandaged and broken, their bodies twisted and mangled—that the trauma of that moment was very much alive in him.

"Man, that is a lot," was all I could say as Kidd finished reading.

"Ya, man, it felt good to get it out, but I had a hard time with it," he said, putting his printout away.

"What was hard about it?" I asked.

"I kept self-correcting," Kidd explained. "My mind wouldn't let me remember certain things about that day, but I kept going back to it, and eventually I put it all together: the little details of leaving the theater, my stepdad's voice, seeing Matt and Tyler in the hospital. I had to beat it out of myself."

"That is why I love writing," I told him. "The more we can unpack from our own experiences, good and bad, the more we can find meaning in the details. Thank you for that. I know it wasn't easy, but I'm so glad you were able to put that day into words for us and yourself."

I could have talked to Kidd for hours about his experience

and its impact on his life, but I could see that the other men had things to share, and I wanted to hear them.

I looked around the room to see who was most eager to go next. I didn't want to single someone out if I didn't have to.

Nate seemed like he was ready, but just as he was about to open his mouth, a crackly voice broke the brief silence in the room.

It was Mr. Craig, and he had something to say. "I have a story."

During my previous visits to the prison, Mr. Craig usually just sat and listened in his wheelchair, sipping coffee and dozing off. I'd seen the guys make respectful jabs at the old man because they knew he would take it with a smile. "Hey, Mr. Craig, what was it like crossing the Delaware with George Washington?" or "What was it like when your village discovered fire?"

This time around I could see Mr. Craig sitting up in his wheelchair a little bit. I could sense that he'd given our assignment some thought and was prepared to share something with the group. As he started to speak, nobody made any old-man jokes or asked him if he needed to be reminded of his own name.

We all just sat and listened.

"In 1959 I was driving from Delaware to Florida, to visit my dad and some other family," Mr. Craig began. He hadn't written anything down, but it turned out he was a natural storyteller. "In a little town in Maryland near the seashore, I stopped to get some gas. I couldn't help but notice that there wasn't anyone around except for the sleepy guy behind the counter inside the shop. I paid him for my gas and was enjoying being out of the car for a little while when I heard music. I finished pumping my gas and parked my car on the side of the main road and got out to walk around and see where the music was coming from. It was some of the sweetest sounds I'd ever heard. I've always loved music, and I wasn't in no rush, so I figured it was worth investigating. I come up on this church sitting back a little bit from the main road, and I swear I could see the sound seeping out from between the cracks in the walls and up through the bell tower. It looked like the whole building was thumping along with the music. I thought nobody would notice if I just peeked my head in and stood in the back. I just wanted to listen for a while. I opened the door, and the sound almost knocked what little hair I got off my head."

Mr. Craig's eyes were beginning to light up right in front of us. As he went on with his story, it was as if he'd been transported in time, back to his carefree youth, exploring the nation with an open heart. I looked around at all the guys in the room, and everyone was locked in on the old man. Nobody made a joke or a sarcastic comment. We were all right there with him, in that dusty Eastern Shore town in Maryland on a hot summer day, listening to the music.

"It was a Black church," Mr. Craig continued.

I realized quickly that I was the only white face in the room. Everyone looked like they'd been at it for hours, singing and dancing. The walls were wet with condensation from all the bodies in there. I'd never seen anything like it.

Just when I thought I'd be on my way, someone grabbed me by the wrist and brought me into a pew. It was a little old lady, and I wasn't gonna tell her no. So I spent the rest of the service singing along as best I could next to this little old gal in a bright red dress with a big fancy hat on. After about an hour or so, the service was over and everyone started making their way to the exit out the front. I shook the lady's hand and thanked her for bringing me in. I thought I'd be on my way, but as I walked out the front of the church, I'd seen that they'd set up a huge Sunday feast in the parking lot. They had oysters, turkeys, and all kinda stuff. Now, if there is one thing I love more than music, it's oysters. My old-lady friend must have seen the drool coming out of my mouth, because she grabbed my hand again and said to me, "You'll stay for supper now," and she led me over to the table. I sat down and ate while she brought me plate after plate of oysters and corn on the cob, and every time I tried to politely excuse myself, she'd bring me another pile of them oysters.

I'd never seen hospitality like that in all my life. She introduced me to all her grandkids and nephews and family members. Everyone was so kind, and I thought maybe I'd just pop the tires on my car and stay forever.

When things started to wrap up and everyone was heading home, I helped clean up and carry the tables back into the church. I thanked the old lady. All she said was, "God's blessings to you on your journey."

I climbed in my old car and made my way outta town with a belly full of oysters. I couldn't listen to the radio for a while because the music I'd heard in that old town was still ringing in my ears.

A day or so later, I made my way to Florida. Just as I crossed into the state—musta been north of Jacksonville somewhere—I come upon a wreck. There were two cars off the road. One of them had rolled at least once, because it was resting on its side, and the other was smashed up pretty good in the front. A white man sat on the hood holding a bloody rag to his head where he had a good little gash, probably from hitting it on the steering wheel. It must have just happened, because the next thing I heard was someone calling for help from the other car that was down in the ditch laying on its passenger side. The back wheel that was up in the air was still spinning a little bit, and dust hung in the air. The guy on the hood just looked at me and shrugged. He didn't say nothin' or even move a muscle. I took off down into the ditch and found two Black men in the other car. One of them was passed out, laying on the other. They were both cut up real bad on their faces. I knew I had to get them out, so I kicked in the back window of the old car—it was already busted up and cracked, so it caved right in. Then the guy who was conscious crawled out, and I went in and dragged his buddy out. I had a canteen in my car and my first-aid kit from when I'd gotten some medic training in the army. I kept it where my spare tire was. I ran up to get it, and as I did, a Florida state trooper pulled up. I said, "I've got two guys down here. One is unconscious, but he's breathing. Let's get an ambulance here quick." What he said next is something I'll never forget: "Leave the niggers be. They take care of themselves."

"I stood in the road in disbelief. I could hear an ambulance coming in the distance, but I knew it was coming for the white man, even though the cut on his head had already stopped bleeding. I needed to figure out how to help the two guys down in the ditch, 'cause nobody else was gonna," he said, his voice now taking on a frustrated tone.

I got down in there with my first-aid kit. The guy who was passed out had come to and was talking to his buddy. I put pressure on their cuts and cleaned 'em out as best I could. Looked like the driver had a busted ankle, too. I could tell by the way his shoe was twisted unnaturally, just laying there in the dirt. I gave them both some water and held a blanket over them to keep the sun off 'em. None of us spoke as we watched the ambulance come and take the white man away.

He walked right in the back of it under his own power. The trooper looked down in the ditch at us and just shook his head before he climbed in his cruiser and drove off. A few minutes later, a black hearse showed up for the other guys. Two young Black men came out and helped me carry them up the hill and lay them in the back where the caskets usually go. I was so mad I couldn't say much other than, "You'll be all right, you just keep them cuts clean," as I shut the door on the two boys and watched the hearse roll away.

"It broke my heart," Mr. Craig said, winding up his story. "I'll never know what happened to them two boys. I'd be surprised if the one with the busted ankle kept his foot after that. It was mangled pretty bad."

Old Mr. Craig, who was known for falling asleep and waking himself up with his own snoring, had been reanimated before our eyes. He'd found emotion and pitch in his voice and expression in his face that he clearly hadn't used in a long time.

"That is an incredible story, Mr. Craig," I told him. "Thank you for sharing that with us."

I could only hope that he would find the energy to share more with the group as the weeks went on.

We talked for a little while about race in our country. Most of the guys were from Maine and the New England area, so they hadn't grown up with a lot of diversity. When I asked the group if they thought racism was still a problem in our country, Calli didn't hesitate. "Absolutely. It's just not as clear. It's baked into a lot of our society."

After a little while, I asked if anyone else wanted to share stories of car crashes. Nate went next, reading from his notebook. He told a story about his older brother pulling him out of a car at the end of a drunken party and feeling like he was going to miss out as his three friends drove off without him. When the car got into a wreck later that night, only one of his friends made it out alive. Calli told another story about a teenage car crash, one that left two of his friends seriously injured. He'd escaped a similar fate only because he'd fallen asleep at home after working all day in his family's lumberyard, a job he hated but one that ultimately saved him.

As I listened to the men's stories, I was struck by something. This was our first meeting, and they could easily have taken the easy way out, focusing on the physical aspect of the events they described. In fact, I'd planned to use what I assumed would be superficial first attempts at storytelling as examples of missed opportunities to examine the more emotional details about their stories. But every one of them had dug deep and shared something that went far beyond twisted metal and shattered glass. Using the kind of compelling details that are the hallmark of good writing, they had reflected on pivotal moments in their lives, even if they didn't realize until years later that those moments were so crucial. If they were faking interest in the class, then they were doing a very good job. I was convinced.

It was clear to me that they had a lot more to share and that my main job was going to be to listen. I looked at the clock. It was time to wrap up. I thanked the guys and reminded them of our subject for next week: "dogs." The men stood and stretched, refilling their coffee cups one last time and grabbing some powdered creamers from the table.

I felt relieved that the first session was over and that it had gone well. Despite my concerns that we'd run out of things to say, I'd been with them three hours and the time had gone by in a flash. It was as if as soon as we'd started the session, we'd entered another dimension, outside the prison. As a group the guys seemed calmer than when I'd walked into the room. They'd all shared something they clearly hadn't talked about in depth before, and I could sense a collective weight lifting off their shoulders.

As soon as the door to the classroom opened, BOOM, the noise and reality of the prison environment beyond came surging back. We said our good-byes, and then Fred and I made our way out of the pod and down The Mile, escorted by a guard. The sun was setting, and its rays cast a warm glow over the yard. On the end of his leash, Fred sniffed the sweet air, taking in the smell of the blossoming vegetable gardens and flower beds that fill the open spaces between the different housing units, awaiting the warm summer weather that was just a few weeks away.

As I climbed into the truck, I called Nora to tell her we were coming home.

"What do you want to do for dinner?" she asked lovingly.

"Oysters and corn on the cob," I replied with a smile as I pointed the truck south, Fred at my side.

CHAPTER 6

Pound Puppies

The following Tuesday dawned cold and rainy. At just past 5:00 A.M., I slipped out the door to head back to Maine State Prison. Fred barely lifted his head from his warm dog bed as I left. He wasn't in a rush to jump back into the truck, and even if he'd wanted to, I couldn't have brought him along. That morning there was going to be a very special delivery at the prison: three new Labrador pups. I wanted to be there for the puppies' first moments with the men and to see how the dogs responded to life on the inside, but if I took Fred with me, he would only cause problems. These VIPs (Very Important Pups) were too young to be exposed to other dogs.

By the time I was leaving to make the drive to Maine State, a van with the puppies and training supplies inside had already departed the America's VetDogs headquarters on Long Island, making its way north through the night. No one was sure exactly what time they would arrive, so I'd arranged to meet Paula, the prison program coordinator for America's VetDogs, and Rebecca, the new staff trainer who was going to be leading the training at Maine State going forward, at a coffee shop in Thomaston, a little town just down Route 1 from the prison. As I walked in, I spotted the two women sitting at a small table sipping hot coffee, their matching black raincoats with the America's VetDogs logo embroidered on them draped over their chairs. I'd met Paula before at the event when Chess had graduated from the puppy program and was immediately impressed by her calm but assertive nature, but this was my first time meeting Rebecca, a quiet but confident twenty-something.

While we waited to get the phone call that the puppies were about to arrive, the three of us chatted about dogs, Maine, and the weather.

It turned out that Rebecca had grown up around dogs—her family runs a boarding and dog-training business.

"I've worked with dogs my entire life," she explained. "The only time I haven't been around dogs every day was during my two years in the army."

As an army veteran, Rebecca had been drawn to the program for the opportunity to help her fellow former service members.

Soon enough Paula got a call on her cell. After exchanging a few quick words to the person on the other end, she hung up.

"It's puppy time!" she told us.

We all took a last sip of our coffees, put on our coats, jumped into our vehicles, and convoyed the short drive to the prison. I followed along behind Paula's van, which had an image of a black Lab in a service vest on the rear hatch and the words LIVE WITHOUT BOUNDARIES inscribed across the bottom.

At the prison I parked my truck next to Paula and helped her carry in some bags of puppy food and a collapsible wire gate she was going to set up so that the puppies could stretch their legs after the long ride. Rebecca met us on the sidewalk, just outside the front doors. She took the awkward wire gate from me and had it assembled in seconds.

"They should be here any minute," Paula said as we all looked up to the sky hoping that the rain would hold off a little longer.

Mike Fournier and Jason Palmer, the two staff members in charge of the puppy program, ran out in raincoats to help just as the first drops began to fall. At that same moment, a van wrapped in America's VetDogs logos turned the corner.

The puppies were almost here. . . .

The driver pulled the van right up to the curb, and two volunteers jumped out. They were both retirees from New York who had chosen to spend their golden years driving dogs around for America's VetDogs. One of them, an older man named Ed, made a joke about being a doggie Uber driver. Meanwhile Paula opened the back doors of the van. Three little puppies spilled out onto the pavement.

First there was LJ, a big yellow pup with paws the size of tangerines. Then came Webber, a chunky black puppy who needed to pee. The smallest was Sayville, a black female who was all business. She marched right over to Rebecca and started playing with her shoelaces. Paula scooped up LJ and Sayville, while I corralled Webber after he'd relieved himself in the grass. We placed the pups in the wire pen so they wouldn't wander off while we unloaded their "luggage." The volunteers had brought the puppies' first months' worth of supplies with them: food, toys, kennels, and some training toys.

LJ watched intently as Fournier carried in an armload of puppy chow.

"This big guy's eyeballin' me," he joked.

The rain was picking up now, and we needed to hustle. Rebecca, Palmer, and I each picked up a puppy, and we headed into the lobby, where the bags of food and other supplies were being fed through the X-ray scanner.

As we shuffled into the sally port and the heavy door slid shut behind us, the reality of what was happening hit me. Despite the fact that Maine State has amazing programs and a progressive approach to corrections, it's still a maximum-security prison. Meanwhile these puppies were adorable, goofy, and innocent. You couldn't take your eyes off them; they were so cute it made your heart hurt. Walking The Mile carrying a squirming, jiggly puppy felt like tossing a marshmallow into a bowl of hot chili. Was it fair to the puppies to bring them into such an unforgiving environment?

We made our way to the Veterans' Pod. The inmate trainers were waiting in the outdoor recreational area, a half-basketball-court-size concrete slab with matching windowless walls, to meet their new students. They were a group of six tough-looking men with tattoos and stern expressions fixed on their faces, one primary trainer and one secondary trainer per puppy. I recognized Nate Nightingale from the writing group and my past visits, but the others were either new to the program or returning after graduating other dogs. To say they were an intimidating bunch would be an understatement.

But as soon as the men saw the puppies, it was as if they melted. They shrank down at the shoulders, lowering their heads and speaking in different versions of what can only be described as baby talk.

"Good boy, good girl," I heard their singsong voices chime, sounding totally out of place in a prison.

Rebecca, Palmer, and I placed the puppies down on the concrete and let them run around the yard. The idea was for the men to observe the different personalities of each dog and for the puppies to have a chance to pick their trainer.

As the little dogs frolicked, each of the men seemed completely focused on them, whispering to one another about little behaviors they'd observed. They took note of how assertively Sayville walked, with her head up, ears forward. She seemed like the wild card of the group, pacing around the rec yard looking back at us to see if we were watching. The men were also paying attention to the dogs' deportment: Did they stick together, did they wander off, how did they interact with their environment?

While most people would have lost total self-control around three wobbly puppies, for these men the training process had already begun.

LJ hopped and trotted his way over to Nate, launching an assault on his bootlaces. I'd gotten to know Nate as a fairly unassuming guy, but watching from a distance gave me a new appreciation for who he was and his dedication to the dog program. He patiently observed LJ as the puppy fumbled with his laces, clearly enjoying the moment.

"I'll take this one, I'm looking for a good challenge this time around," Nate joked, looking down at the yellow puppy who was already tangled up in the brown laces of his Timberlands.

Webber made a beeline for one of the other trainers, Charlie. I'd seen Charlie only a few times around the Veterans' Pod. He was a fresh-faced man in his late twenties, with thinning dark hair and a narrow frame. It was his first time as a primary trainer. Prior to this he'd been a secondary trainer or "understudy," under the instruction of Kidd and Nate. Charlie sat down cross-legged on the concrete so that the sleepy pup could cuddle up in his lap. It was the first time Webber had been still since he'd darted out of the van.

Sayville had found a dried-up worm and was trying to eat it, but Cory, another one of the trainers, was one step ahead of her and put his boot over the tempting snack before she could peel it from the concrete. Cory's skinny but strong build and shaved head made him look like he was still in the military. He had full sleeve tattoos on his arms and a sadness in his eyes that made me wonder how he'd gotten here. He squatted down to Sayville, playfully batting her around. Once he'd gotten her attention, it was clear that the bond between them was starting to form. Paula had noticed this.

"She's looking up at you. That's good," she told Cory. "Make sure you say her name whenever she looks at you. It's never too early to work on name recognition."

"Say-ville, Say-ville," Cory repeated in a high-pitched, excited tone that was completely at odds with his tough-guy exterior.

As well as primary trainers Nate, Cory, and Charlie, there were the three secondary trainers who were learning from the primaries and who could fill in if one of them was unavailable. They stood watching and closely observing as the puppies and trainers were paired up.

By now the three puppies had completely transformed the energy within the rec yard. The men were smiling like proud new parents, showering the pups with attention. It occurred to me that my concerns about the puppies living here for the next fifteen to eighteen months were a result of my own preconceptions about prison being an unpleasant environment. For these puppies Maine State was a kind of paradise. They craved attention, and now they had a team of dedicated trainers completely committed to their well-being. It didn't matter to them that these trainers were convicted criminals. It only mattered that the men were showering them with love and care.

All of a sudden, Nate let out a high-pitched yelp that would have drawn laughter and name-calling in any other part of the prison. LJ had just nipped him slightly with his little puppy teeth. Nate was letting him know that it was *not* okay by disengaging with the puppy, pulling himself away, and holding his hands up.

"Everyone look at what Nate just did," Paula pointed out. "We never tell a dog no. We only offer positive reinforcement. Notice Nate didn't scold LJ. He wanted to make it clear he was in control, but he did it in a loving way. That's how you build a bond built on loyalty and not fear."

I was reminded the men weren't here to play with the dogs.

They were charged with molding them into highly trained service animals that would go on to change the lives of other veterans and their families.

"Good job, Nate," Paula said. "They're going to want to play with you like they would other puppies, but we need to break that habit right away."

It was clear to me that I would not make a good dog trainer. I didn't have the patience to enforce even the most basic obedience behaviors in Fred. I was just happy that he'd sit for me if I asked him really nicely and that he came back to me—eventually— when I called him.

After a few hours observing the men and getting them settled in for their first night with the puppies, we said good-bye.

The next day I was due back at Maine State for our weekly writing class, but I asked Randy if it would be okay for me to arrive a little earlier so I could observe the puppies during their first training class. How would the guys respond to suddenly having a dog in their cells and in their lives? Would they be like new parents after their first night with a baby, stressed and sleep-deprived, overwhelmed with the responsibility they'd just taken on? Or would the presence of such a joyful little creature in their lives help them relax?

Jason Palmer was waiting for me in the lobby, and he took me back to the Veterans' Pod. Paula and Rebecca had already arrived and were waiting in the classroom, chatting near the front while Mike Fournier wiped down the whiteboard with a paper towel, removing notes taken during what must have been a math class held in the same room the day before. I helped place chairs around the perimeter of the classroom for the men. Then I took a seat at the small table in the corner near the door, listening in as Paula and Rebecca went over some final thoughts on their goals for the morning.

"The men should all be taking notes," Paula pointed out, "especially the secondary trainers. We're going to be throwing a lot of information at them, and they need to show that they're paying attention."

"The most important thing we want to see from them is initiative," she continued. "They should be asking questions and genuinely interested in this process. We don't want anyone involved that isn't in it a hundred percent. These puppies are too important to waste on trainers who aren't invested. It's never been a problem here before, but we've got some new trainers in this group, so we need to stay on top of them."

As Paula finished her pre-class pep talk, the men began parading in with their puppies at their heels. LJ was first in the door. I noticed right away that his eyes kept darting from straight ahead up to his trainer, Nate. The way LJ looked at Nate made me smile, reminding me of the first time Fred and I interacted with each other in Sangin, Afghanistan, when he followed me back to my gear after I gave him a fateful piece of jerky. Fred was constantly looking up at me then and still does to this day.

The other two pups weren't quite as focused—they were still going to have to learn the importance of gazing up at their handler, looking to the men for guidance and approval. After they entered the room, the trainers sat down on the floor with the puppies between their legs and the secondary trainers sat in the chairs against the wall, notepads at the ready. The room resembled a Mommy and Me class with toddlers and new mothers—just replace the mothers in this situation with inmates, the toddlers with dopey puppies, and change the location to a classroom with doors that lock from the outside.

Michael Kidd came in just before class began. After deciding not to take on training another puppy following his experiences with Chess and Emma, he'd voluntarily taken a role within the training team as a sort of adviser or teacher-trainer. His expertise and experience were an asset that he happily applied to the group. Next to me at the table, Calli settled in and opened up his laptop. His role was as the note-taker and record-keeper for the dog program, logging the puppies' progress, and jotting down any special instructions Paula or Rebecca had for the trainers.

To begin, Paula reminded the men that Rebecca was soon to be Maine State Prison's new full-time trainer.

"She's going to be here every week, and I want you guys to treat her the same way you treat me," Paula said firmly. It was clear that the men had a lot of respect for Paula, and she wanted to ensure it transferred over to Rebecca. Paula explained she couldn't continue to make the drive from Massachusetts every week to check on the dogs' progress. She was responsible for twelve other programs in prisons all over the East Coast, as far south as Florida. Rebecca was going to take over.

Next Paula asked the men about their first night with the puppies.

"Let's go around and everyone tell me briefly the highs and lows."

Cory, who was paired with the only female in the class, Sayville, went first.

"She's a problem solver, I can tell already," he said somewhat helplessly. "Anytime I try to redirect her from something she's not supposed to be doing, she tries to find a way back to it. She might be too smart for her own good."

Rebecca explained that independence in a dog can be a good thing *and* a bad thing.

"When a dog has a mind of her own, she can buck some of the skills you're trying to teach her because she wants to do it in her own way," Rebecca pointed out. "But on the upside, she's going to be very receptive to training. You'll just have to be consistent, because she'll take advantage of any gaps you give her."

Cory described how the puppy hadn't wanted to go into her kennel after the men were locked in for the night. He'd been trying to get her to go in on her own, but every time he opened the gate on the kennel, she would walk over and paw it shut.

"It was hard not to laugh! She would shut the gate and then just look up at me like, *What you gonna do about it?*" Cory said with an exhausted smile and a shrug. "The only way I could get her to go in finally was to lift her up and put her in. She didn't fight me, but she didn't lay down right away·either. She stood there and watched me brush my teeth and wash my face."

"That's good!" Paula pointed out. "You're all establishing a routine. They need to see how they fit into it. They're observing you just as much as you're observing them. It's why this time is so important for their mental development."

"Once I was in bed, she laid down and only let out a little whine," Cory explained. "It broke my heart, but I knew she was tired and would fall asleep quickly. She woke me up around two A.M. to go out to the bathroom, and that was it for the night."

"Sounds like you're off to a good start, Cory," Paula said encouragingly. "Just remember to keep working on that routine. She's a smart one, and she'll look for opportunities to challenge you, but if you stay true to your routine, it'll make things much easier down the road."

Next up was Webber and his trainer, Charlie. Webber sat between Charlie's legs looking around the room and then back at Charlie. His black coat matched Sayville's, but his chunky body and oversize paws made him look like a caricature of a Labrador.

"How was Webber's first night?" Paula asked with a smile.

"He was really playful after lock-in," Charlie described. "I tried to resist playing with him, but he kept attacking my feet and pawing at me while I was getting ready for bed. I eventually sat on the floor with him and playfully smacked him around a little while working on some name recognition. He just wanted some attention. After that I put him in his kennel, and he was asleep before I was."

As he spoke, Charlie looked down at Webber, who was currently snoozing, his big head resting on his huge paws.

"No accidents in the room?" Paula asked, sounding impressed.

"No, he woke me up around three to go potty outside, and then it was right back to bed," Charlie reported happily.

"That is great," Paula replied. "My only note is to be cautious about too much play after lock-in. That's your time to really demonstrate your role as a leader and to let Webber see that everything revolves around your routine, not his."

Next up were Nate and LJ. The day before, when we'd brought the puppies in, Nate had been immediately attracted to LJ. He had the most energy out of the three and seemed to be the biggest challenge, but that was exactly what Nate was looking for.

"He took a leak on the floor right when we got into my room," Nate said, immediately correcting himself in front of Paula. "Excuse me, he *relieved* himself. And he kept grabbing onto my shorts when I was getting dressed. He tried to tie my shoes together when I was taking them off. Once I got him to settle down, I put him in his kennel, but he started to whine. I could tell he was tired, so I just put a sheet over the top of the kennel."

"That's good," Paula said. "It's a smart way to decrease their stimulation."

The rest of Nate's night was uneventful. LJ woke him up to go potty in the rec area, and then it was back to sleep.

Paula spent the rest of the class going around the room quizzing the men.

"Why is it important that they go to the bathroom in the same place?" she asked the group.

"So they understand the command and associate it with one place first, and then we can begin to branch out to different areas," Cory answered correctly.

"What is recall, and how do we teach it?" Paula asked next. When nobody responded fast enough, Michael Kidd jumped in. He was taking notes and observing the new puppies, preparing for his role as a trainer of trainers.

"Recall is getting the dog to listen and come to you while off or on leash. It's especially important when there are distractions around," Kidd explained. "That's why we teach it using the lure method."

This got a sarcastic eye roll from Nate and the other trainers. Everyone had Kidd's number as the teacher's pet who always knew all the answers.

"Recall is what we'll be working on once they've got their name recognition down," Paula reinforced. "It's the first command we'll be giving them, but it won't work if they don't know their name."

Paula then explained that next week they would be working on the lure method, where the trainer uses a treat to motivate the puppies to perform specific behaviors. "It's how we'll lay the foundation of your relationship with them," she said as she began packing up her things. "They'll start to understand their role through being rewarded for certain behavior."

The class over, the men shuffled out, furry bundles at their sides. Paula and Kidd stayed behind for the next class of the day, with one of the older dogs in the program, Captain.

At that moment the handsome yellow Lab Captain and his trainer, Sean, walked into the classroom. Captain was sixteen months older than the puppies and about to graduate from the program in June. Sean was a dark-haired man in his mid-thirties. He and Kidd were roommates, and the two shared a brotherly bond.

Over the next hour, Sean and Captain put on an incredible display of the skills they'd learned together. The first thing they demonstrated for Paula was "bring." Sean sat in a chair with his back to Captain, who was off leash. A one-pound dumbbell sat on a table on the other side of the room.

"Bring," said Sean in a firm but steady voice.

Captain turned and trotted quickly but calmly to the table, tilted his head to the side as he reached for the dumbbell before gently grasping it with his teeth. Then he carried the dumbbell over to Sean, standing in front of him waiting for his next command. Sean reached up and grabbed the weight, saying, "Give," in the same steady voice. Captain released the weight and took his place next to his trainer.

I wanted to stand and clap right there! It was amazing to see man and dog working together closely and seamlessly. The dog owner in me was blown away.

Paula, however, had been watching closely like a judge at the Olympics, and she had some critiques.

"That was great, Sean, but you still have a lot of kinks to work out," she said.

I did my best to restrain myself from laughing in disbelief. How could Sean possibly improve on that? Captain was just over a year old. When Fred was that young, the most I could hope for was for him to sit still for more than thirty seconds, let alone bring me anything.

"He's still adjusting the weight in his mouth when he grabs it," Paula pointed out. "If that were a bottle of pills, it could pop open, and then you've got a big problem. When he brings it to you, you can't always have him hand it to you in the same place or way. You need to teach him to bring it to both of your hands and also to place it in your lap. What if he ends up with someone with no hands? Or someone in a wheelchair with limited mobility or dexterity?"

As she explained, Sean took notes in his own training logbook.

The rest of the class was more of a display of Captain's discipline and skills. At one point Paula placed a small toy bug on the floor that buzzed and vibrated. Sean walked him around the bug and even right over top of it, off leash the entire time, and the young yellow Lab never so much as glanced at the noisy distraction. They moved together like ballroom-dance partners gliding through a crowded subway station.

Next up Sean started using a clunky metal walker most commonly seen in hospitals to help post-op patients move around as they recover. Despite the new barrier around his handler's bottom half, Captain remained by his side as Sean made his way around the room. I laughed to myself as I noticed the tennis balls that were jammed onto the bottoms of the walker's legs. I knew that Fred and Ruby wouldn't be able to resist gnawing at them, that's for sure. Especially Ruby, who I'd seen sniff out an old, rotting tennis ball in our backyard that had clearly been there since long before we'd moved in.

Paula's only note was when Sean instructed Captain to follow between his legs as he proceeded with the walker.

"I appreciate your extra effort, but there is a reason we don't train them to walk between handler's legs," she pointed out. "A lot of our veterans have balance issues."

Although Paula explained that it was useful for the dogs to

lie between their handlers' legs when they're waiting in line, rid-
ing on a train, or anytime they need a little extra reassurance
that their dog is with them, it wasn't going to work in this situation. Sean had just taken a little liberty with the technique
and trained Captain to walk between his legs, but Paula had to
put a stop to it and remind him to stick to the script, and Sean
completely understood why.

Paula had one last note before finishing up.

"And remember, he's still a dog, and he needs to be reminded
of that as often as possible. He needs to be a playmate *and* a
service provider."

"Ya, he loves to play, but he seems to get most excited when
we start our training," said Sean, looking down at Captain with
a smile. "He's a real pleaser."

Then Paula gave the pair a final pep talk. This was likely the
last time she'd see them before the graduation ceremony in June.

"You've done an incredible job with him," she told Sean. "I
can see that someone has rubbed off on you."

Then she nodded toward Kidd, who was trying to hide the
satisfied grin on his face.

"This was all Sean," Kidd interjected quickly. But it was clear
that the pair had worked together on Captain. The two friends
had been roommates for years, and even before they began training dogs, they'd held each other to a higher standard through
Bible study and college courses. Together they were an example
of what healthy friendships can do.

"Well, whatever you're doing, keep it up, and Captain will go
on to do incredible things for a veteran and their family," Paula
said. "Just make sure to enjoy your time together over the next
few weeks."

"Yes, ma'am," said Sean.

It was time for my lunch break. I made a mental note to ask

Sean how he was feeling about saying good-bye to Captain when I got back. But when I returned to the pod, I spotted Sean in the dayroom playing fetch with Captain, clearly taking Paula's advice to work playtime into their training schedule. I observed the two of them for a moment, just a guy and his dog playing fetch—in a maximum-security prison. It was time for the writing group, and I didn't want to keep the other guys waiting. I elected to leave Sean alone for the moment. If he wanted to come in and share anything with the group, he knew where we'd be, but I didn't want to interrupt this simple but important time he had with Captain.

A week later I was back at the prison. My writing class was in the afternoon, and Paula had said it was okay for me to observe the puppies again in the morning. As the guys assembled with their dogs at their feet, Paula emptied out the contents of her bag on a table at the front of the room near the whiteboard. It contained a small stuffed Chihuahua she'd named Toto, standing erect with a mischievous look on its face.

Paula went around the room and asked all of the men how their first week was with their puppies. Aside from LJ wanting to cuddle with Nate in his bunk and Sayville trying to escape from her kennel, the dogs had all behaved about as well as anyone would expect ten-week-old Labradors to in any environment.

I smiled to myself again, thinking about the degree of discipline required for a person to hold himself back from cuddling a little yellow ball of fur whimpering at the foot of his bed.

"You're starting to establish a schedule," Paula reinforced. "It's important that they know you're the source for everything they need. Their daily routine revolves around you. The more structure you can provide for these puppies, the stronger their bond will be with you and the better you'll be able to train them."

She began to list things on the billboard. In big letters she wrote, "ESTABLISH THE RELATIONSHIP THROUGH ROUTINE AND REPETITION."

Then she placed the small battery-powered toy Chihuahua on the floor in the middle of the room. The puppies all sat on their haunches, observing the little toy with curious faces.

"We'll start with some name-recognition exercises," Paula instructed. "Nate, walk LJ around the room, and every time he looks at the toy on the floor, say his name, and if he looks at you, reward him with a treat."

Nate and LJ began to make their way around the small toy that was now yipping and wiggling around in circles. After every third yip, the toy dog did a tight backflip, landing on all fours. It was more than enough to distract the grown-ups in the room, let alone three excitable puppies. Even so, LJ barely took his eyes off Nate, only glancing at the toy when it yipped loudly. As soon as Nate saw LJ looking in his direction, he used his puppy-praise voice—"Good boy, LJ"—with a big smile, handing the dog a small treat from the pouch on his hip.

Next up were Sayville and Cory. While LJ and Nate were walking around the room, Sayville had been transfixed by the Chihuahua. This was going to be interesting.

"Okay, Cory, remember, this is about name recognition, not just distraction avoidance," Paula explained encouragingly.

Cory was going to need all the encouragement he could get. As soon as he gave his little black puppy the tiniest bit of slack in her leash, she lunged for the Chihuahua like a hound going after a rabbit.

"It's okay, it's okay," Paula said quickly. "This is just an opportunity to practice your positive-reinforcement tactics with her."

Cory did his best to listen to Paula, but I could see the intense sting of failure in his eyes. LJ and Nate had set the bar pretty high. Although LJ's personality was clearly very different from scrappy little Sayville's, Cory still wanted to get off on the right foot with his dog. This was his first time as a primary trainer, and he was taking it very seriously.

Cory held his ground as Sayville tried to pull on the leash, desperate to get to the yipping toy. When she finally looked up at her trainer, he gave her a high-pitched "Good girl!" and offered up a treat.

The entire room watched in suspense to see if she would catch on. After a few moments spent looking back at the mechanical dog and then again at Cory, Sayville bounded back toward her trainer, accepting the treat gracefully. Next Cory tried to get his puppy to take a walk around the room, but Sayville immediately made another attempt to pounce on the Chihuahua. It took almost fifteen minutes, but finally the two made a full circle of the toy, moving only a few feet from where they'd started but covering some important ground in their journey together. Throughout this process Cory had been patient and professional. He understood that each step was a leap in the right direction for Sayville and her training in the months to come. I was incredibly impressed.

As they finished their lap, I glanced up to see a crowd of inmates and staff gathering in the hallway, peering in through the windows of the classroom. Everyone was smiling broadly and pointing happily at the little balls of fur, like grandparents and aunts and uncles visiting a maternity ward in a hospital. The puppies' effect on the culture within the prison was obvious. With a magical wag of the tail, the dogs had transformed a maximum-security prison into a place where people were cooing and smiling from ear to ear. It was impossible to feel depressed or down when faced with a room filled with adorable puppies, and the prison around us just melted away.

Meanwhile as LJ and Sayville put on a show, Webber was snoring on his back between the legs of Charlie, his trainer.

Paula smiled as she looked at the two sitting together on the floor.

"It's my fault," Charlie admitted sheepishly. "I had him up early this morning, because I had to work in the kitchen and I wanted to get him out for his potty break before I left for my shift."

Charlie seemed genuinely afraid of Paula's disapproval.

"That's okay!" Paula responded. "You're starting to establish a schedule with your dogs. That's important. I think he's a good candidate for me to try to demonstrate the lure method with, if you don't mind."

Webber woke up slowly, shaking his big head around as he got up onto his feet.

"The lure method is great to get the dog motivated to move with you or to you, but it's only as good as you make it," Paula explained, taking Webber's leash. "You need to make sure you're making it clear where you want them and how you need them to stand."

The dopey black puppy sprang to life, reanimated at the sight of the Chihuahua and the prospect of a treat. He performed well for Paula, only halfheartedly lunging for the toy dog once or twice.

"You're all doing great so far, but this is just the beginning," Paula told the class as she packed up Toto. "You'll need to continue to create good habits in your training and a solid routine. That is how we take the dog's natural tendencies to be a companion and harness them into methods and skills that change people's lives."

It was time to send the men back to their cellblock, armed with more experience and knowledge, ready to take on the next week's challenges.

CHAPTER 7

Dogs

After the class was over, I took the opportunity to catch up with Kidd. I hadn't had a chance to ask him yet about how he was doing since taking on his new role as "trainer of the trainers."

"Is it hard seeing the guys with these new dogs and not having one of your own?" I asked him plainly.

Kidd took a deep breath and leaned back against the wall in his chair, trying to find the words.

"It's okay," Kidd explained. "Saying good-bye to Emma was tough."

Emma was Kidd's second dog—Paula had brought her from Connecticut so she could finish her training with Kidd.

"You know it going in that you're gonna have to say good-bye at some point, but the work demands a bond that requires you to forget the fact that your relationship is temporary," Kidd went on. "That is what I told these new guys early on when they said they wanted to get into the program. I knew they'd be great at it, but I wanted them to know what it took."

"You did a beautiful job with Emma," Paula noted.

"She was such a sweet girl," Kidd said reflectively. "Saying good-bye to her was actually harder than Chess, though."

"Really? But you only had her for a few months, right?" I asked.

"I got attached to her really quickly," Kidd explained of his time with Emma. "She had a lot of similarities to Chess, and just as our bond was at its peak, she graduated. I didn't have time to prepare myself to say good-bye like I'd had with Chess. It was her sudden absence that hit me harder."

I could only imagine how difficult it must have been for Kidd, integrating Emma into his routine and life, only for her to leave him. My instincts told me to try to ease his pain a bit with some praise.

"Maybe it was because you brought her into your life so completely that you were able to give her the training she needed?"

"I'd say that is definitely the case," Paula added, nodding in Kidd's direction. "Emma needed someone to really bond with in order to break her bad habits. She was just so high-spirited and easily distracted. The only way she was going to get over that was if someone really committed to her, and that is exactly what you did."

"Ya, maybe." Kidd shrugged. "Either way, she was my last. I'm happy to help in the classroom and in the pod, but I can't put myself through it again. Plus, I've gotta focus on school."

"I appreciate that," Paula said, putting a hand on Kidd's shoulder. "You're gonna be a big help to the guys and the dogs. Thank you for sticking around."

"No problem, I'm happy to do what I can," Kidd replied.

Then it was time for us to go our separate ways, Kidd to his prison-issue lunch and me into town for a sandwich.

By the time I got back, the guys were already gathered in the classroom.

"Every day is a challenge in here," Kidd was saying to the group as I settled into my seat.

This week's writing assignment was on dogs, but I didn't want to interrupt the guys who were clearly in the flow of a conversation. Our group was insulated from the rest of the prison.

If our time gave them a chance to vent about the challenges they faced on the inside, so be it.

"What's up, guys?" I asked, sensing that the men could use a few minutes for themselves.

"They tossed our cells," Nate told me from the end of the table.

"They said it was random, but it was only the guys in the dog program," Calli said with a shrug.

"There are days when just being in the dog program makes us a target for both guards and other inmates," Nate explained, clearly frustrated.

I asked why, sensing they wanted to get some things off their chest.

"They just like to send us a message every once in a while," Kidd said.

"It's all because we went above their heads to the warden, but they didn't leave us with any other choice. The guys on the night shift weren't allowing us to take the puppies out for bathroom breaks at night," Calli went on. "So we wrote a letter to Liberty explaining the situation."

It is an important part of training, especially in their initial weeks together, that the trainers establish some basic rules and patterns for where and when the puppies can relieve themselves. In this case there's a small rec yard adjacent to the dayroom that they're supposed to have access to during the night. It doesn't require any more work from a guard than to click a button on a screen to pop the lock on a cell door to let them out. Unfortunately, as with so many things in prison life, the needs of the men are seen as entitlements, even if they are actually the needs of a ten-pound puppy.

"It's not all the guards, just the ones who seem to think we're privileged," Kidd explained to me.

"If it was up to some of them, all we'd have in here would be beds and blankets," Calli said, adding to the conversation. "We're involved in something that elevates us from the toxic mainstream in here. It's great, but there will always be people who try to drag us back down. The guards are the worst at it, because they can just interpret anything you say or do as a violation."

"What is it about the dogs and this program that has such a profound impact on you guys?" I asked, trying to steer the conversation toward our subject for the week.

"You can't be a part of the normal prison culture when you're in this program," Kidd replied.

"Why not?" I asked.

"Because normal prison culture requires you to assert yourself in a dominant and often aggressive or violent way. When you make the choice to be in this program, you have to say good-bye to that lifestyle," he continued.

"Isn't that hard when you're still in here, though?" I asked.

Now Nate chimed in.

"It gets easier, but we're under constant scrutiny from not just the guards but other inmates, too."

This was the first I'd heard of other inmates having a problem with the dog program.

"What do you mean? Are some of the other guys jealous?" I asked.

"Not really, it's more because there's a chance that our dogs could end up getting paired with a police officer or someone from law enforcement," Nate said.

The guys went on to explain that dealing with the attitudes of guards and other inmates was a part of their struggle to be dog trainers in prison. That having dogs to work with every day meant that they were naturally separated from the influences and social traps of prison culture, which was a good thing, but it also came at a cost. What I learned was that when the men agreed to enter into the dog program, they turned their backs on the traditional blow-for-a-blow, eye-for-an-eye mentality of prison life. They'd made a declaration and a promise to themselves that they would no longer get caught up in that kind of toxic behavior. Instead they dedicated themselves to a more disciplined existence so that they could have the opportunity to work toward training dogs. What happened as a result was that others in the prison had clearly become resentful and began looking for ways to drag them down.

For the next fifteen minutes, the guys traded stories of how they'd been tempted to react with violence or anger by certain members of the guard force and other inmates from different housing units. They shared tips on which guards were more likely to escalate an interaction or look for a reason to write someone up. I offered some questions here and there to keep the conversation going, but mostly kept quiet, listening, hoping to understand their day-to-day lives better.

"Training dogs in here seems like it would be difficult enough," I observed. "I never considered that it would bring more challenges because of people's resentment."

"Yeah, but it's worth it," Nate said, as he refilled Calli's coffee cup, passing it back to him.

"Absolutely," echoed Kidd and Calli at the same time.

"Well, that's fitting," I smiled. "Because today's topic is dogs, and I can certainly say that Fred brought me a lot of anxiety in an already stressful situation, but in the end it was definitely worth it."

In my syllabus I had written the following about our next assignment:

"Share a story about a dog that was or is in your life. Did you have a dog growing up? Think about the details and events that led up to your getting the dog. Were you responsible for it? If so, what were your duties? Do you remember what your days were like before the dog came into your life? How did it affect you? Think about the changes it brought. OR: If you're not a dog person, pick a story about any other relationship you've had with an animal. Did you have a cat or another type of pet? It could also be about the first time you saw a moose or a snake. Who were you with? Where were you? How did it make you feel? Why? What made it significant?"

The reason for choosing the topic of dogs was pretty obvious: All the guys in the program with the exception of Mr. Craig were dog trainers. I figured they would be able to relate to the subject. And as it turned out, everyone had a dog story. We started going around the table, each man sharing funny and sad stories about dogs they'd had growing up.

Kidd shared a heartbreaking story about his dad's dog, Bud.

"The first time I ever saw my dad quiet was when he came home from his first chemotherapy treatment," Kidd read from his laptop, not looking up.

He went on to describe how despite his father's sudden shift in energy and enthusiasm after his chemo, Bud never left his side.

"Bud didn't try to cheer up my dad or get him to act differently," Kidd read aloud. "He knew he was sick and just wanted to be near him. It was the first miracle I'd ever witnessed. Looking back, what I learned from Bud is that it's important to embrace the changes in ourselves and in others, even when we don't understand that change or when it's painful. It became clear to me that dogs love us for who we are at that moment, they aren't resentful or judgmental, and they never ask for more from us than we can give. It's a lesson I've learned again through my work with Chess and Emma."

Kidd explained that he loved his father and had been trying to make sense of his passing his entire life. His father had been the center of his world, and when Kidd was fifteen, his dad was gone. Not knowing how to process the loss, he'd buried the pain deep inside, but it manifested itself in unhealthy ways and no doubt contributed to his reliance on alcohol and drugs later in life. Now, as an adult with a son of his own, he was putting in the work to understand not only his father's death and its impact on him but, more important, his life and how he lived it.

When he was done, Kidd closed up his laptop. It seemed like a simple story: A man gets sick and his dog stays by his side, but the way Kidd revisited it gave us all something to think about. His honesty and vulnerability were inspiring.

The rest of the guys shared their dog stories, some of them more funny than heartbreaking. Nate was only ten years old when his neighbor's dog had puppies.

"I remember walking home from the bus stop and they were out on the lawn in a pen, howling and wrestling with each other," Nate said, reading from his notebook. "When my neighbor asked if I wanted one, I said yes without even thinking about how my mom would react."

He'd hidden the dog from his mom for weeks before she'd discovered the new addition to their family.

"She was such a good dog, but I didn't want to name her because I didn't know how long I could keep her a secret," Nate said, smiling at the memory. "I was saving pieces of food from my lunch and dinner every day and feeding her in my room, only walking her when my mom was at work. She never barked or made any noise—she knew how to hide. After a few weeks, I got a little sloppy. My mom came home from work early and found me playing with the pup in my room. When she saw her, she yelled out, 'Jesum Crow!' and shook her head. So I said,

'Mom, her name is Crow. You just named her, now we have to keep her!' and she just huffed a little and told me to clean up after the dog and not to let it on the furniture. Eventually, though, Crow won my mom over, and after a year it seemed like she was more her dog than mine. I'd come home from school and the two of them would be curled up on the sofa watching TV."

I thought about telling the guys about how, growing up, I'd never had a dog of my own. My friend Julie lived down the street, and she'd had a big black Lab named Jake. He was full of life and mischief, and every time I walked into Julie's house after school, I was greeted by that big ball of love and all the slobber that came with him. When my parents split up and my mom left during my senior year of high school, I found myself taking Jake for walks or just sitting with him in Julie's front yard, where he'd often be tied up, napping in the sun. Oftentimes Julie wouldn't even be home, but her mom would let me hang with Jake. His presence was reassuring and consistent during a time in my life when things seemed to be shaky and uncertain.

It might have been a good moment to tell the guys about Jake, but something held me back. Some part of me still wanted to maintain my role of "teacher"—I felt if I gave too much away, the guys might lose respect for me. Their problems were so much bigger than anything I'd ever experienced, so I didn't want them to think for a second that I was comparing my issues with theirs. This group was supposed to be about them.

When it was time to wrap up, I grabbed one more cup of coffee to help get me home, then said good-bye to the guys and collected my things.

Mike Fournier came to escort me out, but first we stopped in his office. It was the end of the day for him, too. His office looked more like that of a phys-ed teacher at a high school than someone who worked in a prison. There was a scale, a rack of basketballs, and a clipboard with a whistle hanging on the wall next to a cliché motivational poster of some football players huddled together, the word TEAMWORK in big letters underneath it. I knew that Fournier had designed a range of CrossFit workouts where the inmates could compete for the best time among themselves.

I was still reflecting on my conversation with the guys in the classroom, and so I mentioned to Fournier how great the discussion had been.

"That's good to hear, Craig," he told me. "We all have our dog stories. I don't know if the guys told you, but my dog is starting to show signs that her time is coming. She's been sick for a while now."

I'd heard Fournier talk about his beloved dog, Shea, a springer spaniel, in the past, but I didn't know she was sick.

"She's fifteen years old," he continued, "so she's had a good life, but she's been with me through some of my toughest times. To say we're connected is an understatement."

"Oh, man, I'm so sorry to hear that," I said, painfully aware that someday I'll have to face the same situation with Fred. "I can only imagine how hard that must be."

"There's nothing easy about it," Mike told me, "but she's such a good girl I can see that she's doing her best to make it easy on me."

"That's love," I said.

"Ya, she'll leave a big hole in our lives when her time comes," Fournier said, "but you know that going in."

We had reached the first series of doors that led to the outside. We both stood quietly for a few seconds as we waited for the big metal slider to open. As we walked through the freshly mopped hallway, I thought about Mike's impending loss, but also about Kidd and the other trainers, about their relationships with the dogs they'd trained. Each dog in the program represented a positive change in the life of a veteran, and that was an incredible gift. But for the guys at Maine State, training the puppies meant forging an intense bond that would then have to be broken. They knew it going in, and I just hoped the knowledge that they were really making a difference in a veteran's life was enough to make it worthwhile. It was a truly selfless act—that they were prepared to bond with a dog and then sever that bond for the benefit of someone else. It was extraordinary to me.

Dogs teach us a lot of things. But one that we might not appreciate is the ability to love without fear, or despite fear, and that is exceptionally courageous. With that thought I started up my truck and pointed it south, heading home.

CHAPTER 8

Traditions

When I arrived for the next meeting of the writing group, there was a staff shortage that day. So when I got to the Veterans' Pod, I found that the usually bustling dayroom was empty—all the men were still locked in their rooms. Michael Fournier popped Calli's cell door first so he could tell us which doors needed to be opened to let out the rest of the guys in the group. Calli rolled over in his wheelchair and recited the room numbers of each of the guys in our class, Fournier automatically unlocking them from the touch-screen computer behind the desk. A little click could be heard each time a latch was released, and I watched as the guys appeared in their windows, checking their surroundings before leaving their rooms.

Standing at the guards' desk, I could see every one of the guys' cells. Unlike the old-style prisons that had cells arranged in rows and tiers, the Maine State Veterans' Pod is built in the shape of a triangle, allowing one or two guards to maintain a visual on the entire unit from the desk. The layout is safer for the staff and the men alike.

"Oh, and 211, that's our last one," Calli said before heading into the classroom.

I looked up to the second tier of rooms just as a large figure emerged from behind the blue metal door. It was someone who hadn't joined our group before and whom I wasn't expecting to see: Chet.

Chet had been part of the group I'd met with on my first visit to Maine State Prison to talk about my book. I'd chatted with him briefly then and learned he used to be in the navy. But I didn't find out any more about his story until April 2018, when I brought Nora along on my second visit to the prison. Randy was giving us a tour of the Veterans' Pod at the time.

The men were out of their cells. Some were watching the news on the TV in the corner, but most were reading or playing cards at the various tables around the large open space. Nora and I made our way toward the wall of windows where the guys were growing various houseplants.

I spotted Chet from across the room, and when he noticed me, he came toward us, meeting us in the sunlight near a large fern that took up an entire window.

"It's Chet, right?" I asked as we shook hands, his large one engulfing mine like an oven mitt holding a teaspoon.

"That's right. Good to see you again," he said with a smile and a nod.

"This is my girlfriend, Nora," I explained as Chet and Nora shook hands.

"You're the musician, right?" Chet said. He'd read my book and recalled that toward the end I'd mentioned Nora's musical gifts.

"I am," she replied. "I was in a band with my sisters for a long time."

I was impressed that Chet had remembered the book in so much detail but also that he was so considerate of Nora. Bringing my girlfriend to the prison, I initially had been worried that the guys might somehow be disrespectful, shooting her inappropriate glances and making her feel uncomfortable, but that hadn't been the case. It very quickly felt like we were visiting with old friends.

"Are you a musician as well?" Nora asked Chet.

"I'm working on it," Chet said with a nod as he tucked a

strand of his long black hair behind his ear. "I love to write music, but I'm learning the guitar and the drums, too."

As they chatted about music, I got a better look at Chet. He stood at around six-two, with a barnlike frame and tattoos that covered every visible inch of his arms, his long, thin black hair pulled back in a neat ponytail. Despite his massive size, he maintained a gentle and approachable demeanor. Still, I got the feeling that he was capable of spectacular acts of violence if provoked. It was the kind of duality of character I'd only seen in people who'd been in combat, men who'd frequently been placed in life-or-death situations. Chet reminded me of some of my RECON marine friends in this respect. They were calm and cool, like a wildcat resting in a treetop without a care in the world but ready to strike with unmatched precision and overwhelming power if necessary. These guys taught me that the toughest and strongest people don't waste time talking about how tough and strong they are; they demonstrate it in very real ways in unimaginable situations.

As Chet began telling us about his time in the navy, the prison warden, Randy Liberty, walked over, giving Chet a fatherly handshake and a pat on the back.

"How are you, Chet?" he asked earnestly. "Anything you need from me?"

"No, sir, I'm right at home here," Chet said.

"You know, I know this guy's entire family," Randy said, turning to Nora and me, talking about Chet as if he were the other man's proud uncle. "I remember the day he left for the navy. We're glad to have you back home, Chet. I know your time in the feds was beyond brutal, but we've got a lot to offer you here, and I hope you take advantage of it."

"You were in the federal system?" I asked with a certain amount of awe.

"Eight years. I wouldn't recommend it," Chet said, shaking his head. "It's a zoo, man, so different from this place. I'm glad to be out of that environment, but it's gonna take some time for me to adjust."

After Randy left to say hi to another group, Chet explained a little more about how he ended up serving a lengthy sentence. It all dated back to his time in the navy.

"I was on a ship. We were on a three-month float, mostly training exercises from what I remember," he told us. "A few weeks in, my appendix burst and they had to helicopter me back to Norfolk for emergency surgery. When I woke up, they discharged me and gave me a bottle of oxy. I was addicted to it before I got my stitches out."

I could see the shame in his eyes as he told his story. It was heartbreaking.

"Wow, the navy issued you the meds that caused an addiction?" I observed.

"Ya, it was all downhill from there," he said plainly. "Once my prescription expired, I started using other means to get it. It wasn't long before they kicked me out with a bad-conduct discharge."

After Chet was thrown out of the navy for his addiction to oxycodone, the powerful narcotic he was prescribed after his appendix burst, he returned to his hometown a shell of his former self. From then on, his addiction dictated every interaction and decision he made. He'd gone into the military as a kid from a small rural town, wanting to serve his country, and he'd come out a hardhearted addict. After robbing a pharmacy in Vermont and going on a crime spree with two other addicts near his hometown in Maine, Chet was sent to federal prison. Like many people in our federal correctional system, he learned how to be a better criminal while inside. Because of his size and strength, he quickly earned a reputation as an enforcer, assigned to inflict bodily harm on "skinners," the prison label given to anyone who'd been convicted of child molestation or sex crimes committed on minors.

According to Chet, in the federal system the inmates govern the facility and the guards just make sure nobody escapes. I guessed that as a result of, in his words, "putting in work" on "skinners," Chet had probably added years onto his sentence. Not to mention the fact that because of his reputation as a tough guy he was moved around the federal system from facility to facility, and with each move he needed to establish himself again and again.

Chet was an open book. He didn't make any excuses, just told us his story. I wanted to give him a big hug and tell him I understood, that I didn't judge him, that he was worthy of respect and a second chance. Instead I did my best to listen and ask questions. That seemed to be what many of the men needed. A sympathetic ear and an open mind went a long way.

We talked a little more about Chet's love for music. Nora told him a few stories from her time touring the world, playing in a band with her sisters in front of thousands of fans. After Randy announced that our prison tour would be moving on in five minutes, we wrapped up the conversation.

The next time I visited, about a month later, I was on the lookout for Chet, but he was nowhere to be seen in the dayroom nor anywhere else in the pod.

I quietly asked Calli where Chet was. Calli always seemed to know the latest news around the facility, and he never had a hard time sharing his opinion on things.

"He'll be back in a few weeks, maybe a month or so," Calli told me. I got the impression that I wasn't supposed to ask too many other questions. It appeared that Chet had been removed from the Veterans' Pod for some disciplinary reasons, but Calli didn't seem to want to elaborate on it. I didn't want to press him for information; I just hoped that it wasn't too serious.

Now that Chet had returned, I did my best to hide my excitement as I entered the classroom, taking my seat next to Kidd at the end of the table.

Chet walked into the classroom behind me. His head was down a little bit, and I got the feeling that he wasn't particularly excited to be with the group. I caught his eye as he took a seat on the opposite end of the table.

"Good to see you, man," I said. "Glad you're here."

Chet lifted his head and shot me a small smile.

"Ya, man. Good to be here. Good to see you."

He had a notepad in front of him, and as the group started talking, he picked up his pen and began to write on it.

This week's assignment was "traditions." I was interested in their reflections on good memories based on traditions they'd had with friends and family. When I'd set the assignment, I'd been expecting the men to write about holidays, birthdays, and other moments that occur every year. For me, growing up, all our family traditions revolved around the major holidays and usually involved receiving and giving gifts.

But the guys had a different relationship with the term.

As usual, Kidd went first.

"Okay, I guess I'll break the ice for you wimps," he said.

Kidd had written about how every summer a group of his close friends would camp in the woods around Moosehead Lake in central Maine. He talked about how they'd collect firewood all year, saving their money for weeks so they could gas up their trucks and have enough supplies to fuel their getaway from the rules and regulations of normal life. It was the highlight of their year, and they wouldn't have traded it for anything. When their senior year of high school came along, most of their classmates were planning on going on a cruise to Bermuda, "or one of them islands," as Kidd reflected with a smile.

"They called us into an assembly, and everyone was talking about how much fun it would be and how they'd always remember their time on this boat. Meanwhile my friends and I just sat in the back of the room, laughing with one another. None of us had the money to go on the trip, but even if we had, it just didn't sound appealing to us. We loved our trips to Moosehead and the freedom we all felt in the woods. You can't put a price on that."

For Kidd, after the death of his father three years earlier, his weekend adventures in the North Maine Woods became his way of connecting not only with his friends but also with the memory of his dad. Kidd's happy reflections of the simple times with his friends brought smiles to the faces of the entire group.

One by one the guys went around the table, each of them sharing stories of hunting, fishing, camping, and just being outside with their friends and family. Not only on holidays or birthdays but every single chance they got. I realized that far from focusing on Thanksgiving or Christmas as I'd expected, the guys associated traditions with being outside with the people they loved. The afternoon passed, filled with campfire stories, minus the campfire.

As the guys told one another tales of their exploits, I noticed that Chet was still quietly writing in the corner. He hadn't really stopped in over an hour. I didn't want to interrupt him, but I hoped he felt comfortable enough to share something with the group.

Calli told a story about his son killing his first rabbit with a .22-caliber rifle he'd given the boy for his birthday.

After that the only one left was Chet.

At the end of the table, he looked up. Maybe he'd been patiently waiting for a gap in the conversation so he could share something.

"I've got a lot of traditions like you guys," he said. "I grew up in the same patch of woods as Nate over there. What I'm most interested in these days is new traditions. Not to knock on anything you guys shared today—I think it's awesome—but for me there is a lot of pain in my past, and I'm doing my best to start some new traditions in here, so when I get out, I can really move forward."

"That's great, man. Everyone here has his own interpretation of the week's topic. There's no wrong way to share," I told him.

The guys were quiet. I could tell that everyone respected Chet, and I got the feeling they wanted to give him as much space to say his piece as possible.

"My new tradition is writing music and learning how to play the drums," Chet went on. "I meet once a week with Jon Fishman—he's the drummer from Phish. He comes in every week and donates his time and skills to me. I always walk away from our lessons better than when I walked in, not just at the drums but in my soul."

Chet touched his chest with his big open hand.

"My other tradition is this group. I know it's my first time, but I can tell that what you've got in here is special, and I'm hoping to continue to be a part of it. Sharing isn't easy for me, but that isn't an excuse to shy away from it. I'll have more to say next week."

He looked down at his writing and held up his other hand, signaling that he was done talking for now.

Before I could say anything, Kidd spoke up.

"We're glad you're here, Chet. None of us know what the fuck we're doing when it comes to writing and sharing our stories, but nothing leaves this room unless we say so."

It was clearly important for Chet to hear that, and Kidd knew it. The culture in the federal facilities Chet had served in was not conducive to any type of personal growth. Instead it was a place where any demonstration of vulnerability on Chet's part would have created more problems than it solved. Kidd wanted Chet to know that Maine State Prison was different.

We wrapped up our group for the week, and as I said goodbye to the guys, Chet hung out in the back of the room. Once we were alone, he slid me a sheet of paper.

"This is a song I've been working on for a while," he explained. "I want you to have it. It's my way of sharing. I'm not so good at writing or talking, but I can put it in a song."

"Oh, man. Thank you. I'm so glad you're back," I told him as we headed to the door.

"I've got a reputation, and it's haunting me a little bit in here," Chet explained, looking me in the eye. "But with groups like this, I think I can start some new traditions and redefine myself. I don't want to be that guy anymore. I want to thank you for taking the time to meet with us. It is an incredible thing you're doing. Don't think we take it for granted for a second."

"I'm getting just as much if not more out of it, man," I told him as we shook hands. "But thank you, I'm proud to spend time up here with you."

Back in my truck, I pulled out the sheet of loose-leaf paper Chet had handed me and read it. His penmanship was astonishing; the words were written in perfect cursive, without a single hesitation or correction.

This is what he wrote:

You left with no warning,
Disappeared like the setting sun,

I'm broken and empty,

Hate is what I've become,

When people approach me, I wish that they would just stay away,

I don't want to feel guilty about the shit that I might say.

Yeah, you could say that I've grown bitter, a little more bitter every day,

And you can claim I've lost my way, I lost my way in yesterday,

Yeah, you could say that I've grown bitter, a little more bitter every day,

And you can pray that I'll get better. I'll get better one day.

My hands are shaking,

I'm so sick of the noise,

I guess I've been forsaken,

No longer one of god's toys,

Dreams from the past keep me living in pain,

They say I need to learn to forgive,

Well, then who would I blame?

Yeah, you could say that I've grown bitter, a little more bitter every day,

And you can claim I've lost my way, lost my way in yesterday.

Yeah, you could say that I've grown a little more bitter every day

And you can pray that I'll get better, maybe I'll get better one day.

You read the words that are written in red and believe they're things that your savior said.

You read the words that are written in red, put your faith into a man that's "shhhhh"

You read the words that are written in red, believe they're things your savior said,

You read the lies that are written in red, put your faith in a
*   man that's "DEAD."*
Yeah, you could say that I've grown bitter, a little more bitter
*   every day*
And you can claim I lost my way, lost my way in yesterday,
Yeah, you can claim that I've grown a little more bitter every
*   day,*
And you can pray I don't pull the trigger, but I'll pull the
*   trigger one day . . .*

Right away I recognized Chet's message. It was as if he were making a declaration to the world: "I'm more than you think I am." I got the impression he needed to hear his own words, just as much as he needed to let others know he was worth a second look.

CHAPTER 9

Liberty

One afternoon, on my way out of the Veterans' Pod after our writing session was over, I ran into Randy in the lobby, and he invited me back to his office to catch up. It was late in the afternoon, and a lot of the staff was heading for the door, but I got the sense that Randy's workday was just getting started. Most of his time in the prison was spent on his feet, in and out of meetings and walking the halls of his prison. It was rare to catch him without at least three or four people hovering around him with various questions and issues that needed his attention.

We chatted in his office about my day in the Veterans' Pod and the progress of the writing-group sessions.

I explained how close I was growing to the guys in the writing group.

"It's amazing how much you find you have in common with them after a little while, isn't it?" Randy observed. "For me it's as clear as day. I could just as easily have ended up on the other side of the wall here."

On a corkboard behind Randy's desk, there was an old photograph, and he pulled it down to show it to me.

"That's me, and that's my eldest brother, Ron," he said, pointing to the two kids in the picture, the younger sitting on Santa's lap. Little Randy was wearing a snazzy clip-on tie, and both he and Ron were wearing their best holiday smiles.

"You know where that was taken?" Randy asked. "At the

Maine State Prison Christmas party in 1971. That's my dad there next to me and Ron."

"It's crazy to think your father was in here," I responded, remembering how Randy had told me about his dad on my first visit. It never ceased to amaze me that the little kid who came to Maine State Prison to visit his father had grown up to become the warden of the place.

"Coming to visit him here is one of my earliest memories," Randy recalled. "My mom used to load me and my three brothers into our car for the hundred-and-ten-mile drive. . . ."

Throughout Randy's childhood he would make routine visits to the prison, his father's home away from home.

"His crimes were usually related to his alcohol addiction," Randy went on. "Burglary, assault, and public intoxication. Perhaps the worst crime he'd committed, however, he'd never been arrested for. He routinely abused and beat my mother—the worst of it all was probably the verbal abuse. One of the first things I remember as a kid is my mother being dragged by her hair across the kitchen floor by Dad. But Ron, my oldest brother, would always take us outside or to a neighbor's house when it got too bad."

"Ah, man, that must have been tough," I told him.

"Ya, my brother is only about a year older than me," Randy said. "But he had to grow up quickly, always ready to protect us from witnessing Dad at his worst. My father never turned his fists on us boys, but the blows to Mom hit us just the same."

There was very little the boys could do to protect their mother. One day, however, Randy did something that stuck in his mother's mind and later helped serve as a catalyst for change.

He was too young to remember what he'd done, but his mother never forgot and shared the story with him decades later.

"This particular day, after Dad had thrown her to the floor, he stood over her preparing to rain down more blows on her. She did her best to protect herself, but I could see that she was helpless, and I had to do something. So I stood over her, making the sign of the cross with my little fingers."

As he spoke, he mimicked the younger version of himself with his fully grown man hands.

"I guess I was trying to summon the power of God to protect my mom."

It didn't work that day, and Ron escorted his brothers outside until it was over. But it cemented something in their mom. Before long she found out that her husband had gotten one of his girlfriends pregnant, and she finally left him.

His father's absence brought some stability to Randy's home life, but they were still dependent on government assistance for basic needs like food and housing. Randy recalled the Army National Guard bus that delivered their monthly rations of surplus food. They'd line up with the other poor families and receive powdered milk, powdered eggs, government cheese, molasses, and whatever else they could get. It wasn't enough to last them the entire month—they were a family of four boys after all—but they were happy to have it. Many of their best meals were the meals at school that came as a part of the free hot-lunch program.

When Randy was seven years old, his mother received some money from Randy's grandmother, Dot, who had cashed out an insurance policy.

"It was enough money to buy an old dilapidated trailer, and for seven years we shared the two-bedroom home," Randy remembered. "In the mornings Ron would crawl under the trailer, which had no siding, with a blowtorch to thaw frozen pipes."

Randy recalled hearing his brother knocking on the pipes and calling up for him to turn on the water when they were thawed. Meanwhile his father refused or was unable to send any child support.

"I don't blame my dad for how he was," Randy insisted. "We learned that our grandfather was a terrible abusive drunk. Unlike Dad, he turned his fists onto his children, even beat my uncle so severely that it caused him permanent brain damage. Eventually my grandparents got divorced but before Granddad left town he forced his children into a chicken coop in the middle of the night and set it on fire. All of them escaped without physical harm, but that did some serious damage to my dad and his siblings, along with poverty and lack of education. It makes sense that he was the way he was."

Randy's mother was his salvation.

"My mom is something else," he said lovingly. "She taught us how to read before we were old enough to go to school and set high standards for our conduct in the classroom and around town. Our greatest fear throughout childhood was disappointing Mom. Each of the brothers wanted to prove to her and themselves that they weren't like the father who'd abused and neglected her."

They took it so seriously that Randy's youngest brother, Ryan, once refused a ride from a police officer while walking home from school in the rain. He didn't want to risk his mother thinking even for a second that he'd been arrested, so he happily finished his walk in a downpour.

"Thanks to her, our father's legacy of hell-raising and alcohol abuse ended with us," Randy continued. "She could easily have blamed her husband for abandoning her with the boys and never following up on child-support payments. She could have thrown in the towel and done the bare minimum required to sustain herself and us boys. Instead she focused on how lucky she was to be a mother. For all his faults, my dad had given her purpose, and she refused to shrink from the responsibility of motherhood.

"She knew how to lead by example. She'd dropped out of high school at fifteen to marry my dad, but she went back and received her GED when we were old enough to understand the value of education. Years later my brothers and I prepaid for her enrollment in college courses for her fiftieth birthday. It was the only way we knew how to repay the woman who had given us everything. Thirty-five years after dropping out of school, Mom was back in the classroom. She received her associate's degree and was hired by the Community Action Program in Maine. She served for eleven years as a counselor to young mothers who were dependent on government assistance, a situation she was intimately familiar with."

"It sounds like your mom should have her own book on parenting," I said with a smile.

"She certainly could. It'd be a real page turner, that's for sure," Randy said happily.

We talked for a little longer about Maine and the struggles families continue to face in the Pine Tree State.

"Most people don't ever escape the cycle of poverty and addiction," Randy observed. "Certainly not most of the kids I grew up with, but none of them had a mom like mine. I still don't know how she did it. I'll forever be in awe of the challenges she faced and the way she overcame the adversity."

The Liberty boys eventually found a stable and loving father figure in their lives. A few years after her divorce, Randy's mom met and fell in love with Carl, a long-haul truck driver. Together they had a little girl, Stephanie, and the boys lovingly welcomed her into their tribe. Their new stepfather was a caring and hardworking man. "He raised us as his own, taught us to hunt, fish, butcher a deer, and to be respectable young men,"

Randy recalled. The money troubles continued, but they no longer needed to worry about the man their mother was married to.

Randy's primary influence, however, would always be Ron. He set the example for his brothers of how to move about the world in a respectful and ethical way. It was no surprise that Ron attracted the attention of an army recruiter his senior year of high school.

"Ron's leadership skills and resourcefulness weren't limited to life at home," Randy told me. "He was active in student government, an athlete, and a great student. Although I gave him a run for his money. . . ."

Before Ron left for the army, he made sure Randy was prepared to continue on the right path.

"He nominated me for vice president of the student council—without telling me!" Randy said, smiling and shaking his head.

"He knew that you'd make a great leader. All you needed was a little shove, huh?" I pointed out.

Just as Ron had, Randy enlisted in the army following his graduation. He served three years' active duty as a military policeman, including a tour in Korea, before returning home and joining the Maine National Guard while taking college courses at the University of Maine. In 1989 Randy graduated and was hired as a sheriff's deputy by the Kennebec County sheriff's department, eventually being elected sheriff. After a tour in Iraq with the Army Reserve left him with PTSD, Randy became an outspoken advocate for treating, rather than criminalizing, vets with mental-health and addiction problems.

All this experience served him well when he retired from the sheriff's office and was handed the keys to Maine State Prison. The young man who grew up visiting his father in prison was now holding the highest office within its walls.

His first order of business was to bring back the gardening program that had fallen by the wayside under the previous leadership. He wanted the men to get dirty, to put their backs, hands, and brains to work. And he wanted a prison garden that was large enough to feed the entire facility. When Randy told his staff what he wanted to do, many of them were skeptical. They shared their concerns, that the men would take advantage of the program and it would destabilize the environment.

"I was more optimistic, but my optimism was based on experience," Randy said. "I knew that the more freedom I gave the men, the more they would value the gardening program. I'd seen it in my work at Kennebec County Jail."

"So how did you deal with people within your staff who openly opposed the program?" I asked out of genuine curiosity.

"I put them in charge," he said with a laugh. Randy chose his most skeptical staff members to head up the screening and vetting process for the inmates who wanted to participate in the gardening program. Before long the men of the gardening program were growing enough food to feed their fellow inmates as well as needy families throughout the state. Over the years the gardening program grew, figuratively and literally, to encompass just about anywhere there was dirt and sunlight within the walls of the prison. It currently covered more than two and a half acres of ground.

Randy also took the classes, right alongside the men.

"The more I learned about gardening, the more I wanted to increase our scale. So the natural next step was bees," he explained. In 2017 Randy asked master beekeeper Walter Kiesow to volunteer to teach his craft to inmates. Six courses later, fifty-five inmates were now tending six hives inside the prison walls, harvesting 130 pounds of honey a year. The men were hooked. They were also busy, working hard, and wearing themselves out every day, especially during the planting and harvesting seasons.

Tired inmates are less likely to get into trouble, but, more important, Randy had found a way to restore their sense of purpose and self-worth. The program also provided an opportunity for the offenders to give back to the community. Gardening was a huge responsibility, and the program was constantly at capacity, so anyone who demonstrated anything less than total commitment was replaced. Randy was also allowing the men to obtain real work experience, experience they could use to get a job at a gardening center, a farm, or a landscaping company upon their release.

"The gardening program saves the state thousands in food costs, and all of the prison's organics are composted in massive bins we've got outside the dining hall. This reduces the prison's waste-management bill by more than a hundred thousand dollars annually," he explained. "The more we grow, the more money the state saves and the more we can donate to families in need. Last year the program at MSP donated more than a thousand pounds of fresh vegetables to food pantries."

Randy had never forgotten what it was like to go hungry, and he clearly took a lot of pride in being able to provide for families in a similar situation.

His next mission was to bring dogs to Maine State Prison, lots of them. After seeing the success of a shelter-dog program that had been established prior to his taking over as warden, Randy once again set out to enhance the environment in his prison. The men in the shelter program were responsible for the dogs' care and some basic training, essentially serving as fosters to homeless dogs until they were adopted. Randy, a former K-9 officer himself, saw the positive impact the dogs were having on the men, and he wanted more of it. He had learned of other facilities in different parts of the country that were having success with programs that provide in-depth training of service and therapy dogs. While he researched different organizations that could potentially bring dogs to his prison for training, he opened up a housing unit designed for his men that had served their country in the military. This was the Veterans' Pod.

The Veterans' Pod became the home of the America's Vet-Dogs program in September 2017 when four puppies were partnered with the first class of dog trainers, Michael Kidd and Chess among them. Within two years of taking over as warden, Randy had transformed a facility that's sole focus was on punishment and security to a much more balanced environment. The once-bleak yard within the walls of the prison was now thriving with crops and busy men buzzing around their plants, carrying bags of soil and working together in two greenhouses. And just past the rows of freshly tilled earth, there were two fenced-in yards serving as outdoor play and training areas for the dogs. In 2018, Randy helped establish an American Legion post within the Veterans' Pod, naming it for Medal of Honor recipient and Maine native Brian L. Buker, who was killed in action in Vietnam.

I knew I could talk to Randy for hours, but I also knew that his time was precious and I should let him get back to work. We shook hands, and I thanked him again for giving me the freedom to contribute something to his prison.

"It's truly an honor," I said.

"You're welcome, Craig," he said with a gracious smile. "You're always welcome here."

CHAPTER 10

Accomplishments

The next week I arrived at Maine State Prison just before 8:00 A.M. I hadn't seen the puppies in a few weeks, and I was looking forward to finding out how much they'd improved and grown. Paula had handed off the responsibility of leading the class to Rebecca, and as I walked into the lobby, I saw Rebecca on her own, waiting near the front desk for an escort back. I signed in, and we chatted until Michael Fournier came to collect us. As we navigated the metal detector, following Fournier through the freshly mopped hallway, he gave her the update on each dog's progress since last week's class.

"They've had plenty of outdoor time since the weather has been nice," Fournier explained. "I've seen the guys working on name recognition and some distraction stuff in the yard. On the training front, everything seems to be moving along on schedule. No news is good news."

The only issue was LJ, who had a little stomach bug.

"His weekend raiser said he had diarrhea all weekend, and Nate has said it's continued over the last two days."

"Any other symptoms?" Rebecca asked quickly.

It felt like we were on one of those hospital TV shows where surgeons get briefed on a patient's condition while quickly walking the hallways of a chaotic hospital.

"No other issues. His appetite and energy levels are all normal," Fournier reported. "He's such a great dog."

We made our way into the classroom, where the men were waiting with their puppies.

I took my seat next to Callahan, who had brought me a cup of coffee.

Nate was sitting on the floor with LJ snoozing between his legs, the puppy's big head resting on his pillowlike paws. It struck me that between the puppy program and the writing group, I had spent a lot of hours with Nate, and yet there was still so much I didn't know about him.

The primary trainers were all on the floor sitting in a circle, with the secondary trainers once again in chairs behind them, notepads at the ready.

Standing in front of the guys for the first time without Paula, I was struck by Rebecca's seeming lack of nerves. Here we were in a state penitentiary filled with guys who'd committed some pretty heinous crimes, and she seemed completely unfazed. I got the impression that the dogs were her number-one priority.

"Okay, guys. How was everyone's week?" she asked. "Let's start with you, Nate. How is LJ?"

"He's such a champ," Nate told her. "He's been sick, but he always lets us know when he needs to go out."

Nate and his secondary handler, Jake, took turns explaining LJ's symptoms, what they'd noticed, and how they'd treated them. Like two worried parents at a parent-teacher conference, they explained their concerns while waiting for Rebecca's response. They weren't grossed out by LJ's tummy issues or frustrated at their lack of sleep—they just wanted to do what was best for him.

"It sounds like you guys are doing everything right," Rebecca reassured them. "As long as he's still got plenty of energy and he isn't vomiting, I'm not too concerned. It's just a puppy thing. He's growing fast, and there are always complications with that."

Her explanation put Nate and Jake at ease for now, and the men began to focus on the training goals for the day.

Sayville and her trainer, Cory, seemed to be doing much better as a team. The headstrong pup was sitting patiently at Cory's feet waiting for her time to demonstrate what she'd learned in the last week.

Rebecca asked Cory to parade Sayville around the room, working on loose-leash walking and name recognition.

"It's important for the dogs to learn how to walk next to their handlers and not out in front of them at the end of their leashes, like most dogs do," Rebecca reminded them. "They need to be close by, connected to you at all times, not focused on the world around them. It's an important distinction between them and a companion dog."

Sayville wasn't distracted by the other dogs, even when Webber playfully lunged at her. She just pranced right by him, never taking her eyes off Cory. It was a significant improvement from the last time I had been there.

"She's doing great," Rebecca told Cory. "I can really see how much work you guys put in. Nice job, keep it up."

As Cory took a seat, the pride on his face was visible. He was sitting up straight and tall as if he'd just gotten a shot of confidence vitamins.

Webber had also improved but needed to be corrected for what Rebecca called a "lazy sit." I marveled at how much these young pups and their trainers were expected to achieve in a short period of time. It wasn't enough that the men had to be able to get a four-month-old puppy to sit and stay—a feat that I'd given up on years ago with Fred—they also had to focus on sitting *technique,* too. If the puppies slumped to one side, resting on a butt cheek, instead of sitting with both hind legs flat, then this was a problem.

"Sit does not mean rest," Rebecca explained. "When they sit, they should anticipate another command to follow. It is not a position we want them to stay in for a long time."

Next up were LJ and Nate. Right away it was obvious that Nate had skipped ahead a few pages in the training manual. He let LJ off the leash and moved around the room with the pup remaining just a few inches from his handler's heel, as if on the end of an invisible leash. It was astonishing to see such a young puppy behaving so well.

"Ah, I see you've started on some of the next-level stuff already," Rebecca told him with a smile.

"Ya, he was getting bored. Hope that's okay," Nate said a little sheepishly.

"Of course," Rebecca responded. "Just make sure you're really establishing the basics along the way. We don't want him to forget more than he's learned."

Next Rebecca placed a small, square section of a rubber workout mat on the floor, just big enough for the puppies to stand on with both sets of paws. LJ had clearly seen this exercise before, because he went right over to the mat and planted his oversize paws perfectly on the rubber square while looking up at Nate with pride.

The rest of the guys in the class all smirked and playfully teased Nate for being the teacher's pet. LJ was clearly a star pupil. Nate had said early on that he wanted to challenge himself, and that was why he chose LJ. He'd been looking for a dog that would bring out the best in him, and it seemed like he'd found one.

It was a great class, and the men left with cheerful smiles and a confident stride that matched that of the dogs at their sides.

I took my break out in town and came back to the prison about ten minutes before the next session of the Purposeful Tails

Writing Group. I was anxious to get back in and see the guys. I hoped Chet would still be in the Veterans' Pod. I got the feeling that last week had meant a lot to him but that he was still struggling.

The week's topic was "accomplishments."

"Share a story about a time you overcame the odds and accomplished something you're proud of," I'd written in the syllabus. "It could be something as simple as hiking a mountain or catching a fish. No matter what you choose, focus on the Five W's: Who, What, When, Where, and Why. No matter what you choose to remember, if it's something you're proud of, it's something worth sharing and remembering."

I had no idea what the guys might talk about, but I had learned that it was best not to have any preconceived notions— they always had more to say and more to give during our time together than I expected.

The guard at the front desk told me I was early and that Fournier wouldn't be up for another five minutes or so. I thanked him. As I waited, I took a look around the lobby. It was a large room with a wooden shelf that ran around the perimeter, displaying a variety of handmade wooden products made by the men, everything from detailed miniature sailboats and ships that looked like they'd been made by expert craftsmen to children's toys like trucks and cars with bright colors and shiny paint. A little plaque advertised the retail shop in town where visitors could purchase things made by the men inside. I'd been there a few times and always walked out with something unique and beautiful, even if I didn't know who I'd be giving it to when I bought it. I was proud to give gifts made by the men in the prison, because it gave me a chance to talk about my time there and the friends I'd made behind the wall.

The lobby was pretty big, and I wasn't usually there for very long, so I'd never wandered around it before. I noticed, tucked away on one side of the room, a children's area. There was a little desk with board games, puzzles, picture books, and faded wooden blocks that fit into the desk. Two little wooden chairs sat neatly in place, as if a well-behaved child had just tidied up his or her play area before dinner. It looked like it belonged in a doctor's office or in the waiting area of a Jiffy Lube—except here it was in the middle of a state penitentiary that was home to eight hundred men serving lengthy sentences. It was just about the saddest thing I'd ever seen, a staggering reminder that living with a parent behind bars is the norm for so many children across our country.

Before long, Fournier came and escorted me back to the Veterans' Pod.

It was time to get to work.

The guys were all ready when I walked in. Right away I noticed that although Mr. Craig was missing—apparently he was taking a nap in his room—there was a new member of our group: Marcus.

Marcus was one of Kidd's best friends—his co-conspirator in crimes that put them both behind bars. The two of them had been close for years. I knew they were in prison for offenses they'd committed together on Halloween night in 2011. Marcus and Kidd received the same sentence, fifteen years for kidnapping and robbery followed by four years of probation and eight years suspended. From what Kidd had told me, Marcus's addiction had been out of control for much of his adult life, and when he met Kidd in 2010, the two of them were the wrong kind of friends for each other.

Kidd had said he'd been working on getting his buddy to come spend time with us but that Marcus was the kind of guy who needed to make the decision for himself. In the past, Marcus had popped in and out of the group a few times, including our first-ever meeting, but always just to crack a joke and say hi. I was glad to see that word about our little writing program had made its way around the facility and that our gatherings were something Marcus wanted to be a part of now.

Marcus was one of a relatively small number of Black men in the facility, a reflection of the demographics of Maine, which is overwhelmingly white. But in many ways his skin tone was his least remarkable characteristic. His quick wit and inviting smile put everyone around him at ease wherever he went, and he lit up any room he was in. It was easy to see why he and Kidd had become so close during their time on the outside. Marcus was a cutup but at the same time knew when to dial his personality back. As the group began talking about our topic for the day, Marcus quickly settled in and gave all the men at the table the time and respect they deserved. To me it was the mark of a good friend: someone who keeps a smile on your face but also listens when the time is right.

The guys were ready to share stories of their greatest accomplishments. I'd selected this theme because I wanted the men to recall a time in their lives when they felt they were on the right track. I wanted them to remember what they were capable of. Some of my most significant accomplishments took place between August of 2010 and March of 2011, when I was serving in Afghanistan, the greatest one being bringing Fred home. Since then my little Afghan dog served as a reminder to me of what I was truly capable of when I put my mind to something.

As the men began to share, I noticed that Chet was quietly writing in the corner again, his pen barely visible in the clutches of his meaty hands. I hoped that this would be the day he'd feel comfortable enough to share a little more with the guys, but I wasn't going to push him.

For the first time in the history of our group, Nate volunteered to go first. He seemed eager to share his story this week, and we were all excited to hear it.

"In 2002 my job at the paper mill was cut during an economic downturn," he read. "Because of the layoff, I was given a stipend to attend college courses to learn a new trade or further my education. I always loved to cook, so I enrolled in the culinary-arts program at the community college.

"I didn't know the first thing about actual ingredients and recipes. I just always felt comfortable in the kitchen," he continued with a smile. "I'd make my mom dinner all the time with whatever we happened to have around the house.

"I did okay in the class," he went on, turning the page in his notebook so I could see where he'd made notes to himself in the margins. "We learned how to bake and make pasta from scratch. I really enjoyed the lessons and learning by doing. At the end of the semester, the professor offered an extra-credit assignment for anyone who wanted to do it. It was a contest to see who could make the best tomato sauce. A bunch of the other professors would judge the sauces, and the winner would get bumped up a full letter grade."

"This story is making me hungry," Marcus joked, and all the guys agreed.

"Ya, I know," Nate said with a quiet smile. "Now I'll have to cook more for you guys next time I'm in the kitchen. Believe me, I thought of that already."

Then he went back to his notebook. "I didn't really know what I was doing. I just knew that every cooking show I'd ever watched about pasta sauce, they always talked about garlic and fresh tomatoes, so I added lots of garlic and smashed-up fresh tomatoes to my sauce. I just kept tasting it as it cooked and adding more stuff that seemed like it would complement it. When I'd look around at the other students, it seemed like they all knew what they were doing, so I stopped looking at them and just followed my taste buds as best I could.

"We all cooked our pasta, and our plates were brought in front of the judges one at a time. It was like being on a cooking show. When they got to my plate, I tried not to let them see me sweat. If it was bad, I didn't want them to know it was mine. To my surprise they all seemed to really like it. One of the judges even took the plate back after the others had tried it and started eating it all by himself. They sent us back to our desks while the professors deliberated about our cooking. For me it felt like I'd already won because none of them spit out my sauce.

"After a few minutes, they called us back up and announced that my sauce was the winner overall. I couldn't believe it. My professor called me up to shake the hands of the judges, and they all wanted to know what I'd done to make mine stand out so much. At the moment I couldn't remember what I had done. I never took any measurements or wrote anything down—I just cooked by taste. So I just said, 'It's an old family recipe!' and that got a laugh out of them, so I went back to my seat."

Nate let a huge grin spread across his face, then put his notebook down with a satisfied sigh.

"I love that story," I said, giving Nate a fist bump. "Guys, what did you like about that story?"

Chet spoke up quickly. "I like how you just threw yourself into something new, not knowing how it would end up. You lost your job at the mill, but you didn't lose yourself. I think that we could all be reminded of that more often."

The other guys agreed and offered similar sentiments about Nate's story. I took note. Perhaps the men could use more reminders of things that had happened to them that didn't revolve around pain or suffering.

Calli's story took a similar theme to Nate's. He talked about how he was the first person in his family to go to college. Sadly, his father made him change his major from history to business, so he could better serve the family company. Even so, Calli felt a lot of pride for taking steps to further himself through higher education.

The rest of the guys began chiming in. They all seemed to feel that their children were their greatest accomplishments. Everyone in the group that day was a father. Kidd had a son, as did Marcus. Chet and Nate were both fathers of daughters, and Calli had a son and a daughter. The men explained that they found consolation in the hope their kids would lead better lives than they had. It broke my heart a bit to hear them speak this way about their children, as if they themselves were beyond hope, unworthy of redemption.

The only one who hadn't shared yet was Chet. As Marcus wrapped up a story about his son and how Marcus knew he was going to be a better man than his father because he was always telling his dad to stop joking around so much, I could see that Chet's notebook paper was full and his pen was flat on the table. It looked like he was ready to share something with the group.

As the guys quieted down, Chet took his cue.

"I'd like to share a song I wrote," he said, looking around the room, making sure everyone was listening. "It's for my sister. She died when I was eleven."

He began to read, but it was clear he knew the words by heart:

"Letting Go"

I stopped by to see you today, as I talked and cried you had nothing to say

I don't know why I don't stop by more than I do, I don't
believe there is a better person for me to talk to, for I know
that you hear every word that I say and you continue to
love me though you're so far away.

No, there is no stronger bond than the one that we share even
though you're not here and it's yet my time to be there. As
I drove away from my spot in the earth I cried out to God
for all that I'm worth, "How could you do this to me! Can't
you see that I'm living in misery!" I asked him, "Where can
I turn! What can I say, how do I let go of yesterday?"

Well, tomorrow isn't looking so bright, me and drugs are at
war, and the drugs are winning the fight.

The war I started with my misery, I thought of drugs as an
ocean, I tried to drown in the sea, anything, just anything
to escape from the cold reality.

The war isn't over, no, this war's just begun. This war won't
be over, until this war I have won.

I'll never say good-bye, but, sis, I have to let it go. For it's the
only way that I'm ever going to grow.

I just can't keep living my life this way, that's why I need to
let go of that October day.

I love you, how I miss you, thankfully we will be together
again one day.

I truly believe that's what God had to say.

As Chet read his song, his voice was tight and measured, as
if he needed to remove himself from his own lyrics so he could
actually say them out loud. It sounded more like a confession
than a song, as if the rest of us just happened to be lucky enough
to overhear him talking with his God.

"It was important to me to read those words out loud before I
talk more about my greatest accomplishments," he said, looking

around the room at his fellow inmates. "I don't talk about this, not to anyone, but if there were ever a time or a place, this is it."

For once I thought I could detect a little emotion in his voice.

"She was my older sister by just two years," he said, as a big solitary tear ran down his cheek. "We did everything together. One fall day we were out on four-wheelers, buzzing around the property like we always did. I was younger and lighter on the quads, so I could always outrun her on our races back to the house.

"The last thing I remember was looking back over my shoulder as I went around a bend. I saw her reach her right arm out and open her mouth to shout something. I just assumed she was joking around, trying to slow me down. . . . I'll never get that image out of my head. It was the last time I saw my sister alive."

I could see the years of pain, like rings in an oak tree, showing through on Chet's face.

"When I got back to the house, my dad and my uncle were skinning a buck they'd shot earlier that day," Chet went on. "They asked where my sister was, and I made a joke about how I left her in the dust before heading inside to get washed up for dinner. After about a half hour or so, when she didn't come back my dad and my uncle went out looking for her. The sun was starting to set, and they were worried she might have gotten lost or run out of gas. The rest is too painful for me to talk about. I've never seen grown men cry like that, and I never want to again."

Chet was looking down at his notebook. After a short pause, he continued.

"So from here on out, I want to make sure I live my life without the pain of that day. Because now I have a daughter, and she, like a lot of you have said, is my greatest accomplishment. She has taught my own mom and dad how to love again. They see my sister in my daughter, and they love her with all their hearts. But she has only known me in prison. I want that to change. I'm not done. I've got a lot more to accomplish in life, and knowing that my daughter is out there without her daddy is reason enough for me to put all this behind me. Because after my sister died, my parents always kept me close by, babied me a little bit. That's what made me want to get out into the world, to join the navy and be a man. But the drugs and my mistakes took away the kid I was. I always apologize to my parents for what I did to their baby boy. I want to be their son again. That will be my next great accomplishment."

As he finished his speech, Chet nodded and pointed to his chest with an emphatic self-affirming poke.

"That's beautiful," Kidd said before anyone else could speak up, looking Chet firmly in the eye. "I know we don't know each other very well yet, but I can tell you right now that we're proud of you today, for sharing something so deep and difficult. That takes a lot, and I have even more respect for you after today than I did before."

"Chet, you've given us a lot to think about," I told him. "Thank you for putting it all out there for the group. I don't think any one of us will ever forget it."

I wanted to heap more praise on him, but I could see that he was tired of having so much attention focused on him. He had done what he set out to do, and he didn't need our approval.

"What do you guys think your accomplishments say about you?" I asked the group, taking the heat off Chet.

After a few seconds, Kidd spoke up. "I'd say that they reveal more about who we really are than say our low points do."

"That's a good observation. I'd have to agree," I said. "We can eventually outrun or learn from our mistakes if we want to, but our successes and accomplishments are evidence that we can do more."

"We just need to do a better job of reminding ourselves of the good stuff we've done in our lives," said Nate, chiming in, "so we don't constantly feel like all we can ever amount to is a fuckup."

"That's exactly right," I replied. "When was the last time you thought about your tomato-sauce victory?"

"I had completely forgotten about it, to be honest, but it felt good to relive it. I could almost taste it—"

"Okay, stop, you're making me hungry again," said Calli.

We all laughed, and the guys began to collect their stuff. It was time to say good-bye.

On my walk out, I passed by the children's corner in the lobby again, and again I thought about the sons and daughters of my friends in the writing group. They had a difficult road ahead of them, that was certain. Many of them were going to spend their whole childhood visiting this prison, until eventually they outgrew the toys in the corner. Their lives would go on without their fathers, but they'd be forever affected by that absence, even when their dads were released. The thought occurred to me that whenever we detain someone in our country, we're simultaneously handcuffing those who depend on them. One other thing was clear: Chet, Calli, Kidd, Marcus, and Nate were loving and dedicated fathers—I just hoped their love and devotion was powerful enough to transcend concrete and razor wire, too.

CHAPTER 11

Bubble Boy

It had been a month since the first writing class. In the weeks that followed, I'd quickly shaken off any skepticism I once had that the men might be using their time with me as an excuse to get out of their cells and goof off. Instead our sessions together had become an opportunity to explore their lives in ways that were often profound. In this respect, they reminded me of the philosophy classes I'd enjoyed at college. The guys had faced so many challenges, many of them unimaginable to me. But they'd made a choice to use their time in prison to better themselves by reflecting on the twists and turns their lives had taken. They weren't looking for excuses or scapegoats. They were dissecting their experiences and choices, finding purpose in their pain, and a way forward.

Although I rarely shared my own personal stories with them—I never wanted the guys to feel as if I were hogging the mic or comparing my problems to theirs—it was perhaps inevitable that being around them and learning about their stories would inspire me to reflect on my own journey. During my long two-hour drives to and from the prison for the sessions, I found my mind drifting back and forth in time, to how far I'd come to get to Maine State Prison.

As a little kid or even as a young man, I don't think I could have ever predicted that one day I would find myself excited to spend hours with a bunch of men in a cramped prison classroom.

I was raised a long way from Maine, in Burke, Virginia, a

picture-perfect suburb of our nation's capital. It was an environment that was altogether different from the disadvantaged rural areas where Randy Liberty and the guys had grown up. Burke was filled with properly proportioned middle-class homes, occupied by mostly white families with stable incomes and neat lawns—it was a fortress of virtue. As a kid, the only time I felt unsafe was when I accidentally took the wrong bus home in first grade. I rode it to the last stop, hoping that the houses around me would suddenly become familiar or that the bus driver would turn into my personal chauffeur and shuttle me home. Instead she forced me off the bus and into a strange and foreign suburban maze. I found my way home with the help of a friendly older boy with a sweet Mongoose BMX bike. Burke dwellers prided themselves on our lack of crime, lack of danger, or any visible symbols of economic disparity. In fact, for me, the lack of problems *became* the problem. It was as if I were living in the perfect bubble—and I couldn't wait to escape from it.

My only windows into the outside world were my occasional trips into D.C. with my family. We'd go in every so often to walk around the monuments or check out a museum. I remember seeing homeless people for the first time in D.C. and feeling a sense of panic and helplessness. How could we just drive by them? They needed help! We had money, we had food. Why didn't they? And why didn't anyone seem to care?

Then there were my annual trips to the auto show every March with my dad. Even as a kid, I was obsessed with cars and trucks, and so once a year we climbed into my father's secondhand Volvo, braved the D.C. traffic, and went to the show. As we neared the convention center, my dad would find a street spot a few blocks away. We didn't mind walking, and it was cheaper than paying for the underground lot. One year, on our walk from our parking spot to the convention center, I remember passing a dark alley and hearing two men shouting. I looked down the alley and saw that they were fighting. I was able to watch for a few seconds before my dad grabbed me by the arm, but it was enough to sear into my brain the image of a man striking another man in the face, an image that outlasted the memory of any shiny car or truck I also saw that day. Until then I'd only seen fights in cartoons or action movies. Where a single punch would send a man flying through the air or knock him unconscious while the hero escaped. This fight was different—it wasn't pretty. The men's bodies twisted together as each tried to gain the upper hand. Just before my dad pulled me away, I heard one of them scream out that he was going to kill the other. I believed him.

When I tried to ask my dad about the scene I'd just witnessed, he dismissed my concerns, changing the subject to the car show. But I never shook the image of those two men and the feeling I had watching them. It was a combination of fear and a sincere desire to help, to make them stop and see that there was a better way to solve their problems. I hated that they were fighting, and I hated how dirty they looked.

I returned to Burke that night forever changed. There was a whole world outside my suburban bubble, and now I knew it.

As I got a little older, I continued to seek opportunities to go beyond the Burke bubble. I became obsessed with the reality show *Cops*. I was fascinated with the men and women who were trained to uphold the laws of our society, to respond to everything from fistfights to gunfights to hit-and-runs. When officers responded to a domestic dispute, the reality of the situation was all laid out there for the viewer. The messy house, the husband in a dirty T-shirt and the wife screaming at him from the porch, the officer testifying from the dash camera in his cruiser as he talked about why he became a police officer. The world of *Cops* was clear-cut and without any moral ambiguity. There were good guys and bad guys, saints and sinners, cops and robbers.

I saw a side of our society that I'd been protected from in my suburban middle-class world, and I was hooked. Inevitably my dad would come into the room at some point and ask me to change the channel. "This is the worst of society. Why would you want to watch that?" was his standard dad line. But it was too late. I'd already decided I wanted to be a cop. It wasn't that I was looking for action or to assert authority over people. I genuinely felt that being a police officer was a calling, a job that took more than an education—it took a special type of person. I wanted to be that person. I didn't want to pretend that there weren't problems in the world, I wanted to do my part to fix them. I understood at an early age that being in the police force was a challenging job, but if nobody signed up to do it, what would our world look like?

My aspirations were fueled further a few times a year when we'd visit my Aunt Donna and Uncle David in Hampton, Virginia. Uncle David was a career police officer in the area, and spending time with him was always the highlight of our trips. He was full of stories from his time on the job, and when I got old enough, he'd bring me into the station to meet his fellow officers. Uncle David was unlike anyone I'd interacted with back home in Burke. He exuded authority but spoke in a kind and gentle tone, with a laid-back Virginia accent.

Then there was my dad. He was a completely self-made man. He'd left home at seventeen for the air force, the start of his career in aviation, service to his country, and the world. In his career at the National Transportation Safety Board, he dedicated himself to making air travel safe, painstakingly reconstructing some of the worst aviation accidents in history. Through the data collected from the flight recorders or "black boxes" and material gathered at crash sites, he'd figure out what had gone wrong and devise a plan to make sure it didn't happen again. Although his passion for flight and engineering hadn't rubbed off on me, what my father did manage to get across to me was a sense of duty, loyalty, and service to something bigger than myself. He taught me that doing the right thing is often a thankless job, but that doing the right thing was *always* thanks enough.

The problem was, I was turning out to be a terrible student, and that frustrated my dad. I coasted. I didn't care much about my grades. This enraged him at times, because he equated success in life with success in the classroom. While I never found my academic footing during my high-school years, I was a natural at speaking in front of large groups of my classmates, often making them laugh with my skits and humor. My mom was always on my side. She served as a constant cheerleader for my antics and exploits. A father's approval, however, is an elusive and tempting thing, and I craved it deeply.

My senior year of high school, I enrolled in a satellite program at a neighboring school that taught trades and specific skills for industries like auto repair, hotel management, hospitality, and law enforcement. Every day I'd carpool with some other students from my school to the satellite school, where we'd gather in a trailer with our teacher, Mr. Kerr, a retired Fairfax County police officer.

This class was the only one I'd ever taken that I could directly associate with my future. We examined real-life cases and situations faced by law-enforcement officials across the country. Every week Mr. Kerr brought in a different guest speaker. Some were former military members who went on to join police forces, others were career cops with decades of experience. All shared stories and experiences from their time in uniform, and I soaked up every bit of it. I was trying to piece together what my own career and life after high school would look like. My friends were heading off to four-year universities and were already talking about their careers and plans after college. The end of high school felt like a looming cliff that I was just going to drop off in June 2001, if I didn't have a plan.

By the time high school drew to a close, I'd decided that what I really wanted to do was to join the marines. To appease my cautious father, I'd agreed to enroll in a semester of college classes first, just to see how I liked it. The summer after high school, I floated around Virginia. I worked on my cousin's farm in Marshall with my friend Mike. Mike was heading off to college in Ohio in the fall, and I was enjoying spending time with him before we parted ways.

Before we knew it, it was September, and we were both trying not to talk too much about the end of summer. On the morning of September 11, 2001, Mike and I were listening to our local morning radio show. At around 8:50 we could tell by the uncharacteristically nervous tones in the hosts' voices that something very bad was happening to our nation. The chaos of that morning played over the small speakers in Mike's old Dodge pickup truck. We sat silently, hanging on every word. I remember saying to myself, *I wish I'd joined the marines. I should already be in the marines. . . .*

We spent the rest of the day huddled around my cousin's television watching through tears and rage as the towers collapsed and the Pentagon burned. I had grown up in a bubble that was predictable and accommodating. I no longer saw the world that way. There were people who hated us, who weren't interested in a peaceful existence, and I wasn't interested in allowing them one. My country had been attacked, and I had to do something about it.

That fall I attended my college classes to appease my dad, but I was just going through the motions. College wasn't for me. I'd enrolled in a law-enforcement and criminal-justice program but was required to take biology and remedial mathematics. It was everything I hated about high school but without the consolation of my friends. I sat in huge classrooms with tired-looking adults who weren't interested in laughing at my jokes and clock-watching professors who read from textbooks and answered questions by condescendingly telling students to "read the syllabus."

I felt alone and unaccomplished. I was living at home and working as a pizza-delivery guy a few nights a week, doing my best to avoid my dad. I know now that most of what I felt stemmed from my own insecurities, but at the time I felt like I was nothing short of a total disappointment to him. I wanted to make my dad proud, but I wanted to do it in my own way. The first step in forging my own path was to break free of the northern Virginia bubble I'd been peering through my entire life. To me it represented safety, predictability, and mediocrity. I had developed an allergy to my hometown. I was itchy and uncomfortable with how comfortable I was. I became confrontational and cynical. Northern Virginia didn't feel like home anymore. It felt like a hole that was trying to suck me in.

I proudly failed most of my classes at community college. I had tried, but it wasn't for me. My miserable grades weren't evidence of failure, they were the proof that I needed to forge my own path.

In March of 2003 I finally shipped off to USMC Recruit Training Command, Parris Island, South Carolina. I'd joined to be a military police officer, thinking that I'd gain some valuable experience, serve my country, and be able to transition into a career in law enforcement without having to go to college. Boot camp was three months of yelling, sweating, shooting, and marching. I loved it. I was proud and focused, but mostly I felt like my life was on track for the first time. The best part about coming home for my post-boot-camp break was knowing that I'd be leaving again, off on another adventure.

Later that summer I began my training as a military police officer in San Antonio, Texas. When I received my orders after boot camp, I was surprised. I was going to be working in a military prison—or "brig," as they were called—a corrections institution operated by the military where service members are locked up for major and minor crimes. I hadn't known that being stationed at a brig was even an option, and I wasn't particularly thrilled about it. I'd assumed I'd be learning about traditional law-enforcement roles on a base or overseas. I didn't realize I could end up working in a prison.

With no other choice, I decided to make the best of it. During training we were taught that every day in the brig would be like going to war. Only our weapons would be our eyes and our minds. We'd have to stay mentally rigid when interacting with the inmates and keep our eyes open for infractions and security risks. The instructors did their best to make it seem like a life-or-death situation. We heard horror stories about prison guards getting killed and assaulted by angry and entitled inmates. It was us versus them, good versus evil. It didn't matter what someone was in for—every inmate had the potential for violence.

While I was in San Antonio during military police training, I had my own brush with the law when I was caught underage drinking and driving over the limit—an offense that could have landed me in the brig, ending my career before it began. But even after this happened, I refused to see the line between myself and the men I'd be charged with detaining as anything less than definitive. It was me against them.

I arrived at my first duty station in September of 2003. I'd requested to be sent to Iraq or Afghanistan, a request that was met with laughter by the training staff. "You picked the wrong job, devil dog," one of them said with a smile as my heart sank into my feet. Most of my classmates were heading to Marine Corps brigs at Camp Pendleton, California; Camp Lejeune, North Carolina; or Camp Hansen in Okinawa, Japan. I was somehow selected to serve at a marine detachment on a navy base in North Charleston, South Carolina.

The brig I was assigned to was a consolidated facility. It housed inmates from every branch of service and required a detachment from each branch to serve as the guard force. I showed up ready to learn and prepared to do the job I'd been given to the best of my ability. I discovered I was going to be guarding an inmate population doing time for crimes as serious as murder and rape, down to infractions that are only enforced in the military, such as being late for work (which was considered dereliction of duty) and desertion.

The horror stories of physical altercations on the job I'd been told by the training staff in Texas bounced around in my head. "These boys have nothing better to do than pump iron and think about ways to beat on skinny little guards," one instructor would always bellow during our morning workouts. "Your first line of defense against attack is to keep your body hard and your mind harder," the same instructor would say as he counted our push-ups.

We heard stories of guards being blackmailed into sneaking everything from money and drugs to women and alcohol into facilities. The ultimate punishment was that you could end up being incarcerated next to the same men you'd once guarded.

It was a terrifying fate that kept me up at night. I'd already had my brush with being thrown into the brig, and I didn't want to come anywhere close to letting that happen again. I considered myself to be a nice guy, I enjoyed talking to people and getting to know them, but I was going to have to change that about myself if I were going to make it through my first four years on the right side of the bars.

Every day I showed up to work, prepared mentally and physically to do battle against an enemy that I believed wanted to exploit any sign of weakness. During my interactions with prisoners, if they didn't stand at parade rest, their arms folded behind their backs, three feet from my desk, I wouldn't allow them to get a word out. I'd send them back to their cells or tell them to start over. In my mind if I allowed them to relax around me, it would set a dangerous precedent. I needed to keep up an unbreakable wall between them and me if I wanted to survive. I'd been told that these men would do anything to get under my skin, that they would try to lull me into casual conversations so they could learn about my background, my family, my likes and dislikes, in order to exploit them at a later date. It never occurred to me that they just might want to have a friendly chat with the new marine.

My early days in the Marine Corps only reinforced the idea that when it came to morality and law and order, things were clear-cut. I found comfort in seeing the world in black and white. There were good people and bad people. I wasn't interested in learning about the circumstances and factors behind people's actions, especially if they were criminals.

I'd wanted to be deployed ever since I enlisted; it was why I joined the marines. About six months into my time in Charleston, I got what I'd been asking for . . . kind of.

I was heading to the U.S. Naval Station in Guantánamo Bay, Cuba.

We were shipping out from the Marine Corps base in Quantico, thirty minutes from where I grew up. I arrived there and checked in to the barracks where the rest of the marines I'd be deploying with were staying, all sent from other Marine Corps brigs. Altogether there were around twelve of us, led by a staff sergeant and a warrant officer. After everyone had checked in to his room, we assembled in formation. Looking around, I remember thinking, *Where is everyone else? How are we supposed to guard the entire inmate population in Gitmo with only twelve guards?* It was a question none of my fellow guards seemed concerned about answering, so I assumed there was something I didn't know, and to prevent myself from looking stupid, I kept my concerns to myself.

In fact, as our commanding officer explained, we were going to be serving as augmentees to the army's guard force that was made up of reservists from the New Jersey National Guard, before getting shipped to one of the most dangerous prisons in the world. We were to serve alongside them as "experts in our field" to make sure they didn't cross any lines or endanger themselves or others with their inexperience. I'd been working in corrections for only six months, but I was supposed to be the expert, guiding and instructing others in the proper handling of some of the world's most dangerous and hateful people? If I wasn't nervous before, I was certainly feeling it now.

On the day before we shipped off to Gitmo, my dad hosted everyone at our house for a cookout. We all laughed and joked in my backyard over burgers. My father loved meeting everyone I'd be serving with on my first deployment.

That night my new friend Sean, who was the only corporal in the group, pulled me aside.

"I knew you were a rich kid from the first moment I met you," he said with a grin.

"What?! Are you serious?!" I replied in genuine shock. I never considered us to be wealthy. Our house wasn't small by any means, but by northern Virginia standards it was average at best. I'd known kids who'd grown up with pools that fed into other pools and garages bigger than my entire home. What I would later learn was that by national standards I *was* a rich kid. Sean had been raised by a single mother in the Seattle area. His meals were never guaranteed, and he'd often end up stealing cans of soup for him and his siblings just to get through another week. When he arrived at boot camp, it was the first time he'd ever had three real meals a day in his entire life. Every month he sent almost half his paycheck home to help support his mom and her other children. While I had joined the marines for guidance, direction, and adventure, Sean—and many of the people I served with during my career—had joined because they had no other option. Our nation's poor communities provide the bulk of bodies for our enlisted ranks, kids like Sean whose only way up is to sign up.

The next day Sean and I, along with our fellow MPs, set off for Cuba, flying via Miami. When we landed on the island, the heat punched us all in the face. It was unlike anything I'd ever experienced. The base was mostly dusty rocks with iguanas running around like squirrels. If I hadn't seen the ocean from the runway, I'd have sworn we were in the middle of a desert, not the Caribbean.

On our first day, we were given a walk-through of some of the cellblocks before being assigned to our team of guards. We passed long rows of steel mesh cages with metal bunks and squatting-style toilets that I'd never seen before; they were stainless-steel openings in the ground with elevated foot-shaped holds where the inmates could squat to do their business. Each cell also had a little black arrow painted on the floor indicating the distance and direction to Mecca, the Holy Land for Islam and the direction in which they were required to pray five times a day. The cells in the first block housed low-level detainees who didn't pose much of a security risk to the guards. Most of them were still asleep underneath white sheets on thin mattresses. The ones who were awake just stared at us and uttered things under their breath that we didn't understand.

The next block would be a different experience altogether.

This block housed one of the highest-level Taliban fighters the United States had captured so far. He'd served as Osama bin Laden's personal driver and security guard during his time in Afghanistan. We'd been warned before that the rest of the detainees felt a fierce loyalty to him and did whatever he commanded. As we stepped onto the block, we heard one of the detainees shout, "Marines! Marines! Fuck you!" in a thick Middle Eastern accent. We continued onto the long walkway, parading ourselves in front of what felt like the angriest mob in the world, as if we were camouflage-wearing models in the world's worst fashion show. The men screamed, stomped their feet, and shook the doors of their cells, some even hanging off them. One man with a prosthetic leg held it up and shook it at us. He pointed to it and said, "Marine! Marine!" indicating that he'd suffered the loss of his leg thanks to U.S. Marines.

We made our way past the man who'd served as bin Laden's driver. He was tall and thin, with a long black beard that matched his dark eyes. He stood with his arms crossed, staring back at us silently. The two detainees in the cells on either side of him screamed like banshees and tossed their mattresses around, using them as punching bags. As we left the cellblock, we heard shouts and cries of, "Marine go home!" and "Fuck your mothers, marine!" coming from the surrounding cellblocks. I began to wonder how we'd be able to work on the blocks at all if our mere presence nearly incited a riot.

We did our best to shake off what we'd just witnessed on our walk back to the trailers that housed the admin offices.

I began working right away as the day shift took over for the night shift. My team of weary Army National Guard soldiers had already been in Gitmo for a month, but they looked as if they'd been there for years. I wondered if I'd look that way, too, in a few weeks, like a coal miner descending into a dark and dreary mine.

I quickly learned that being a guard at Gitmo meant dealing with two very different populations. The first group was made up of the hard-core fundamentalists on the higher-security blocks. These men watched me like birds of prey waiting for their opportunity to pounce on any weakness or mistake I'd make.

Most of these detainees were at a "lower-incentive" level, which meant they had only the bare minimum in their cells: a mattress, a pillow, sheets, and a Koran. As a result the most effective weapon they had against us was the cup. The men would fill it with bodily fluids throughout the day, waiting for the perfect moment to strike. When a guard was bending over to reach a paper plate that had been tossed through the bean hole—the name we used for the opening in the door—the detainee would grab his toxic weapon. As the guard stood up, he'd receive a face full of piss, shit, and anything else the detainee could squeeze into the cup.

These men would often flinch at the very touch of an American. To them we were unclean, unbelievers, unworthy of even looking them in the face. The most stressful times for us guards were during meals and showers. This was when we'd have to interact with the men and make ourselves even more vulnerable to their verbal or physical attacks. During dinnertime on the cellblocks, I'd often end up wearing more food than I served that night.

Other times our daily operations would escalate to a brutal and savage place. I'll never forget fighting hand to hand with someone who wanted to kill me. It reminded me of the two men fighting in the alley on my way to the car show. They were ugly and desperate battles.

When I interacted with this population of men, it was clear they were the enemy and that they belonged off the battlefield where they couldn't violently enforce their toxic worldview on innocent people and launch attacks on American and coalition forces.

But then there was another population of detainees. For these prisoners the battle was already over. You could tell they were broken men who didn't have a fighting bone in their body. Either they'd gotten caught up in a conflict that they didn't have much choice about or they were half-assed fighters who'd signed up to shoot at coalition troops in order to make a fast buck. It was clear very quickly who was a true jihadi and who was a bargain-basement mercenary or an innocent bystander in the wrong place at the wrong time.

My time in Gitmo seemed to be full of contradictions. There were moments where I felt proud of what I was doing, like when my fellow guards and I found plans to overrun an entire guard force—along with a stash of metal shanks—in a camp that was supposed to be for detainees who were cooperative and ready for release. Or when I stood up to the verbal and physical abuse of detainees who took every opportunity to strike me or hurl some nasty cocktail of bodily fluids in my face. I took great pride in reacting with the absolute minimum amount of force necessary to safely defuse the situation. No matter how much the detainees hated me and my country, they were under my care, and if anything happened to them, the responsibility would fall on my shoulders.

But there were many moments during my time at the controversial base when I felt confused and saddened by the circumstances we'd created for the men in our custody. There were many detainees who just seemed to miss their families; it was all they wanted to talk about. I often found myself spending extra time with them, pushing the boundaries prescribed by my duties. I remember one detainee in particular who claimed he'd been a farmer in Afghanistan when American forces came and captured him in his home. His eyes would fill with tears when we spoke about his kids, his village, and the life he'd been ripped away from. He'd received letters from his family that he kept neatly folded in his Koran. Whenever we'd speak, I'd bring him Jolly Rancher candies from the chaplain's office and slip them to him through the cage that separated us. I missed my family, but I knew I'd see them again soon. As far as I knew, this man's fate was uncertain. But one thing I was willing to bet my life on was that he wasn't a fundamentalist Islamic terrorist. I'd spent enough time up close and personal with men who hated our country and our culture to their very core. Hate that strong is difficult to disguise.

One day I was assigned to work on the cellblock where my farmer buddy was housed. I filled my pocket with Jolly Ranchers and made my way toward his cell, feeling as if I were going to see an old friend. When I reached his cell, it was empty. I asked the guard on the outgoing shift where the man had been moved to but received just an unconcerned shrug. My only option was to look up the man's ID number in the computer system we used to report our count throughout the day. To my surprise I'd remembered his assigned number, and when I punched it in, I learned that he'd been transferred to the camp designated for detainees who were being flown back to their home countries. My friend was going home.

I smiled as I walked away from the computer and continued with the day's duties. I thought of the man reuniting with his family, hugging his kids, and walking in his fields. Then I realized that even if he was returned directly to his village and his family, Afghanistan was still a war zone, his village likely occupied by NATO forces and Taliban operatives. He was arguably safer at Gitmo, where his every need was addressed and he could receive adequate medical care. The situation made me sick to my stomach. There didn't seem to be any kind of peaceful resolution for anyone. What was the endgame of the war on terror? How did we hope to bring peace to places like Afghanistan and Iraq? We weren't fighting an enemy with a flag or a nation, we were fighting an idea, a deep-seated belief that the world, not just the Middle East, needed to be ruled under sharia law.

While I slept well on the nights after a shift on one of the high-security cellblocks where the fundamentalists were housed, on the days that I guarded the broken men, I would stay awake wondering what the hell we thought we were doing. My deployment to Gitmo created more questions than it answered for me. At the time I had a relatively simplistic mind-set, but even I was having a hard time believing that we were gaining more than we were losing in Gitmo.

During my time in Guantánamo Bay, a layer of ignorance was peeled away from my young mind. The division between the guys who clearly belonged there and those who were caught up in the wrong place at the wrong time was obvious. I also saw very clearly that all of this was a symptom of a different kind of global conflict from those we'd fought in the past. What I worried about was that we were essentially creating new enemies by detaining people in this way. Most of the detainees were held in their cells for twenty-three hours a day, only coming out for an hour of recreation time in a caged area the size of half a tennis court and for showers and medical appointments.

Returning to my duties in Charleston was a relief. It felt great to drive around the Low Country in my Jeep and be alone in my kayak paddling through the deep, dark waters with the alligators and birds. In many ways things made sense again. Except when I got to work. After spending nearly a year handling and interacting with some of the world's deadliest terrorists, men who'd killed Americans and who wanted nothing more than to do it again, I had a hard time enforcing what seemed like insignificant rules and regulations within the brig. If an inmate wanted to stay in bed for an extra hour, I didn't care. If I found an extra pillow or an unauthorized number of socks during a cell inspection, I ignored it. I had a new standard for what actually constituted a threat to security. As long as the inmates in Charleston weren't harming one another or attempting to escape, I left them alone.

Post-Gitmo it was tough for me to judge my fellow service members and treat them like criminals, especially the ones who'd spent time in Iraq or Afghanistan. The war was only a few years old, but the regulations were complicated, and it seemed like a lot of the things guys were getting locked up for were a result of murky rules of engagement and leadership that forced people into life-or-death situations without proper guidance or direction.

Our military in the early 2000s was stretched thin, and our enlisted service members were finding themselves in increasingly stressful situations, both before and after they came home. The guys who got caught using drugs or assaulting people after returning from Iraq or Afghanistan didn't deserve to be locked up and disregarded—they needed treatment. The best I could offer them was a little extra time in the weight room or an hour or two of sleep during "active hours." I no longer cared about enforcing inconsequential rules governing uniform regulations or grooming standards. Many of the inmates had been discharged from the military while still serving their sentences. It didn't seem fair that they were forced to shave and wear a uniform just because they were incarcerated in a military facility.

I remember speaking to one inmate who'd just been sentenced to eighteen years for gunning down civilians during a firefight in an Iraqi village. When I read his charge sheet and the small amount of media coverage his case had received, it was easy to develop an opinion that the soldier was a savage and careless killer. Hearing his side of the story, however, broke my heart. During the firefight his friends were being shot and killed all around him. Meanwhile he'd had to figure out the difference between enemy and civilian, and he'd failed. It seemed to me that this was an incredibly complicated situation for any soldier, let alone a junior enlisted man on his first combat tour. It doesn't matter how much training you've had, there are some things you can never fully be prepared to face. Now this young man's life had been changed forever because of his inability to properly function in circumstances that most of our military would never find themselves in. How could any of us condemn him?

My concept of crime and punishment had been compromised. I no longer saw things in black and white, right and wrong. I saw them from the perspectives of everyone involved, especially the person who went to prison. It didn't mean I automatically sympathized with the men behind bars I was charged with detaining. Some of their cases were open-and-shut. They'd been criminals when they joined the military, and they'd continued their criminal activity while in uniform. It was the first-time offenders who made me think twice. The men who'd led otherwise upstanding lives as fathers and co-workers, serving their nation while raising a family. Through a series of events, however, some their own fault and some consequences of poor leadership and unimaginable stress, their careers and lives were utterly compromised.

My philosophy when it came to the inmates in Charleston became one of mutual respect—and indifference. My days in the brig became much easier to get through once I stopped looking for infractions to enforce that only served to create a more stressful environment for me and the inmates.

If Guantánamo opened the door for me to develop a more understanding and compassionate worldview, then my experience in Afghanistan and my training as a human-intelligence officer pushed me through that door. After my first four years as an MP, I knew two things: I loved being a marine and I wanted a different job. Eventually I found my way to the field of human intelligence and counterintelligence. It was the perfect fit, a deployable job that played an important role on the battlefield. The training was difficult, but it was worth it to finally be in a role I loved.

One of the first tests we had to pass as human-intelligence trainees was the interrogation screening. This involved weeks of training and researching the rules and techniques for successful interrogations. By the end of this phase, we'd lose almost half our class. The rigorous process was the instructors' way of trimming the fat early. If you couldn't hack it in the interrogation booth, then you weren't worth their time.

For the training we were placed in a simulated environment in a fictional country that was dealing with the fallout of a civil war. The training ground was the Virginia Beach area, where we'd have to navigate a network of surveillance-detection methods to meet with our sources and a mock town on base where we'd conduct patrols through crowded markets and village streets packed with role-players. Then we were locked in a room for hours with an instructor assuming the part of a terrorist so that we could simulate interrogating him. When it was my turn, all I knew was that the instructor in front of me was playing a thoughtfully scripted role. He had information for me, but he would reveal it only if I identified and used the right interrogation approach. It was up to me to figure out what that was.

During the first three hours, I did my best to run a "fear-up" approach, describing every terrifying scenario that would befall the man if he didn't comply with my every question. After three hours of listening to me paint the gloomiest picture I could for him, my subject had only managed to cry and piss himself. At first I thought these were good signs. *I'm getting to him,* I thought as I watched urine drip down his pants and onto his shoes. The goal of the interrogation was to get him to "break," meaning I'd identified his breaking point and could now bend him to my will. After reducing my subject to losing control of his bodily fluids, I thought I was on the verge of getting my first break. The way you determine this is by asking a pertinent question, something he wouldn't want to give up under normal circumstances. When I asked the man this question, however, he froze. He had nothing to say. For a while I sat there waiting for him to speak. I began trying to ramp up my fear approach, talking about what would happen to his family while he rotted in jail. But it felt like kicking a deflated ball. I wasn't getting any reaction. I decided to take a minute outside the room and rethink my strategy.

In the hallway one of the other instructors leaned out of the control booth where they watched our interrogations.

"Stick with the fear-up—maybe he'll shit himself!" he told me.

I knew that my instructors weren't looking for marines who needed their hands held. When I faced this situation for real, I would likely be alone on a battlefield with no one around to tell me what I was supposed to do. I felt that my time in the course was beginning to be measured in minutes, and if I couldn't figure this out, I'd be gone.

Then I remembered how in Guantánamo I'd once seen an interrogator letting a prisoner watch DVDs in an air-conditioned room—all in order to get the information out of him that the interrogator had needed. They had shared laughs and a hookah together; they'd gotten to know each other over snacks and small talk. I hadn't heard of anyone using this approach during our training. All my fellow classmates seemed to be bragging about their epic fear-up interrogations. But this seemed like the only option after taking such a hard line with the man.

Before I walked back into the booth, I grabbed two bottles of water from a cooler outside. Without saying anything, I handed one to the man along with some tissues. I even opened it for him. I watched as he drank down half the bottle. When he put it back on the table, he looked at me and said, "Thank you, I needed that," looking down at his urine-soaked pants.

We both burst out laughing, and I joked about getting him some toilet paper if he needed it. I asked him about his life before the conflict, what his childhood was like, what he envisioned for his children, and I shared some of my own story. Before I knew it, we were bonding over our shared struggle as people in the world, searching for meaning and purpose. We paid each other sincere compliments and each heard the other's deepest fears. That was when I saw my opportunity.

"It seems like your biggest fears are related to the forces that are trying to take over the government," I said, leaning forward in my chair a little bit. The man leaned forward, too, and let out a big sigh.

"You're right. Whatever I can do to stop them, I should do, because it will make a better life for me and my family."

He proceeded to tell me about his neighbor who was secretly building bombs in his basement and handing them out to rebels at a café in town. As I followed my training for asking follow-up questions, I felt a sense of accomplishment I'd never felt before. I'd thought on my feet, used my head and my heart, and gotten myself through the situation.

A little over a year later, when I found myself face-to-face with a real-life interrogation situation just outside Marjah in Helmand province, Afghanistan, I already had a road map for how to deal with it.

The subject in question was rumored to be a Taliban commander who had lobbed grenades into people's homes, killing entire families for cooperating with Afghan government and coalition forces. We raided his house and found IED-making materials like blasting caps, homemade explosives, wires, and jugs, along with ammunition and an AK-47 with a bright red buttstock.

The man was huddled in the corner of the chicken coop in the compound we'd turned into our base, with a blindfold on. He was shaking and terrified. His hands and feet were zip-tied together. I was surrounded by RECON marines and Afghan commandos who were all looking at me. With the help of my translator, Ali, it was my job to get this man to divulge what he knew to me. I thought about the families he'd killed, the fear he'd instilled in people's lives, and the wounds he'd inflicted that would never heal. I was consumed with rage, but I knew that would be what he was expecting.

Instead I stood him up, cleaned him off a little bit, and had one of the RECON marines bring a crate for him to sit on. I removed his blindfold and smiled at him. Over the next three days, I built a relationship with the man. There were moments when I screamed at him and took away what little comfort he had and moments when we laughed together. We shared meals and talked about raising children in a war zone. While I never achieved a "break," I did get enough information to justify his further detention. A helicopter came and whisked him away to where he could be further processed and interrogated. I didn't have the same sense of accomplishment that I'd had in Virginia Beach, but we all slept better knowing that one more Taliban fighter was off the battlefield.

My training and experience in human intelligence taught me the value of asking questions and listening. I saw that putting myself in someone else's shoes was more than a courtesy, it was a necessary skill. Especially when it came to people who were enemies of the free world. I realized I always got further when I started by trying to figure out where someone was coming from. It left me vulnerable at times, but the gains usually far outweighed the risks.

It had been more than fifteen years since I'd first left home to start my career in the military. I had joined as a fresh-faced nineteen-year-old with an unflinching view of right and wrong. Before long my experience in the marines helped me realize through firsthand experience that the world of crime and punishment isn't clear-cut and transparent, it's muddy and inconsistent.

Now Randy's approach to prison and prisoners had shown me a way to help offenders find a sense of purpose and self-worth, to give them a second chance and opportunities for redemption. Despite some residual skepticism on my part when I'd first arrived at Maine State, I was now convinced that Randy's philosophy was the right one. By coming up to the prison and volunteering my time, I felt that I was doing something to positively affect the guys. I was spending three hours every week sitting with the group, telling stories, sharing fears and feelings, and bearing witness to the heartbreak that comes with every prison sentence. What I didn't realize yet was the profound level on which the guys were beginning to affect *me*.

In the early days after my return from Afghanistan, it had been difficult for me to talk about myself and my experiences in the military. I saw every well-intentioned question from a counselor or a concerned friend or relative as an attempt to get me to "break," to let my guard down and share something I wasn't prepared to reveal about myself. Fred was my outlet. He helped me see that being open and sharing my story with others meant finding a purpose in it. Through the writing process and going out to talk about my book, I learned that the more I could be honest and vulnerable with others, the more I understood myself and my place in the world.

But there was still part of me that was closed off, frozen, scared of what would happen if I truly let people see me. As my therapist at the VA had pointed out to me, I might be permanently altered from what I'd experienced in Afghanistan. I remained fiercely protective against letting anyone see that. I had too much to be grateful for to have any problems I couldn't handle on my own. I'd been born into a loving and supportive family, I'd made it home from Afghanistan with my life, all my limbs, and a great dog. And I'd accomplished my goal of writing my first book. Why was I still struggling with the same issues?

The men of Maine State Prison had taken down their walls, and slowly they were chipping away at mine.

CHAPTER 12

Acts of Kindness

By the time I saw the puppies again, I almost didn't recognize them. It had been a month since I'd last visited the prison. All through May, Fred had been in high demand. Together with Nora and Ruby, we'd spent the month traveling to appear at speaking events, from Minnesota to Wisconsin to Maryland. Returning to Maine always made us fall in love with our new home state all over again. After weeks on the road—often involving a lot of time spent in crowded cities—crossing the state line into Maine sent a calming wave to our core. The pine trees seemed to lean forward, pointing us home. After unpacking the truck and restocking the fridge, my next priority was getting back up to Maine State Prison. I'd missed the guys, and I didn't want them to think for a second that I'd forgotten about them. And I couldn't wait to see how much the puppies had grown.

I decided to head up early in the morning without Fred. He'd done enough time in the truck, and he could happily sit this one out. I arrived a little late after getting distracted by the siren song of Moody's Diner, a Maine institution, famous for their doughnuts and home-cooked classics. As I walked into the puppy classroom, I could see that the lesson was already under way, with Rebecca and Paula at the helm, Paula having made a special trip to see how the puppies were coming along.

At first glance the pups had each gotten so much bigger it was hard to tell which dog was which. Their legs were longer, but the rest of their bodies hadn't caught up yet, so they looked like pups on stilts. The guys all gave me a nod when I walked in and then turned their attention immediately back to the class. I took my seat next to Callahan, who patted me on the shoulder and whispered, "Welcome back," between taking his notes.

The lesson today was about how to teach the dogs to handle distractions. As each guy walked his dog around the room, Paula tried to divert the pups' attention by playing the part of an excited bystander:

"OH! WHO'S A GOOD BOY!? ARE YOU A GOOD BOY!? COME HERE, PUPPY! HELLO, HELLO!!"

It was funny to watch Paula, normally the disciplined trainer, speaking in high-pitched baby talk, but clearly this was an important aspect of the dogs' training. These puppies were going to need to be prepared to deal with all kinds of distractions once they got out into the world while staying completely focused on their owner.

Despite Paula's best attempts to distract Sayville, the strong-willed female in the group, the dog stayed on task, with only a flicker of side-eye every now and again. I was glad to see Cory working so well with her after what seemed like a challenging start.

Nate and LJ navigated Paula's gauntlet of diversions, LJ remaining unfazed as he pranced around the room at Nate's heel, his eyes darting from straight in front of him up to meet his handler's eyes.

Next Paula squeaked a stuffed gorilla in LJ's direction, waving it wildly at the puppy.

"You're not going to get him with that, Paula," Nate said proudly. "I'm notorious for not letting people engage with LJ. Everyone in here knows that. I won't even tell people his name, because I don't want them calling out to him when we're in the yard training. Most people think his name is 'Nate's dog.'"

The class continued with Paula introducing more and more distractions to the room. By the end there was a clapping monkey banging cymbals while marching in circles, that flipping stuffed Chihuahua again, a vibrating lizard, and a two-foot-long wooden teeter-totter that slammed into the ground when the dogs walked over it. The men all paraded their pups around the chaotic classroom, calmly navigating the cartoon-ish obstacles.

The whole thing looked so silly that I had to suppress a laugh—but the guys didn't even break a smile. Instead they stayed focused on the pups, making sure to offer praise and encouragement at the right moments. From the outside it was easy to see the humor in a bunch of grown men guiding puppies around squeaking and squawking toys, but the guys knew that this was serious business. If the puppies could be easily distracted, they wouldn't be able to safely pay attention to their future owners. Their professionalism was exemplary.

The puppy class wrapped up as Paula offered her insights into each dog, observing each one's strengths and what each would need to work on most.

"Overall you guys are doing a great job," she said as the trainers collected up their dogs for the walk back to the Veterans' Pod. "As long as we continue to create good habits and stay consistent, you'll continue to improve. Keep it up."

After leaving the puppy class, I took my short break before heading in for the writing session.

I spent my break walking off my Moody's doughnuts around Rockland, enjoying the warm spring air while exploring one of Maine's most popular coastal towns before the tourist season. It gave me some time to think about today's topic with the men, "acts of kindness." I had instructed them to share stories about a time in their lives when they were on the receiving end of an act of kindness and what that felt like.

Here's what I wrote in the syllabus about the class:

Compassion is a powerful thing. It allows us to understand one another and often replaces anger with tolerance. Think of a time when compassion was displayed in your life. It can be a time you were compassionate toward someone or when someone else showed compassion to you. What were the circumstances? Why was it meaningful to you? How has it affected your life since? OR: A truly kind act is something bigger than holding the door for someone or wishing them a happy birthday. It takes extra thought and effort to be kind. Think of a time when you witnessed true kindness. It could be something someone did for someone else or for you or something you did for someone. What made it different from just being nice?

Back inside I sat with the men and listened. With the exception of Mr. Craig, who was snoozing again, everyone else was there. Nate volunteered to go first. The same guy who rarely spoke at length in our writing group sessions, and who had just shown me how accomplished he was with a five-month-old puppy, now began sharing more about his story than he ever had before.

"My story about kindness is from my trial," Nate started. "I knew I was going up before the judge, and I knew I was going to be facing some serious time. I felt completely helpless. Like my life was over."

Although he'd brought his notebook with him, Nate was speaking from his heart. The memory was crystallized in his mind, as was the pain that came with it.

"Two ladies from my hometown got together and decided to buy me a suit," Nate continued, looking down at his cup of coffee. "They knew what I'd done, because it was in all the newspapers, and even so they found it in their hearts to help me. I didn't even know them. They just asked my mom for my measurements and told her they'd take care of it."

I'd never asked Nate about the crime that had put him away in here—I usually left it up to the men to decide how much they wanted to share with me. But as he rarely talked about getting out, like the other guys did, I assumed he must have done something pretty serious.

"I knew I was going away for a long time," Nate said, looking back up and around the room. His face was blank, as if he'd just gotten some very bad news and was still in shock. "But there was something about putting on that suit that has stuck with me and always will. I was starting to believe what the media and the prosecution was saying about me, that I was some kind of monster. It was the darkest place I've ever been mentally. But the suit reminded me I was still a person and I was worthy of redemption, even if just within my own mind, even if the judge and the media didn't think so. A true act of kindness often comes from strangers."

"That's beautiful, Nate," I told him. "I don't ever want to forget that story. I guess strangers are often the only ones capable of truly selfless and kind acts, because they don't know or care about our past, they just want to help another person."

"Ya, strangers and dogs," Nate agreed. "Dogs don't care about our pasts, they just want to be there for us, no strings attached."

"That's for sure," I told him.

Nate looked up from his coffee and I could sense that he was about to tell us more, maybe even more than he'd anticipated sharing before coming into the session.

"Looking back, I think my biggest mistake was not going active duty," he went on.

I knew that Nate had been in the National Guard, but I couldn't imagine how that was his biggest misstep. The Guard and reserves are an attractive option for anyone looking to join the military. You receive the same training as active-duty personnel, and you can work on building your civilian career while going to school and getting valuable experience in the military. For Nate and many other members of our military force it was a way to serve without leaving too much behind.

"Why was that a mistake?" I asked.

"After the mill closed and I was out of work, I knew that the army would be a good option for me, and it was. It was the first time in my life I'd felt like I was on track. I was a good soldier. Then I came home from training, and all my demons were waiting for me," he said, the regret clear in his voice. "It's nobody's fault but mine. But I'm not a monster. I just got off track and never found my way back."

Nate explained about how hard the opioid crisis had hit his hometown, how few jobs there were available. All his training and newfound discipline as a soldier weren't enough to save him from addiction and lack of opportunity. The reality was, he was left with very few options in the weeks between his stints of National Guard duty.

It was clear to me that Nate wasn't looking for pity. He was still trying to forgive himself for his mistakes, and looking back on the decisions he'd made throughout his life, like joining the Guard instead of going active duty, was a part of that.

"It says a lot about where you're at now, man," I said. "That you can trace it back to one decision that really changed the course of your life."

"I'm doing the most time out of anyone here," he continued. "So I've got nothing but time to think about where it all went wrong."

Then he sat back in his chair, opening up the discussion to everyone else. A tortured look fixed itself on his face.

Next up was Kidd. He had printed out his writing, and he shuffled it like a news anchor getting ready to deliver a breaking story. Everyone refilled their coffee cups and shifted their attention to him. Kidd's story was from January of the year before. Sadly, his grandfather had passed away, and Kidd had decided to put in an application to be released to go to his funeral. Kidd knew it was a long shot and that the administration would probably decline the application, but he figured he didn't have anything to lose. Eventually, to Kidd's disbelief, the request was granted, in large part thanks to a transport officer who volunteered to come into the prison on his day off to bring Kidd to the funeral. Just as Nate had been positively affected by the kindness of the two women who'd bought him the suit, the guard's act of selflessness meant that Kidd was able to say good-bye to his grandfather and see his family at the funeral. Kidd got to speak during the service and eulogize his grandpa. And he even got a little taste of the freedom that awaited him in the future when, after the service, he was allowed to attend a reception with his family in the church basement.

"I found a seat and plopped down, and immediately the table was full and people were hovering around me," Kidd described, conjuring up the memory. "Everyone was showing me pictures on their phones—'Look at this'—and simultaneously someone else was snapping a picture: 'SMILE!' I was too overwhelmed to eat despite dreaming about the time when I could eat real homemade food again. I ate some chocolate-chip cookies, and that is it. It was blissful. I never wanted it to end. Eventually the officer told me the time had come, and I walked around the entire basement saying good-bye to everyone there. Actually saying 'See you soon.' If I'm honest, I never left that basement. I am still there in my mind and am reminded of how joyous that day is going to be. Free from anxiety and worries that surrounded me before. The way I feared people perceiving me is replaced by the knowledge that I am truly loved, welcomed, and known by those who matter most."

"That is an incredible story, man," I said as he finished. "It really is proof of how powerful kindness can be in the life of another person who really needs it, don't you guys think?"

"Ya, I mean, a part of me was hoping I'd get denied the request so I'd have a good excuse for not being there. I was terrified of facing my family," Kidd replied.

"Same with me and my suit," said Nate, "It made me uncomfortable at first to have strangers do something for me, but once I opened myself up to their generosity, I realized how meaningful their gift really was. I can't undo what I did, no matter how bad I want to. I'll be filled with remorse for the rest of my life. But their gift reminded me that I still had some good in me."

"Who we are at our worst isn't who we really are. At least it doesn't have to be," Chet chimed in.

"That's right," agreed Kidd.

We talked a little more as a group about kindness, compassion, and our evolving relationships with these concepts. But as I left the prison that day, I couldn't shake the look of anguish on Nate's face as he finished telling his story.

Later that night I decided to do something I hadn't done with any of the guys yet. I Googled Nate. I wanted to see for myself where his decision to join the Guard had led him. I found various newspaper articles from the time of his trial, as well as court documents. The more I read, the more my heart sank in my chest. Nate had killed two people and was convicted of manslaughter for one victim and murder for the other. From what the court documents said, it seemed like a horrible accident. The two people he'd shot were his neighbors and the parents of one of his closest friends. He'd taken an old pistol into their home to try to sell it to them in return for money to buy drugs—according to the friend, Nate also owed the father money. While Nate was there, the gun went off in his hand, killing the father, and then when the man's wife ran into the kitchen to help him, Nate panicked and shot her. Nate had been sentenced to over forty years. I did the math. He wasn't going to be released until he was in his sixties.

I tried to reconcile what Nate had done with the man I knew him to be: the man who trained puppies and told stories in our writing group. It was hard to make the two fit together in my mind. Yes, he had committed murder—he'd killed two people, there was no getting around that—but as far as I could tell from the documents I found online, and his statement during the trial, when he entered the house that night, that had not been his intention in any shape or form. He clearly wasn't a career criminal or a cold-blooded murderer, just someone who'd made a terrible mistake while in the throes of a serious addiction.

It made sense to me why, sitting in our classroom, many years after his crimes, it seemed as if it was still a shock to him that he'd ended up in prison, as if his life were a bad dream that he'd eventually wake up from. No wonder the gift of the suit from two strangers had been so important to him. It was proof to him that he was still human.

I also considered the fact that Nate was even showing up for classes. Of all the men in the dog program and our writing group, Nate had the least amount of incentive to participate. While Kidd, Marcus, and Chet were all reaching the end of their sentences and were focused on improving themselves in preparation for returning to the real world, Nate was going to have to serve every day of his forty years. No ifs, ands, or buts. It didn't matter that he was sorry, that he spent his days training dogs for disabled veterans, and he certainly wasn't getting out any earlier for spending his time sharing his story with me in our group. In fact, you could say that he was making his time in prison more difficult by participating in programs that involved self-improvement and growth. It would be much easier on Nate mentally if he shut down and spent his time getting high and disengaging from the world outside the walls. But that wasn't who he was. Through his story Nate had shown me who he was before he came to Maine State and before he was ever put on trial—a kid who'd made the mistake of joining the National Guard so he could return home instead of getting shipped out to wherever the army decided to send him.

CHAPTER 13

Second Chances

"So how did you end up in prison?" I asked with a smile.

I was standing in the lobby at Maine State with Rebecca while we waited for Michael Fournier to come and escort us back for the puppy class. I'd wanted to ask her for weeks how she ended up getting the job of prison puppy-program trainer. After all, it was far from a typical career choice.

"I heard about it from someone else in the dog-training community," she replied, her dark hair pulled up into a bun on top of her head. "America's VetDogs is a really respected organization within the dog-training world, and they know how to get the word out to the right people."

"Had you ever been to a prison before working here?" I asked.

"My first time in a prison was the first day we walked the puppies in," she replied. "I was nervous, but I was nervous when I joined the army, too, and that was one of the best decisions I ever made. After my first day here, I realized that most of my fears were in my head. It's just a place for me to do my job now."

We took turns passing through the metal detector. "I wanted this job because I felt like it was my purpose, and I was missing that after the army. I've been training dogs my entire life, but this felt like a chance for me to use my experience to serve and give back in a more meaningful way."

I learned that Rebecca had been forced to leave the army prematurely because she'd developed a medical condition that affected her breathing. After her first year in the military, she was medically separated and returned to Maine. It was a blow to her self-confidence, as it would be for any young person trying to find their footing in the world. For a long time, like many veterans, she struggled to obtain the same sense of self-worth she'd had in the army. Working at Maine State Prison didn't make a lot of sense on paper—she had to drive almost two hours from her home and her own dog-training business, and the pay wasn't anything life-changing—but it gave her an opportunity to serve others, to be a part of something bigger than herself. In many ways the dog program at Maine State Prison was Rebecca's second chance.

Through the window in the metal slider door, we could see Michael Fournier coming down the long hallway. The big blue door jolted open, and we both smiled and shook hands with Fournier, who had a lot to tell Rebecca about on our walk back to the classroom. I let the two of them talk.

The education area of the prison was buzzing today. There was a yoga class going on in one room, a meditation group in another, and a band singing Christian rock songs in the chapel area. If the men hadn't been wearing the same prison-issue blue jeans and white T-shirts, the place could easily have passed for the campus of an all-male community college.

As we walked by the classroom next to where the dogs were, I heard someone call my name.

"Hey, Craig! Good to see you, man!"

It was Troy. He and I had talked a few weeks earlier when I was visiting with the guys in the Veterans' Pod. Troy was an inmate in his late thirties and the head of a program called Fly Time that taught the guys how to make lures and flies for fly-fishing. Kidd and Nate had taken to it, and he'd just dropped by to deliver some of their supplies. The group members were responsible for making intricate flies on their own time that would then go to nonprofits that take people on fishing trips around Maine. Each fly took a great deal of time and concentration to get just right. Looking at some of the ones Troy had in a small box he carried around with him made my brain hurt. The knots and loops in each one looked like they'd been tied by tiny elves, not grown men.

I waved to Troy from the hallway, saying I'd catch up with him later. It felt good to be recognized by other guys in the prison, outside my normal groups.

In the dog classroom, I said hello to the guys and took my place next to Calli, who already had his laptop out.

Rebecca seemed pleased with the progress the puppies had made since last week. All except Sayville, who was still finding ways to resist her training.

"She won't give me any eye contact, or when she does, it's just enough to get me to praise her a little, and then she goes right back to doing her own thing," a frustrated Cory confessed to Rebecca.

"It's okay, she's just a very independent dog," Rebecca said with a smile that seemed to provide some much-needed encouragement to the frustrated Cory. "I know it's difficult to see LJ and Webber moving along in their training, but you're going to have to take it back to the basics. Just focus on eye contact, sit, and stay until she gets it. Don't introduce anything new. She'll come around. I'll tell you when it's time to get discouraged."

The men were getting excited for the upcoming demonstration at the prison on June 22. Each of them would be responsible for demonstrating a few skills with their puppies. Before the class was over, Rebecca had them do a run-through of the program. It was just what the men and the puppies needed, to end the class on a high note.

Each dog and each man had a responsibility. Since Kidd was

the best public speaker and wasn't attached to a dog, he would serve as the emcee for the demonstrations. From his notebook he pulled out a typed-up script and reviewed it while the rest of the guys and dogs got ready.

The first team up was Cory and Sayville.

"Here we have Cory and Sayville. They're here to demonstrate up, down, and sit," Kidd said in a clear and confident tone. As he spoke, Cory led his little black pup toward a wooden box they used during their training. He gave her the command "Up!" and as she hopped up onto the box, she slid on the slippery tile floor, making a loud *thwonk* that made all the dogs jump—including herself. Cory immediately looked down at Sayville reassuringly saying, "It's okay, girl, good girl." Then he looked up at Rebecca.

"It's not her fault. The floor is so slick in here," he said defensively.

"It's okay, just try again, and hold your foot against the box if you need to," she replied patiently.

"The room where we're doing this is carpeted, so it won't be a problem," Kidd reminded everyone before resuming his explanation of Cory and Sayville's skills.

"The up command is useful for the veteran if he or she needs the dog to jump or climb onto an elevated surface. We condition our dogs to become accustomed to a variety of heights and surfaces so they're comfortable with whatever the world throws at them."

On the second try, Sayville executed it without a hitch, as well as a perfect down and sit. She was done. Cory could take a deep breath.

"Next up we have Charlie and his dog, Webber. They'll be demonstrating sit, stay, and fetch," Kidd said, continuing his emcee duties.

Charlie and Webber made their way to the center of the room.

Charlie gave the sit command, and his little black pup sat perfectly. As Charlie backed away and began to give the stay command, however, Webber took the opportunity to flop down on his belly, resting his head on his oversize paws. It was really cute, and as far as I was concerned, he hadn't technically violated any rules. He was right where Charlie had left him, after all. But he hadn't been given the command to lie down and look cute. He was supposed to stay in a sit until he heard another command from his trainer. Charlie patiently leashed his pup and walked him around the room to try to wake him up a bit so they could try again. That did the trick, because after a quick lap around the room, Webber executed a perfect sit, stay, and fetch, bringing Charlie a small Kong toy he'd placed on the other side of the classroom.

"The skills that Webber is demonstrating are the building blocks for important functions the dog will go on to learn," Kidd read. "Fetch eventually becomes bring, which is a useful skill for veterans who need assistance around the home."

Next up was LJ, the star pupil of his puppy class.

"Finally we have Nate and LJ. They'll be demonstrating kennel, head into vest, and body handling," Kidd recited from his script as Nate and LJ began their maneuvers. "The head into vest is one of the more crucial and difficult things to teach a dog."

Nate held up the vest for LJ, and I watched in amazement as the young puppy inserted his head through the opening in the vest, practically putting it on himself.

"It is important for the dogs to be able to assist in getting themselves ready for the day in case their veteran is incapable of doing so unassisted," Kidd went on, reading aloud.

After that, Nate opened LJ's kennel and gave the command "kennel" to the puppy. To my astonishment LJ went right through the open door and stood inside the kennel, looking up at Nate confidently.

That'll be a hit with the crowd, I thought. I couldn't believe I was seeing a dog as young as LJ essentially put on his own vest and walk himself into his kennel.

But LJ wasn't finished yet. Nate released the door of the kennel, and LJ stayed put, standing in the open doorway. Just because the gate was ajar, that didn't mean he could run out. Nate gave him the command to leave the kennel, and then LJ went right over to the wooden box. After hearing "Up!" from Nate, LJ hopped up onto the box. The trainer then got him into a down position and began inspecting his paws, belly, and mouth in a practice known as "body handling."

"It's important for the dogs to develop trust with their handlers," Kidd explained. "The practice of body handling teaches them to allow their handlers and veterinarians to inspect and treat any issues they might have, without resistance."

Of all the skills the puppies were learning, that might be the one I wished I'd taught Fred. Fred is a good dog, and I have a strong connection with him; he knows when I'm upset, and our shared experience in combat is something that binds us together in a unique and powerful way. But Fred is still very much a wild man. If he's off leash and he sees a squirrel, he's gone, and there isn't much I can do to stop him. Although I love his adventurous spirit—even when I've had to chase him through the woods—it causes problems when I have to examine him. Fred is very particular about his hygiene and his body, but anytime he has something—whether it's a tick or a doggie zit—and I need to inspect him, he squirms and fights me, making it very difficult to figure out what's going on. I don't hold it against him. He was born a stray and was used to taking care of himself before I came along, but it would be nice if occasionally he just let me take a look without forcing me to wrestle him.

What was becoming obvious to me as I watched the prison

puppies progress from week to week was that the skills they were developing were more than neat tricks. They were methods of harnessing the natural instincts of dogs—of loyalty, companionship, and trust—and taking them a step further. Rebecca and the trainers were fine-tuning the human-dog bond and transforming it into a superpower. They were making sure that the veteran the dog went on to serve would be that dog's number-one priority at all times. If the dogs saw another dog or a critter that was begging to be played with or chased, their first instinct was going to be to look up at their handler. If they didn't receive the command, they didn't go. That is the level of dedication and loyalty our veterans deserve.

After a quick break, I was back at the prison, hanging with my guys in our little classroom. One by one they made their way in. Each of them had a glow from spending the afternoon outside in the June sun. Kidd rode on the arm of Mr. Craig's wheelchair across the dayroom, the two of them wearing matching white tank tops. Mr. Craig looked like he was ten years younger than he'd been the last time I'd seen him. All that napping must have done him good.

"Oh, boy, here comes hell on wheels," I said as they cruised through the classroom door, skidding to a halt just before the table.

"Had a great workout in the yard today," Kidd told me with a big smile. "Marcus and I crushed a training workout for The Murph. It's one of the memorial ones for a fallen Navy SEAL."

In his white tank, Kidd raised a fist to show off his swollen biceps.

"And I got a workout just watching them," Mr. Craig said jokingly, wiping his forehead with a towel.

I knew about The Murph, a workout dedicated to Michael P. Murphy, a SEAL who was posthumously awarded the Medal of Honor for his selfless acts of courage and bravery on an Afghan hillside in Kunar province. The workout consisted of a one-mile run, one hundred pull-ups, two hundred push-ups, three hundred squats, and another one-mile run. The guys were going to compete against their fellow inmates for the fastest time.

Marcus and the rest of the guys barreled into the room, bringing all their energy with them. It was clear that they were having a good day.

Today's topic of discussion was "second chances." I was interested to see in what direction the guys took this theme. I wanted them to really examine their lives and understand how the good and the bad played an equal role in their journeys.

"Think about a time when you gave someone a second chance," I'd written in the syllabus. "Or when someone gave you a second chance. What did it mean? How much of a risk was taken? Was redemption found? Do you regret it? Why or why not? More often than not, we need more than one second chance. Write about one, or all of yours."

For the first half hour, however, we were just a bunch of boys in a locker room. We talked about our biceps and how to get the best pump. The guys laughed when I told them my workout regimen that was important when I was young and single.

"I used to do curls-for-girls, but now I call them curls-for-Nora," I said with a smile, knowing that Nora didn't care one way or another how many curls, pull-ups, or push-ups I could do. Like most of the silly stuff we do to attract someone, it was all for our own benefit. What Nora found the most appealing were the things I was trying to hide behind the muscles and hair products.

"How are you going to run the mile portion of The Murph?" I asked, wondering how someone runs a mile inside a prison.

"Fournier has it mapped out. I think it's like forty laps around the gym or something," Marcus said.

"I tried it already. It felt good to run a mile," Kidd chimed in. "Can't remember the last time I did that. I think I'll start running when I get out. I love the idea of just being able to run uninterrupted over a long distance."

"Ya, right, dude, you'll be hacking up a lung after fifty yards," Marcus jabbed. "Who do you think you are, Forrest Gump?"

And the trash talk continued.

The upcoming Murph had given the guys something physical to focus on. It was Michael Fournier's idea; he organized similar events throughout the year. On the surface it seemed like a distraction for the guys, to give them something to occupy their minds and bodies. But on a deeper level, Fournier was creating natural ways for the guys to discover how good habits paid off in the long run. He was showing them that when they focused on something, making changes in their daily routine to accommodate a training schedule, it was worth it. It was more than just a diversion from their lives in prison, it was *therapy* disguised as a workout.

Kidd and Marcus were most interested in their own friendly competition. Like two brothers they bickered about how each one's method of training was harder than the other's and how their strategy would give them the edge.

Just when I thought I was losing control of the group for this session, Marcus spoke up.

"Hey, guys, I'm going first this week. I really liked this topic," he said loud enough to cut everyone's sidebar conversations short.

"Okay, Marcus, what did you like about it?" I asked, grateful that someone else had stepped up to start the session.

"Well, when I think about it, my entire life has been a second chance," he said, his voice taking a more serious and reflective tone than I'd ever heard from him.

The guys grew quiet as everyone realized that for the first time since many of them had known him, Marcus was serious.

"I was adopted. Both my birth parents are drug addicts and have been in and out of prison their entire lives," Marcus explained. "My mom and dad, I don't call them my adopted parents or anything like that. They're my true parents in my mind, without a doubt."

As he spoke, he looked at me to make sure I got that part right.

"My mom and dad gave me a second chance by adopting me," he went on, reading from his notes now. "I could have ended up in foster care or something like that. By bringing me in and treating me like one of their own from day one, they showed me what a family is supposed to look like.

"Even so, I've had a fear of rejection and a cycle of anxiety throughout my life. I knew my mom and dad loved me. They adopted me, and to me they are my parents, but there was still this feeling that at some point they'd change their mind or feel that they'd made a mistake. I think that I used that as an excuse throughout my life to make bad decisions or just not care about the consequences of my addiction. I didn't have to fear being rejected if I was high.

"What I like most about this week's topic is that you talked in the syllabus about how more often than not we need more than one second chance. Well, I think it's safe to say that I blew my first one. All the love and support my parents gave me, I threw it all away. They tried to save me from a life of addiction and crime, a life my birth parents are still in today, but I found a way to screw it up."

As he spoke, Marcus looked around the room at the rest of the guys, his voice taking on a raw tone, as if he were admitting this out loud for the first time.

"What I see now through my time in prison, getting off drugs, and spending more time with quality people like Kidd and the guys in this group is that it's easier to stay on track when I surround myself with the right people. I see that I have value, and I see it most when I talk to my son. He is better than me in every way. He's only eight, but he tells me all the time that I need to behave, that I need to follow the rules, so I can get out and spend time with him. I know that my family loves me. Despite all I've put them through, my parents tell me they love me every time I talk to them. I know they'll be there for me when my time is up. I know my son will be ready to go fishing and camping, and he'll be ready to have his dad for the first time in his life. The hard part is giving *myself* another second chance. I've lost faith in my own abilities to make the right choices. I see clearly where I've gone wrong, but sometimes I worry that it's too late. Like I'm just destined to be a fuckup forever."

The group sat in silence for a few seconds, each of us waiting to make sure Marcus was done sharing his handwritten notes. Marcus was one of those guys everyone looked to for a quick joke and a big smile. He was the class clown, but today for the first time he let his guard down. It was obvious by the change in his voice and the fact that he hadn't smiled or cracked a joke in a record-breaking fifteen-minute stretch.

Finally Kidd spoke up to his friend.

"I know it's hard to see it from in here, man, but you're on the right path," he said bluntly. "It sucks that it took us coming here to get it right, but I've known you a long time, and this is the first time I can honestly say that you're on the right path."

Kidd had a way of cutting right through the bullshit, his words hitting like body blows of truth.

"I know, man. I'm starting to see it," Marcus replied, shrugging a little. "But at the same time, I've been so wrong for so long, sometimes it just seems like I'm too far gone."

Kidd wouldn't let it go, however.

"No, you're never too far gone. We're in here for the same crimes, man," he insisted. "If I can find it in myself, then so can you. The most important second chance is the one we give ourselves."

"Ya, maybe you're right," Marcus relented. "I'm not saying I'm giving up. I'm just saying if I focus on all this shit I've done, then it just seems like it's too much to come back from."

It was Chet's turn to offer some encouragement.

"You're preaching to the choir here, my friend. We've all felt that way at some point, and I still do. But as long as we're alive, we have to see the value we offer. I apologize all the time to my parents for what I did. It's my way of saying I'm sorry for what I've done to myself. I can't imagine what it must be like for them to see me go from an innocent child to where I am now. But like you said, I see my second chance in my daughter. She's given my parents new hope and taught them how to love again, and she's doing it for me, too. I'm finally ready to focus on the work it takes to be the best version of myself, for her. She's only known me in here, and that breaks my heart, but I have to make sure I make the most out of this time so she can know me out there."

As he said the words "out there," Chet pointed toward the wall on the other side of the pod.

The guys took turns lifting Marcus up. The role of the group had shifted. The guys weren't just gaining confidence in their writing and storytelling abilities, they were becoming better versions of themselves by reflecting on their experiences. And perhaps most important, they were listening to one another and helping one another. I realized that in many ways I was a part of a support group masquerading as a writing session.

My only piece of advice to Marcus was to make sure he didn't bend to peer pressure in the prison.

"You've got a big personality, man," I pointed out, "and it's your biggest gift to the world, in my opinion. But people expect a lot from you, and if there's even the slightest change in how you behave, even if it's what's best for you, you'll be made to feel like you're doing something wrong."

I could tell that Marcus was getting uncomfortable having the group focus on him for this long, but I wanted to make my point.

"I only say that because I've seen it happen in my life in recent years," I explained. "I've made a few changes to my habits and behaviors that were really important for my mental and physical health. I've stopped drinking in excess, and I've really committed to my relationship with Nora. Most of the people in my life have seen the changes and been happy and proud of me, but it's also been difficult for some people who knew me in my drinking days, and I wasn't expecting that.

"I've always been a light for others, and I take a lot of pride in that. But after Afghanistan my light was dimmed a little bit, and I needed help. I didn't ask for it because I was worried people would think I was broken. I was used to getting attention for being the life of the party. I didn't want to draw attention to myself for what felt like selfish and negative reasons. But that's the wrong approach. In the end it's never selfish to focus on yourself. It's the opposite, because when you're the best version of yourself, you can be there for everyone else."

As I spoke, I was looking directly at Marcus, but the reality was that these words were as much for myself as they were for him. In the past the only time I'd shared anything from my life with the guys was to move the conversation along or provide context for our topics. I felt silly complaining or comparing my problems to theirs; I was there for them, not the other way around. But hearing Marcus tell his story for the first time made me feel connected to him and the group on an entirely different level. I'd played that same role of the class clown and people pleaser as Marcus, and I saw myself in him. Eventually I understood that I wasn't doing myself or anyone else any favors by consistently putting my own feelings second. I had a hunch that Marcus knew what it meant to have his needs overlooked in the interest of making those around him comfortable. It felt good to discuss this dilemma with him, one that I'd never really verbalized before.

We were about two hours into our meeting, the point where Mr. Craig usually took an involuntary nap in his wheelchair, his wide chin resting on his chest like a scarecrow in a field of corn. On this day, however, I noticed he was listening to every word the men were saying. Chet had started to talk about his struggles with addiction and how hard it was to get clean when people around you wanted to drag you back into their world of robbing, cheating, stealing, and partying. Chet finished his thought, and Mr. Craig took advantage of the gap in the conversation.

"I feel sorry for just about everybody in this room," he said, his big eyes looking around the table.

"Why's that?" I asked.

"Well, when I was coming up, all you needed to worry about was alcohol and maybe smoking pot," he said, leaning forward a little in his chair. "But it wasn't addictive to most people like this shit y'all got hooked on. It don't alter the chemistry of your brain after just one go."

The guys silently nodded.

"As far as I'm concerned, y'all don't have much to be ashamed of," he said, the color rushing to his cheeks. "These drugs made you into somebody you ain't. Now, I killed a guy, but he had it comin', and if I hadn't killed him, he sure as shit woulda killed me."

The weight of what he'd said sank into me like a heavy fog. Some of the guys had talked a bit about what they had done, but I never pressed them for more information. If they wanted to talk about it, that was part of what we were there for, but I wasn't so much concerned with their pasts, more with their presents and futures.

"Do you want to tell us what happened, Mr. Craig?" I asked as respectfully as I could.

"I choked him out," the old man said matter-of-factly. "We got in a fight, just two men in their eighties duking it out in the backyard. Leo was my friend. We rode up to his place in Maine together from Florida, and I was staying with him. But things got out of hand, and I was just defending myself. Next thing I knew, I was on top of him choking the life out of him.

"I deserve to be in here. I don't deny that. But I'm an old man. This ain't much different than what I'd have if I was in an old-folks' home. It breaks my heart to see you young men in here. You're good boys, and you should be out livin' your lives."

"Will you tell that to my caseworker?" Calli said with a smile, patting his roommate on the back.

"I'd testify on behalf of any of you boys," Mr. Craig said, holding his right hand up and placing his other over his heart as he sat back in his wheelchair.

He'd made his point, his words hanging in the air with the smell of sour coffee.

Before the guys left for the day, I let them know that this was the last class listed on the syllabus.

"We made it through the first six weeks," I pointed out. "So do you guys want to keep going, or are you good?"

"I mean, if you're still down to come up here and hang out with us lowlifes, then I know I'd like to keep going. . . ." Kidd said.

"Ya, me, too," echoed Marcus, Calli, Nate, and Mr. Craig.

"You're stuck with us now, bud. You've created a monster," Chet said with a laugh.

"Ah, I feel the same way. I just wanted to make sure you guys know you're under no obligation," I said, grateful for the positive responses. "So what do you want to talk about next week?"

They chatted among themselves for a bit before coming up with a topic: "alcohol."

Mr. Craig's observation had clearly sparked something in them that they wanted to talk about.

"Okay," I said. "That's a subject I could probably say a few words about, too. I'll see you guys next time."

CHAPTER 14

Graduation

The date was June 22, 2019. A beautiful sunny Saturday, one of the first Maine had seen in the often unpredictable month of June. While the rest of the East Coast eases into summer, June can be somewhat of a weather wild card up here, but today it felt like the sunshine was finally beating back winter.

That morning Nora and I climbed into the truck for another visit to the prison. It was time for the doggie graduation ceremony, and we couldn't wait to see the puppies strut their stuff in front of a crowd. We decided to leave Ruby and Fred behind. Even though they were pretty well behaved, we didn't want them to detract attention from the dogs in the program and the people responsible for raising and training them. There were also a few very special guests scheduled to be there—this was shaping up to be a day to remember. On the drive up, Nora and I joked about Ruby and Fred changing the locks on the doors while we were gone to get back at us for leaving them home.

I'd heard from Paula that Prince Denson, the veteran who had received Michael Kidd's dog, Chess, was going to be the guest of honor. This would be the first time a graduate dog had returned to Maine State to see his trainer. Last time I'd spoken to Kidd about it, he was trying not to get too excited. In addition to the prospect of seeing Chess again and meeting Prince, Kidd had requested that his ten-year-old son be able to attend the event since Kidd was the emcee. It was a big ask for the prison staff, who would have to make an exception to the rules for Kidd, and as of last week they hadn't given him a definite answer. The concern was that it would cause problems with the other guys, who might also want to have members of their family present.

As we pulled in to Maine State Prison's parking lot, I saw Paula unloading pee pads and bags of dog food from the America's VetDogs minivan. And there was someone helping her. The man was on the shorter side and stocky. Next to him was a black Lab on a leash wearing a service-dog vest. I guessed the dog was Chess, and that meant the man holding his leash must be Prince, his veteran owner.

Nora and I made our way toward them and introduced ourselves.

I learned that this was the first time Prince had visited Maine State Prison or any prison for that matter. He lived with his wife and kids outside Philadelphia and had come all the way up to Maine to thank the man who'd trained Chess. He told me about the drive up and commented on the beautiful weather. Prince didn't offer any further details, but I knew from Paula that he was a former army helicopter pilot who had flown medevac flights as a civilian until he started having anxiety attacks.

We chatted some more as we walked toward the building together. I asked how Chess was doing.

"He's great. He's an amazing dog. I'm very grateful," Prince replied.

Prince had a kind of soft and confident way about him that reminded me of my dad and other people I knew who worked in the aviation industry, people who didn't speak until their words had passed a series of preflight checks. I felt instantly comfortable around him.

I asked Prince how he was feeling about meeting Michael Kidd, the trainer who shaped Chess.

"I'm excited to thank him in person," Prince responded quietly. "I want him to know he's not worthless, at least not to me."

We began to make our way toward the prison entrance, each of us carrying a bag of dog food and bundles of pee pads.

The lobby was packed with people, volunteers, and community members alike. The energy of the crowd reminded me of a church congregation chatting before the beginning of a service, everyone catching up with neighbors and learning about one another's lives. I had to remind myself we were in a prison and these people were here voluntarily on a Saturday, when they could be literally anywhere else.

One by one we all signed the logbook and walked past the metal detectors and through the large metal sliders. The jolting clicks of the doors went almost unnoticed amid the friendly chatter. Nora and I smiled at each other as we waited for the last door to pop open in the cramped sally port entrance to the Veterans' Pod.

We made our way into the large, open visitation room. It had high ceilings and big windows, giving it an inviting feel. Along the walls there were murals and paintings done by inmates depicting scenes from fairy tales and biblical stories. If it weren't for the uniformed guards standing near the front of the room with radios buzzing on their belts, the space could easily have been mistaken for a church community room.

Sheila O'Brien, the director of external relations for America's VetDogs, was chatting with Michael Kidd and some of the other inmate trainers from the program. She'd made the trip up from the organization's headquarters on Long Island especially for this ceremony. The puppies were all romping around playing with one another while the men did their best to corral them and remind them that they were supposed to be on their best behavior.

Kidd and the rest of the men spotted Nora and me and immediately began to taunt me about my haircut. I'd forgotten that I hadn't seen them since getting my long hair trimmed a bit. The result had given me a look that resembled a little boy's bowl cut. Nora had teased me about it but then assured me that it didn't look that bad and that my hair grew so fast that nobody would notice it within a week or so. It just took one trip to see my friends in prison to reveal the truth: I had a haircut better suited to a seven-year-old.

"You know picture day was last week," Kidd said with a grin, much to the delight of Nora.

"I told him he looked like a little boy," she piled on, laughing.

"Just because they gave me a lollipop and a sticker afterward doesn't mean this is a kid's haircut," I chimed in, laughing along while making a mental note to have my head buzzed at the barbershop ASAP. It was time to say good-bye to the long hair.

After he and Nora had had their fun at my expense, Kidd took a second to direct our attention to one of the tables at the front of the visitation room.

"That's my grandmother and my son over there," he said proudly.

"Ah, man! They made it. I'm so glad." I hadn't wanted to ask what ended up happening in case the news was bad. "This is gonna be such a cool memory for your son."

"Oh, I can't wait to meet them," echoed Nora.

At that moment Prince walked in with Chess. Right away the dog spotted Kidd, who did his best not to make eye contact with his old friend, instinctively understanding he shouldn't distract the dog from his work, no matter how difficult that might be. After all, this was Chess, his former dog, the dog he trained for eighteen months, the dog he'd taught how to sit, stay, bring, follow, turn on lights, and wake someone up from nightmares.

The dog that taught *him* how to love again. Kidd was going to have to wait a little longer, until the end of the ceremony, to be reunited with Chess, but it would be worth the wait.

People took their places at the tables arranged around a podium. There was going to be a demonstration of skills from the puppies, and then the graduate, Captain, the handsome yellow Lab trained by Sean, was going to perform the whole symphony of skills he'd acquired over his year and a half at the prison. Sean was his primary trainer, but he'd been assisted by Kidd and the volunteer weekend puppy raisers.

Out front there was a wooden platform, a kennel, a few chairs, and various items the dogs regularly used for their training.

Michael Fournier took to the microphone first to kick off the ceremony.

"I'd like to welcome everyone and thank you for coming. We're very proud of the dogs and the men we have here who are completely dedicated to their training. Their hard work is an inspiration to me and the rest of the staff here, and we're looking forward to sharing a bit of what goes on here with you. We'll have refreshments afterward. Without further delay I'd like to hand it over to Henry, our American Legion post commander."

With that, Fournier stepped away from the podium and veteran inmate Henry took to the mic.

Another achievement of Randy Liberty and his staff was working with the American Legion to establish the Veterans' Pod as a formal post. It brought resources to the veterans in Maine State Prison that they wouldn't have access to otherwise and provided a greater sense of structure and community. I'd seen Henry around the Veterans' Pod during my weekly visits. He was an army vet, and he carried himself like a master sergeant, checking in on the men and making sure they were being productive. He always made it a point to say hello and to thank me for coming to spend time with the men.

"So many of us have been on the wrong path for so long it's difficult to see any other way of life," Henry said, looking down at his speech to avoid eye contact with the crowd. "But through things like the dog program, we're able to regain positive momentum in our lives and see for ourselves that we're worth something, that we can contribute to the world in important and profound ways."

His thick New England accent couldn't hide the emotion in his voice when he was talking about the Veterans' Pod and the different programs helping the men regain their sense of value and purpose.

Henry closed by thanking the volunteer puppy raisers, the staff from the prison, and America's VetDogs for giving the men a chance.

I looked around the room and could see that a few people were getting a little teary. On the floor at Nate's feet, LJ lay flat on his belly, chomping loudly on a Nylabone. Kidd's son was sitting straight up in his chair, next to his grandmother. The two were quietly listening, but I noticed that the boy's eyes were fixed directly on his father.

Kidd was sitting patiently with his fellow inmate trainers. Soon it would be his turn to speak.

Next to the podium was Bill Palmer, a retired marine master sergeant and father to Jason Palmer, the lead Correctional Care and Treatment worker in the Veterans' Pod. Bill was wearing one of his signature Hawaiian shirts, this one yellow with white hibiscus flowers and tropical birds. He opened with a joke about how his son had given him a puppy to raise on the weekends and that he had no other choice but to accept since he was retired. He continued with a story about taking his assigned puppy, Sayville, to Lowe's with him to pick up some lumber for a project when the two of them ran into Maine senator Angus King.

"I proceeded to talk his ear off about the program and all the good it's doing for veterans across the country and right here in Maine," Bill said. "Then I looked down, and Sayville had completely untied the senator's shoes!"

The story drew a laugh from the crowd. Bill finished his remarks by turning to the men and saying, "These dogs are a reflection of the good inside each of you. Never forget that."

Next up to the microphone was Michael Kidd. I glanced over my shoulder to the table where his son and grandmother were sitting. His grandmother's eyes were already filling with tears, but his son was on the edge of his seat, eyes wide and chest puffed up with pride, as if he were getting ready to meet his favorite athlete or superhero.

As planned, it was Kidd's job to emcee the demonstration portion of the program and walk the audience through the different training techniques, explaining the value of each one.

"I'm not a very good public speaker, so I wrote it all down. I guess that makes me a public reader," Kidd joked, drawing a giggle from the crowd. I watched his son realize that his father had just made a roomful of people laugh out loud, and I wondered if it was possible for someone to pass out from pride.

Kidd introduced the first puppy in the room, Sayville, and her trainer, Cory. The sight of the puppy alone drew an "awwwww" from the crowd.

Sayville was a little distracted by all the people and other dogs, but eventually she did a perfect sit, stay, and down for Cory, and the two took their seats.

Next up was Webber with his trainer, Charlie. Webber hopped up onto a wooden box, sliding a little bit on his big black paws. He performed a sit and then hopped back down, heeling perfectly at Charlie's side before executing a fetch and give with a small rubber toy. I laughed to myself seeing ten-month-old puppies perform tasks that Fred would never allow me to train him to do.

Now it was time for LJ, the big yellow Lab, and his trainer, Nate. LJ was the furthest along in his training, and it showed. Nate instructed him to put himself into the kennel, and he did so right away. The crowd buzzed with disbelief. Then LJ lay down in the kennel for a few seconds before Nate opened the gate. But instead of bursting out of the open kennel as any young pup might do, LJ paused, looking up at his trainer, waiting patiently to be told to come out. After receiving the command to exit the kennel, LJ moved directly to Nate's side and looked up at him as if to ask, *Okay, what next?*

Nate directed him up onto the box and demonstrated body handling, pulling on LJ's loose puppy skin and big paws to the delight of the crowd.

"Body handling is an important skill that enables the handler to examine the dog, trim its nails, and strengthen the bond between the two," Kidd explained over the microphone.

Nate and LJ wrapped up their demonstration, and the crowd clapped for all the puppies. The noise drew a curious look from LJ, who tilted his head and looked out into the audience as if taking a bow before following Nate back to his seat at the front of the room.

Next up was the graduate, Captain, and his trainer, Sean.

Sean stood up from his seat next to the other inmate trainers and sat in a chair directly in front of the audience. Captain didn't move but watched his trainer intently, waiting for his first command. It had been a while since I'd observed the pair work together. I was looking forward to seeing their skills on full display.

"Rest," Sean said, looking back at his dog.

Captain got to his feet and walked confidently over to Sean. He gently placed his big head on the man's knee, looking up at him with large, caring eyes. Kidd explained from the podium that the "rest" command was taught to help soothe a stressed-out handler, reminding him or her they weren't alone.

After a few seconds with Captain's head on his knee, Sean gave another command.

"Under," he said quietly.

Captain then crawled under the plastic chair, his big body wedging its way between the legs until his head popped out from between Sean's feet, finding its place on his right foot.

"Similar to the rest command, 'under' can be used during meetings, at dinner in crowded restaurants, and other stressful situations a veteran might find themselves in," Kidd explained.

I looked around the room and noticed that even some of the guards were wiping the corners of their eyes. Kidd's son was still watching intently.

It was clear to me that the men who trained these dogs and shaped them into instruments of change were the first to be affected by them. Sean and Captain's connection was on display to everyone in the room, and it was beautiful.

The duo demonstrated some other skills they'd learned together. For their big finish, Sean handed a one-pound plastic barbell to Kidd's son, who was standing rigid with excitement to be involved in what he clearly saw as his dad's show. I got a good look at the youngster for the first time as he awaited his next instructions. His little blue polo shirt was tucked into a pair of jeans, and his short-cut blond hair was combed neatly, clearly the work of his grandmother. He held the barbell horizontally between his small hands like a tiny magician's assistant.

Sean took his seat with Captain by his side.

"Bring," said Sean calmly.

Captain trotted toward Kidd's son, who was doing his best not to giggle and squeal at the dog heading straight for him. Captain, standing at almost eye level with the young boy, gently took the weight in his mouth, cradling it as if it were made of tissue paper, not hard plastic.

Kidd narrated the exchange:

"'Bring' is one of the most important and difficult commands we teach the dogs, because it can often be used to bring someone his or her medication, or a phone to call for help, or other necessary items that may be fragile. It is also important that the dogs know where specifically the person needs the item. For example, if they are in a wheelchair or are missing limbs, it is important that the dog place the item in a way that the handler can reach and use it."

After retrieving the weight from the boy, Captain turned and calmly brought the item to his handler, placing it in his right hand, just as carefully as he'd taken it from Kidd's son at the other end of the room.

There was emotion in Kidd's voice as he watched the exchange between Captain, his son, and his fellow handler Sean. He'd trained Chess to do the same thing for Prince, and today his son was seeing exactly what his dad had been up to while he was away from him.

Now that the skills demonstration was complete, it was time for Captain to graduate. That meant removing his training vest and putting on his official service-dog vest. Sean gave his dog one last command, "Up," and with that he leaped onto the wooden box next to Paula.

Paula removed the vest he was wearing that read SERVICE DOG IN TRAINING in big bold letters on the sides, and she held the new one above her head for all to see. This one said simply

AMERICA'S VETDOGS SERVICE DOG in blue letters against bright yellow fabric. She slipped it on over Captain's big head and fastened it just under his shoulders.

"Congratulations to Sean and Captain and all the inmate trainers on successfully graduating another dog into our program," Paula said, shaking Sean's hand. "Captain will go on to change the life of a deserving veteran and their family. You should all be very proud of the work you've done over the last eighteen months."

Sean's eyes were filled with tears—his time with Captain was in its final minutes—but a smile crept its way through as Paula encouraged him to take his dog on one last victory lap around the room. The two were serenaded by applause and cheers from the group of attendees, all on their feet.

There was one more item on the agenda, however. Paula stepped up to the podium and pulled the microphone down so she could speak directly into it.

"I'd like to introduce our first graduate from Maine State Prison, Chess, and his veteran handler, Prince," she announced with a smile.

Prince and Chess made their way toward the podium through the crowded room. The Labrador's eyes darted quickly from Prince to Kidd and back again. The dog could wait no longer, and Prince gave him the command "Free" as he released the dog's leash from his collar.

Chess cut through the crowd, heading straight for Kidd, suddenly transformed from a highly trained working dog into a puppy reuniting with his family. After a few minutes of excited rubs from Kidd and tail wags from Chess, the two settled down, Chess sitting on Kidd's foot, looking back at him and over at his handler.

Prince took his place at the podium.

"Good afternoon, my name is Prince, and I'm a former army warrant officer and CH-47 pilot," he said haltingly. I could see that he wasn't very comfortable speaking in front of a group of mostly strangers. "I joined the army in the nineties after high school and separated in 2000. I wanted to serve my country and follow in the footsteps of my dad, who was a helicopter pilot in Vietnam. He didn't talk much about his time over there, but I was proud of him, and like so many boys I wanted to make my dad proud.

"After I got out of the army, I started flying medical-evacuation helicopters for a hospital in Philadelphia, but after a few years I began to suffer from panic attacks and severe anxiety. My mind was consistently anticipating the worst outcome in every situation. It was crippling. I was ready to give up a few years ago, and I wouldn't listen to anyone.

"After three days in the hospital, I came home and began to isolate myself. I was ready to die. Then I got the call from America's VetDogs, and for the first time in years I felt a little bit of hope. I was paired with Chess just a few days before Christmas, and since then the fog of panic and anxiety has been lifted from my mind. I think, besides me, the people who have benefited the most from Chess are my wife and kids. They feel like they've got their father back."

Prince's voice had begun to crack a little. I wondered if he'd ever shared this much about his struggle in public. He bravely went on to describe his experience at the training facility on Long Island, how Chess began to identify his signs of stress within just a few days.

"When I first met Chess, I didn't think he liked me," Prince said, the emotion in his voice lifting somewhat. "But after the second day, I realized that it wasn't him who had the problem, it was me. I needed to open up my heart and allow myself to be loved, allow myself to be accepting of what Chess could do for me. It was only then that Chess's instincts and superb training kicked in, and our bond began to form. It was the first way he saved me, but there have been countless others since. By the time we left New York, I knew my life was forever changed. For the first time in a long time, I was excited for a new day, a new chapter."

Then he turned and looked at Kidd, who was rubbing Chess's ears and smiling.

"And I owe that all to you," he said, locking eyes with Kidd.

Kidd nodded in return. I hoped Prince's words made the pain of saying good-bye to Chess worth it for Kidd.

"Everyone in this program is a lifesaver," Prince said, turning back to the group and wrapping up his speech.

I glanced over at Kidd's grandmother, who had her head in her hands. She was weeping uncontrollably. One of the guards took a seat next to her and gently placed his hand on her back. I couldn't imagine what it was like for her to see her grandson go from a troubled young man to a convicted criminal to a loving and hardworking member of a team of people dedicated to training such important dogs. It had to be an intense combination of pain and pride.

Prince left his place behind the podium and shook Kidd's hand while Chess sat happily between them smiling from ear to floppy ear.

Walking over to the microphone, Kidd pulled it toward him.

"This concludes our program. Thank you all for coming. Please help yourselves to refreshments and snacks," he said with a smile and a wink directed toward his son, who was now sitting on the floor next to Chess.

Everyone stood and clapped for the men of the Veterans' Pod and their life-changing dogs.

Then we made our way toward the refreshments table for coffee and snacks. I watched as Prince headed over to speak with Kidd's son. The big army veteran crouched down on the floor at eye level with the young boy, who started peppering him with questions about Chess. The son of an incarcerated veteran, another veteran, and his dog, brought together by a program that fosters love and change in everyone involved.

CHAPTER 15

Alcohol

The next writing session topic, as selected by the guys, was "alcohol." I was interested in the men's experiences and stories with the substance and how it affected their lives. Since I'd moved to Maine, the amount of alcohol I consumed had decreased considerably, and I didn't miss it. Like a bad relationship, it had been manipulative and toxic for me—but I only saw this after it was out of my life. I wondered if the guys had similar feelings or if they couldn't wait to get out of prison and have that first cold beer.

This time I'd brought Fred with me. He'd happily trotted into the classroom at the end of his leash, excited to see his prison buddies. I settled into my regular seat at the corner of the table with Kidd to my left at the end. Michael Fournier took a spot away from the table at the back of the classroom. He didn't always join our sessions, but every now and again he checked in on us, which was fine by me. Kidd's laptop was open, and he was playing a familiar song that I recognized as Sturgill Simpson's "Life of Sin." When I discovered that Kidd and I shared a love of authentic country music, I'd suggested he try to get his hands on some of Simpson's stuff.

"Hey, you got it! What do you think?" I asked, flattered that he'd taken my suggestion to heart.

"He's awesome," Kidd replied, turning the volume down as everyone got settled. "I've only been able to get a couple songs, but my buddy is working on getting me more. I thought this one kinda played into what I wanted to talk about today."

By the time class started, my little Afghan dog was at the opposite end of the table, already asleep on his friend Chet's size-thirteen sneakers. Calli sat in the corner, while Nate's puppy, LJ, settled in under the chair next to me.

"Well, why don't you start us off today, then," I said to Kidd, happy that everyone seemed ready to dive in.

"Ya, sure," he said casually as he closed his laptop and shifted to his notebook, where he'd written out a few pages by hand.

"I guess my relationship with alcohol started when I was young," Kidd said with a grin. "Like most of us, I remember my dad and his buddies having beers around the fire on camping trips and after doing work outside. It just seemed like what men did. So naturally my friends and I wanted to do it, too. When we were probably twelve or thirteen, we started sneaking beers from our parents' fridges and bringing them with us on weekend camping trips. I honestly hated the way they tasted. Most of the time, the beers had been rattling around in my backpack for a day or two, so they were warm and foamy, but I didn't say that to any of my friends. I'd just drink 'em down as fast as I could and smash the bottles into the fire.

"After my dad died, though, I think I started to use alcohol for the wrong reasons. I realized that when I drank enough, I didn't feel the pain, I didn't miss my dad, I just felt good. But eventually, after discovering Twisted Tea and Mike's Hard Lemonade, I realized I didn't have to fake enjoying beer anymore. I could have twice the alcohol in an easier-to-drink package. Those brands weren't hard to get either, because most of the time convenience-store workers just thought they were sodas or energy drinks. By age sixteen I was drinking to excess regularly.

"During the week my friends and I would meet up on the same dirt roads and ATV trails we always had, drinking and cutting loose. I liked how drinking made me feel—it just made me a more fun version of myself, at least for the first couple of drinks—but I would eventually turn into somebody else. I think I would have been dead or in jail much sooner if it hadn't been for my friend Jeff. He always partied with me, but he seemed to have a better grip on alcohol than the rest of us. I never saw him get drunk or out of control. Whenever I would make that turn, whenever I started saying things I would normally never say, hateful and nasty things, Jeff would grab my keys, knock the drink out of my hand, and drive me home. He knew I was hurting, and no matter how many insults I hurled at him or how hard I fought him, he would always make sure I got home okay. He looked out for me when I wasn't looking out for myself."

Kidd was clearly grateful for his friend but remorseful that he'd put Jeff in that situation.

"I'm glad you had a friend like Jeff. Are you guys still close?" I asked, wanting to keep Kidd going.

He clearly had more to share.

"He's the only friend of mine that testified on my behalf during my sentencing," Kidd said, tears now forming in his eyes.

"Oh wow, he never gave up on you," I said.

"Not even close. When I came back from the army, I lived with him for a little while. He tried so hard to get me out of my funk. He got me a job and kept me fed. I was in too much pain to see that his friendship was my way out. When I started selling drugs from his house, he had no choice but to kick me out. I'll never forget the look on his face when he told me to leave. It hurt him all the way to his core. So for him to come and testify and plead with tears in his eyes to the judge to take it easy on me, that broke me. It took me years, but I finally see now that he is the truest friend I've ever had. He saw the good in me and never let me get away with anything that wasn't consistent with who he knew I really was. I'll always regret putting him through what

I did, but at the same time his loyalty to me has been one of the most consistent things in my life. It's almost enough to make me '*thank God for this here life of sin.*'"

I smiled, knowing that he'd just quoted a line from his new favorite song.

"I see a lot of my own struggle with alcohol in yours," I told Kidd. "At first it was just this fun thing that made me feel good. I was just a happier version of myself. But as I got older, it became a crutch. Especially after Afghanistan, when I had a lot of pain and trauma that I was repressing, alcohol brought it all to the surface in an unhealthy way."

For the first time ever in class, I began telling the guys about the period after coming back to the States. Even with Fred at my side, I often felt lost. In Afghanistan, despite the imminent danger that surrounded me, I knew at any given moment what I was supposed to be doing and where. I spent my nights patrolling, then my days sleeping until it got too hot, before writing reports from the night's patrols, taking meetings with locals, or interrogating captured fighters. Every day felt different, but at the same time my routine was anchored in a sense of regimented duty, and I loved that. When I came back, I went to work for the Defense Intelligence Agency (DIA), where I was responsible for weekly reports and metrics that dealt with intelligence collected from human sources all over the world. It was important work that had an effect on intelligence and security operations in some of the most sensitive and hostile environments of the time. But the job very quickly became dull and tedious to me. I no longer felt as if my actions were contributing to a bigger picture. In my mind I was out of the fight, but I still had a lot of fight in me, and that left me feeling frustrated and without direction.

"In a lot of ways, going to war was the easy part," I told the guys, revealing more about myself than I had in any other session. "You didn't have time to think about fear during a fight or a patrol. You just did what you had to do. I spent years preparing to go to war. I trained my body and my mind as best I could. But when it was time to come home, I didn't give it nearly enough attention. Because to me that would have meant admitting things to myself that I was afraid to admit. Coming home, I tried to keep that going. I stayed busy, and when I wasn't busy, I drank."

I told the guys about how every Monday, when I had to staple myself to a desk chair and reprogram my mind and body to focus on Excel spreadsheets and emails, I lost a little bit of hope. In the evenings I spent time in bars with people who seemed just as angry and lost as I was. Most of my friends from high school were married already and working on starting families. I didn't want to bother them with my problems, and I wasn't sure I could have articulated them to anyone even if I'd wanted to. It didn't seem to me that I had much to complain about. I'd made it home in one piece, I had a good job with a decent salary, a new truck, and a really cool dog. But the reality was that I was behaving in ways that were unbalanced and unhealthy.

My drinking was out of control. It was just that I was good at disguising it and pretending it wasn't a dependency on a very addictive but highly acceptable drug. Alcohol became a part of my routine. It made the weekly drone of my work life go by easier when I knew that my problems and feelings of inadequacy could melt away with a few shots. Coming home from combat and as a survivor, it's like a permanent excuse to party. You're alive, you made it out; nothing seemed to have any consequences anymore.

"I could call it pride but in reality it was fear," I went on. "I was afraid to admit I was different, I was afraid to admit I wasn't happy, I was afraid to admit I was in pain. I was afraid of unpacking what I'd done in Afghanistan. To everyone around me, I was a tough marine combat veteran with a Purple Heart and a dog plucked from the battlefield. I had great stories from my time overseas. It was easy just to tell those and not let anyone else see the pain behind them. I wanted to be someone I couldn't be anymore, so I felt like an outsider in my own life."

As I spoke, I realized I'd never really shared these thoughts with anyone else before.

"Nora was my Jeff," I told the guys, referring to Kidd's friend who had always looked out for him. "She didn't hold my feet to the fire or make me feel bad about myself. She just held up a mirror so I could see how far off the mark I was. I'm starting to see that this is what real friends do. They don't judge or make you feel like there's something wrong with you. They support the best version of you by not enabling the toxic behaviors that compromise your character."

Continuing to drink heavily was the easy road, and that has never been the path I've wanted to take. The challenge, then, was overcoming the habit I'd created for myself. I had to get my drinking under control if I wanted to retake command of the rest of my life.

"I guess I know what it's like to feel rejected and lost in your own skin," I told the men seated at the table. "You guys separated yourselves from the world around you through your addictions and are now spending years segregated from the world. It makes total sense that you'd fear rejection from a society that has all but condemned you."

If alcohol was my crutch, then cutting it out of my routine would mean other parts of me would grow stronger. And that's exactly what happened.

"After just a few weeks with no alcohol, I began to see my challenges as opportunities," I told the guys. "Especially the ones that stood between me and writing my first book. But it wasn't easy to get there."

I wondered if I'd said too much. My speech had been longer than at any other time I'd shared with the guys. Would they think I was unfairly comparing my struggles to theirs?

To my relief Chet chimed in with a tagline of his own.

"Alcohol is a drug with a kick-ass marketing campaign," he said with his usual poetic simplicity. "It's just as addictive as heroin or any other drug out there. The difference is that we've allowed it to become a part of our culture, so for a lot of people their addiction is socially acceptable. It isn't treated like a drug—it's as natural as a cup of coffee in the morning. We just accept it in all its forms, despite its proven ability to destroy lives. I know when I was just drinking, I was way more impulsive than when I was on heroin or oxy. The addiction was stronger to those drugs, but when I had my dose, I was good, I wouldn't harm a fly. On booze, though, I was far more impulsive and reckless."

"That is fascinating and terrifying," I said in response to Chet. "Do the rest of you guys agree with his theory?"

"I definitely think it's more addictive than we realize. I'm not sure it was equally as addicting as oxy, but everyone is different," Marcus said after giving it some thought.

"I gotta say, guys, every time I go to the grocery store and I walk past the liquor aisle, I get nervous for anyone who suffers from addiction. . . ." It was Michael Fournier, speaking up from his spot in the corner. "The bottles of booze are right there, in between the chips and the ice cream, shelves and shelves of the stuff ready to be bought and consumed. You don't have to break any laws to get it. All you need is a little bit of money. For me alcohol was always this forbidden and alluring thing. I didn't really respect it until I joined the army and started seeing the damage it was doing to people's lives. In the military it's practically issued to you. At unit parties and in the barracks, if you weren't drinking until you puked every weekend, there was something wrong with you. I'm just lucky I made it out of the army without any DUIs."

"I can say that I'm more afraid of alcohol on the outside than I am any other substance. Because it can very easily lead me down a dark and impulsive path," Kidd echoed.

"Alcohol is the real gateway drug," Chet continued, dropping another poetic bomb on the group.

"You're right about that," a few of the guys said, nodding.

"We can't blame our problems on it," Nate pointed out, taking a break from combing his fingers through the fur on Fred's back. "But at the same time, we can't help but notice that the decisions we made and the direction our lives took were partly because of our relationship with booze. I agree with Chet, it really is the real gateway drug. I take full responsibility for everything I did on the outside, but that wasn't me. I would have never done those things if I hadn't been high."

"I'm not sure I can have a casual beer anymore," Calli said, speaking up for the first time today.

"Well, that raises another question I guess," I told the group. "Do you guys miss alcohol? Do you find yourself craving it or looking forward to that first cold beer—or Twisted Tea in your case, Kidd?"

"For me I mostly miss the people and places," said Kidd with a smile. "I miss off-roading with my buddies, fishing and hunting. I realize now that alcohol doesn't really enhance those activities—if anything it hinders them. I don't need a bunch of Twisted Tea to have a good time anymore. I'd like to remember the rest of my days."

Kidd talked about getting his truck stuck in the mud and watching his buddies slip and slide, falling again and again as they ran a rope from his bumper to another truck that would eventually pull him out. Chet spoke about carrying beers in his backpack on a long hike up Mount Katahdin and how good it tasted even though it was foamy and warm from bumping around on his back all day. Everyone agreed it was the people and places that made the memory, not the substance we drank. Alcohol was an accessory, not a main attraction. At least that's how we all saw it now.

I glanced up at the clock. Our time was getting short. Soon enough Fournier was going to have to lead me out, back into the lobby, so I could hit the road home.

But before the session ended, I wanted to get the guys' input on another subject altogether. For a long time now, I'd been waiting for the right moment to propose to Nora. Ever since we'd started dating, I'd known we were meant to be together. She brought out the best in me, and I like to think I did the same for her. We were a unit, and it was time to make it official. We'd never really talked about getting married. Nora wasn't waving her ringless hand at me. It was more important for me to demonstrate to her that I couldn't imagine my life without her. I'd decided that after the summer was over, I was going to ask her. It felt like it was time. In fact, it was long overdue.

The guys had been bugging me for a while about tying the knot with Nora.

"If you don't ask her, I'm gonna when I get out in a couple years," Chet had said only half jokingly more than a few times. I was glad whenever they brought her up, because I didn't want to make them depressed by reminding them about their lack of a female connection. Most of the guys hadn't been with a woman in a very long time, and some of them likely never would again.

"I haven't told anyone else yet," I explained to them that day in the classroom. "I've got a ton of planning to do, and I figured you could help me. I know my secret will be safe with you—it's not like you can tell anyone. . . ."

"Ya, there are no snitches in here," Chet said with a laugh.

I filled them in on my plan. It was elaborate and risky and required a lot of things to go right. But with the guys' help, I knew I could make it happen.

"It's possible, but only if you don't tip her off," Calli said knowingly. "She'll figure it out right away if you start acting funny. Women have radar for stuff like this."

"Thanks, guys," I said. "I'll keep you posted on how everything develops. I've got a lot of phone calls to make. . . ."

On the walk out, Fournier congratulated me on finally deciding to make things official with Nora.

"You know Randy is going to be pleased," he reminded me. "He's always telling you to hurry up and put a ring on her finger."

As we walked back along The Mile, Fred trotting ahead with his snout in the air, we talked about the session, and Fournier shared some more of his story with me.

"The conversation about alcohol really hit home," he confessed. "When I came back from serving in the Balkans, most people didn't even know we had troops over there. It made it really difficult to deal with what I'd seen."

It turned out that Fournier had dodged a serious bullet while he was in Bosnia, where he'd served as a tanker. One morning he'd opted for a roving patrol instead of a refueling mission. It was a decision that saved his life. The man who rode where Fournier would have if he hadn't been assigned a different duty that day was killed when the truck slipped off a bridge into a ravine, crushing the passenger side of the fuel truck completely. Fournier knew that it could just as easily have been him.

"When I got back, I buried the memory of it and tried to move on, like so many veterans do," he told me. "But it didn't work. My marriage fell apart, and I started drinking and reliving the past. From childhood right up until the present day, everything that had ever happened to me in my life that left a scar came flooding back. Depression got hold of me until it felt like I couldn't breathe. I even thought about ending my life."

I was stunned. Fournier was someone who always seemed so calm and upbeat. It was hard to imagine him on the brink of suicide.

Eventually Fournier's mother walked him into the VA and stood by his side until he got help.

"It was a struggle after that, finding happiness again," he confessed. "I spent a lot of time at the VA, found some new approaches to dealing with emotional stress. I started digging into my past, trying to make sense of it. Hearing the guys talk about alcohol and how it affected them really made me grateful that my mom didn't let me go any further down that route. Not that I've had it easy, but I could've had it a lot worse, that's for sure."

"Ya, man, at the end of every visit up here, I always come away more grateful than when I arrived," I told him. "I had no respect for alcohol, even after a few close calls. I honestly don't know how I didn't end up in jail or dead. It's almost like I have survivor's guilt after talking to the guys."

It was a thought I'd had for months now, but this was the first time I was hearing myself say it out loud.

"Well, it never hurts to be grateful. I know I sure am," Fournier said, looking down at Fred as we waited for the big metal slider door to open.

"Absolutely. I'm grateful every time I walk outta here," I agreed as we made our way through the lobby and said our good-byes. "Freedom is fragile."

Fred and I hopped into the truck and headed south toward home, Sturgill Simpson playing on the radio, *"Thank God for this here life of sin. . . ."*

CHAPTER 16

Dear Self

"The warden wants to see you," Turner, the guard at the front desk, bellowed as I walked through the front door of the prison. The way he'd said it made me a little uneasy. My mind immediately began to search for anything I might have done wrong. Had I forgotten to clear something with Randy? Had the guys done something and I was implicated? Was my writing program causing problems? Things had been going so well that I was almost waiting for it all to go south.

I heard the jarring pop of the large metal slider door opening. On the other side stood Michael Fournier. I searched his face for a clue but couldn't find anything that indicated the reason for my being summoned by the warden. I hadn't seen Randy in a few weeks, but I'd assumed he'd been busy running the prison. Maybe he just wanted to check in to make sure I was doing okay?

"Apparently the warden wants to see me?" I asked Fournier, trying and failing to hide the concern in my voice.

"Ya, I'll take you back to his office. Should just be a sec," Fournier replied, nodding hello to Turner.

As we walked into the administrative offices, one of the women who worked inside popped her head out of her hallway office.

"Hey, where's Fred?" she asked, genuinely disappointed that I'd left my sidekick behind that day.

"Last I saw him, he was napping in the sun," I said, noticing that she had a Fred calendar hanging in her office.

"Well, you be sure to bring him in to see me next time," she said as we continued down the long hallway toward Randy's office. "He always brightens my day."

"Yes, ma'am," I replied, as cheerfully as I could.

We reached Randy's office, and Fournier gave the door a little knock with his knuckle.

"Ya, ya! Come in!" we heard from the other side of the door.

As we walked in, a few men in suits were gathering up their things. I'd never seen them around the prison before, and I tried not to make any assumptions about why they were here.

"Hi, Craig, good to see you. No Fred today?" Randy asked from behind his desk, buying some time while the strange men made their way to the door. "I'll see you next week, guys, thanks for coming in," he called to them before I could respond. One of them nodded and closed the door behind him as they left.

"Good to see you, Randy. Is everything okay?" I asked, unable to conceal my concern.

"Ya, ya, everything is fine," he replied, sitting forward in his chair and resting his elbows on the desk. "I just wanted you to hear something from me before you heard any rumors or anything in the media."

Right away I wondered if there was some kind of political scandal going on. I knew that Randy had butted heads with the previous governor.

And then Randy laid it out for me.

"If all goes well, I'll be leaving Maine State Prison next month for another position," he told me. "Our new governor, Janet Mills, will be nominating me to serve as her commissioner of the department of corrections."

"Oh, man! That is incredible news!" I replied, my excitement for Randy washing away any anxiety I had about why he'd wanted to see me. "I mean, I'm sure everyone around here will miss you, but you'll really be able to do so much more in a position like that, right?!"

"Ya, I'm excited," he told me. "I have a lot I want to accomplish still, and I'm ready to get to work."

It meant a lot to me that Randy had wanted me to hear the news directly from him. He didn't owe me that, but what he said next showed me that he clearly saw value in the work I was doing with his men.

"I wanted you to know that whoever takes over as warden will be under my instruction to allow you to continue your program with the guys in the Vets' Pod," he explained, looking me in the eye. "There will be no interruption to your work, and your access to the men will remain at your discretion."

"Thank you, Randy, that means a lot to me," I said, trying to make it clear that I didn't take his trust in me for granted. "I love coming here, and most of the time I feel like the guys are teaching me more than I am them."

"Well, that just means you're paying attention. They can certainly teach us all a thing or two about what *not* to do," Randy joked as he stood to shake my hand.

I laughed and thanked Randy again for the opportunity to be involved in his prison. Then Fournier and I made our way back through the lobby and to the Veterans' Pod. As we walked The Mile together, he revealed the identity of the men who'd been in Randy's office when we arrived: They were from the governor's transition team.

"When he told me the news this morning, his next instructions were to make sure that your program with the men didn't get lost in the shuffle," Fournier explained. "The handoff is already starting, and he's going to be very busy getting prepared for his confirmation hearing in Augusta."

"It goes without saying that I need to keep this close to my chest?" I asked as we entered the building containing the Veterans' Pod.

"Ya, for now. You might hear rumors," Fournier replied, holding the door for me, "but just play dumb until it's in the media."

"Playing dumb is never hard for us marines," I said with a smile to the former army guy.

The men were waiting for me in the classroom, and I took my seat. Today's assignment was for them to write a letter to their teenage selves. After the success of the last session, where they'd selected their own topic, Chet had come up with the idea to write a letter to their younger selves. It was the kind of assignment that clearly fit with his mind-set as a songwriter.

As I took my first sip of coffee, Calli spoke up. "Did you hear that the warden is getting a promotion?"

I almost shot coffee out of my nose, but I managed to hide a smile behind my cup just long enough to deny having heard any such rumor. The prison news network did not qualify as a legitimate media source, accurate as it might be.

Luckily, I was able to change the subject quickly and naturally by introducing myself to a new member of our group. His name was Del. Kidd had invited him to the group after getting to know him in Bible study. He was a dark-haired man in his mid-forties, with sleeve tattoos and broad shoulders. As Del said hello back to me, his thick Boston accent told me he wasn't from Maine, but that was pretty much all I knew about him for now.

The men spent the first half hour of the session venting about some new guards who were enforcing unnecessary rules just to aggravate them.

"They busted me today," said Mr. Craig sarcastically.

"What'd you do?" I asked with a laugh.

"They come in and tossed my cell, made a mess of it," he

said, explaining with his hands. "Some new guard. He dumped out all my Tupperwares and counted my ketchup packets, had 'em all lined up on my mattress like a drug bust. He wrote me up! Makes no difference to me, I'm gonna die in here, but what the hell was the point of that? What's an eighty-year-old man in a wheelchair gonna do with some ketchup? I forgot I even had them in there!"

"It was ridiculous," echoed Calli, who was Mr. Craig's room-mate. He'd also had his stuff searched, but he seemed more upset that they had harassed his elderly friend.

"It's not a coincidence that they only searched the guy's cells who are in the dog program," Kidd said with his arms crossed at the end of the table. His room had been tossed, too. "Luckily, I ate all my ketchup the night before," he joked with a roll of his eyes.

"I get the rule, it's there for a reason," Mr. Craig said. "They don't want us stockpiling stuff and using it as currency. But whatever I can get in here for a pile of ketchup packets, I don't want!"

"Most of the guards in here would have seen that for what it was," Calli pointed out, looking around the room. "They don't enforce the rules to the letter like that. But some of these guys just like to remind us that they're in charge—as if we could forget."

I was learning that an instance like this constituted one of the greatest sources of stress within the prison environment. Little mistakes or infractions that did not pose a security threat were enforced in a way that had a lasting effect on the men that far outweighed the actual offense. Even the smallest infraction went on their permanent record and was taken into account during review boards that determine when someone can be transferred to a minimum-security facility or if they can participate in a program like gardening or dog training. For Mr. Craig it was a joke—he knew he wasn't getting out of prison until the day he died, but for the rest of the guys every cell search put their fate into the hands of the officers. I was happy to let them vent about it whenever they wanted.

It was frustrating to them that no matter what they did to better themselves, certain guards would always treat them like irredeemable scum.

Once they all had taken their turn getting things off their chests, we began talking about the assignment for the week: a letter to our teenage selves.

For the first time, I'd completed my own assignment. It felt like something I needed to do. I wanted to put into writing a feeling I'd been wrestling with for months. I'd realized that I'd made some changes in my life in recent years and was the happiest I'd ever been. The problem was that some people saw the changes I'd made as a threat instead of growth. It was a frustrating reality that I needed to write out on paper and share with the guys to really understand. I'd written it down the morning of as I waited for my coffee to brew. My letter was very short but said everything I needed it to. I went first by sharing mine. I felt comfortable with the men, and I wanted to make sure they knew I was a part of the group, too.

"Dear Craig," I read. "Don't worry so much about becoming someone else. Who you are right now is valuable. Do not compromise it for anything or anyone. Ever since your high-school years, you've felt like you needed to become somebody else. You were made to feel that your strengths were actually weaknesses. That your energy and short attention span were flaws that needed to be corrected. That because of these 'flaws' combined with your poor grades and failure to develop a plan after high school, there was in fact something wrong with you. Everyone around you seemed to have found their place in the world, and you were failing to find yours. For eight years the marines will provide you with that place, but afterward you will feel like you're right back where you were after high school. What I've figured out now is that my years in the marines combined with my natural ability to connect with people and the world around me through stories have finally merged. I've found myself reconnected with the fearless and confident eighteen-year-old I used to be, while also having the experience and education that come with time. I guess I'm just starting to see that a lot of the things I was told were flaws are actually my strengths."

"Ya, I think that's important," Calli responded, looking down at his own letter. "I wish I could communicate that to my son. I never wanted him to feel like he needed to be anyone he didn't need to be."

"Do you want to go next?" I asked, raising my coffee cup to my lips. "Sounds like you've given this one a lot of thought."

"Ya, absolutely," Calli replied. "This one got to me for sure, because I feel like a lot of the decisions I made early on in my life were influenced by other people's expectations of me."

Calli pushed his thick-framed glasses back up his nose, preparing to read his letter to himself.

Michael,

This letter is not easy for me to write and is probably even harder for you to read and fully comprehend. I am writing this from prison, so I hope you will put some thought into what I say. I am not going to write pages and pages about how I got here, but I will say that I put myself here, and it's not somebody else's fault. Let me pass on some advice and a little knowledge you wouldn't have if I wasn't writing this.

You're going to spend way too much time trying to get your father's approval. You're not going to get it, and it's a waste of your time and energy. Your grandfather was a poor parent and passed those poor skills on to our father. I did not see it at the time, but while our father is putting a hurting on your self-confidence, our mother will be there for you, and she is going to try to be supportive of your decisions. I did not know it at the time, but you trying so hard during your early years to get your father's approval, while you already had your mother's, really hurts her, so you know. Trust me on this point: You might not understand this now reading this, but she will be way more important to your future or the way mine turned out.

I need you to understand that our father is going to push you into a life that he thinks you should follow, for the benefit of the family business. If you listen to our father, you will change your college major from history (which you have a passion for) to business (which fits into running a family business). If you do that, it will start you down a path that will get you to my seat, writing this letter. If you do not listen to our father, you will miss out on not only the misery that I know will come into your life but also you will lose having the two most incredible children. Who knows what will happen if you decide to change that one decision, but I am sure if you do, you will have less for a while. You will not meet your first wife. Some will say that's a good thing. You will probably get married and have kids, but not the ones I know and love. You most likely will not go to prison or meet your second-wife-to-be.

There are a host of decisions that I could tell you about. You might want to change them. The problem is I cannot tell you what those changes will bring. No matter what, you should make your mother a bigger part of your life. If you change nothing else, do that. She will be there when our father walks away from you, when you need him the most.

I am writing you this letter to give you an option that if you want to take the easier course in life, knowing that you will end up in prison if you do exactly what you think is right at your age. Most likely only our father will think negatively of your decision, but you will not have to deal with what I did, and your mother will support you. As much as some of my life has really sucked, today I would not change my life or my decisions. Although I wish some things had turned out different, they made me the person I am and got me the things that I have in my life. You might want to be a different person than the one I turned out to be, that's all right also. Your decision is yours to make. Choose wisely, for they have their own consequences. Good luck.

Truly,
Michael

"Thanks for listening, guys. This wasn't easy for me to write, but I'm glad I did," Calli said as he sat back in his chair.

"I thought it was really honest, man," I told him, wanting to keep the focus on him a little longer. "It shows that you've really grown as a person. A lot of people would only express regret and anger in a letter like this, but you found the purpose, even in your mistakes."

"Ya, it's hard to have too much regret when you've got kids," Calli responded as Nate handed him a cup of coffee. "Because if you hadn't made the same choices, they might not exist, and for so many of us they're our sole motivation to get outta here and not come back."

"So it's almost like you're glad you're in here because the alternative is them not being in your life at all?" I asked tentatively.

The guys all laughed.

"I wouldn't go that far, bud. None of us are glad to be in here," Kidd chimed in.

"Well, ya, I guess—" I started to reply, but Del interrupted me.

"I guess for me all I've ever known is crime," he said, staring at the floor as he spoke. "I'm lucky to have a daughter that's being raised outside of that life, but I was born into it. I've never even had a real job, but she . . . she is good. . . ." His voice started to shake, and I could see tears begin to flood his eyes. Everyone in the group gave him a minute.

It was Del's first time, and he'd jumped right in, sharing thoughts that he'd possibly never verbalized before.

"I'm sorry, guys, it's just that I've struggled a lot with this," he told us, wiping the tears away with his big tattooed hands. "I'm no good, never have been, but I've got this little girl who has a shot at a real life. And it breaks my heart that I'm not out there with her, but then I realize that she's probably better off without me. I'm not sure I'd be of much use to her."

"Children always need their fathers," Kidd told his friend, doing his best to comfort him by patting him on the back. "You've got a lot to offer still. You've just gotta focus on yourself while you can."

"I know, it's just hard to see any value in myself when she's the only thing good that I've ever done in my life," Del replied, taking a deep breath.

"Well, that's enough: She's your purpose," Calli pointed out firmly.

"Thanks, guys, sorry for crying on my first day," Del said with a smile.

"That's okay," I reassured him. "We're all here to work through this stuff. There is no judgment here."

The group affirmed what I'd said. It was important for Del and all of us to be reminded that our meetings were bound by a covenant. No matter what, we'd always respect one another's stories and feelings. Unlike every other interaction in prison life, their words and thoughts in here would not be used against them. Vulnerabilities, dreams, and fears were not currency to be manipulated by others. The guys were safe to share for the benefit of themselves and the group.

Kidd, Chet, Nate, Marcus, and even Mr. Craig all had their turn, sharing their letters that were filled with sound advice for any young person. Words of encouragement and caution such as: "Don't give in to peer pressure." "Don't drink so much." "Be true to yourself." "Don't worry about what other people think." "Don't get in your own way, you've got enough obstacles as it is." "Whatever you get in this life is going to come from you, and the same goes for the mistakes you've made. The good and the bad fall on your shoulders." "The things you think are important aren't going to be important later." "Above all else, talk to someone. You don't have to suffer in silence."

I realized that this was the first time every one of the men had contributed something in writing. Each week they all had a lot to say, but usually only Kidd, Chet, and Nate took the time to write their thoughts out on the page. Not this week. The men clearly found the letter project inspiring, and they wanted to record their thoughts, the things they wished someone had said to them, pieces of advice that seemed so simple to them now that could have saved them years of pain.

"I just want to point out that not many of you would change much about your lives," I told them, trying to share my observations of the session. "You just want your younger selves to know that the things they thought were so important might not turn out to be quite so important after all. None of you wish you hadn't gotten caught or hadn't done what you did. You just seem to want your younger selves to see the value in your family, your God, and yourself. Things that you see now were taken for granted and that you didn't appreciate when you were younger. I think that is beautiful, because you can clearly see that if you'd focused on those things at an earlier age and not compromised yourself for the sake of others, your lives would have naturally gravitated away from the situations that ultimately led you to prison. That is my big takeaway from today. What do you guys think?"

Calli spoke up. "I think we all have regrets, regardless if you're in a place like this or not. But I think most of us have realized that holding on to regret is a waste of time. Things are going to go wrong in your life no matter how you live it. The important thing is that you take accountability for your mistakes. The more you put the blame elsewhere, the more likely you are to repeat them."

I'd never asked Calli about his past. I had a feeling that one day he'd feel comfortable enough sharing the details with me. It turned out today was that day.

"Look at what happened to me," he went on. "I was afraid of disappointing my father and failing the family business. I didn't stand up for myself because of that fear. I thought eventually I'd outrun it, but it just came out in other ways. I felt trapped in my life, and I reached a point where the only way out was suicide. But I guess I failed at that, too.

"I had a nervous breakdown, I burned my own house down, and I tried to hit my ex-wife with my car. Then I holed myself up in my bedroom and fired my rifle at the cops when they came to get me. I wanted them to shoot me. It wasn't attempted murder, it was attempted suicide. I was ready to die but not ready to admit that I was responsible for the mess I'd made of my life."

I knew our time was getting short, but I hoped Michael Fournier was running behind today. I didn't want Calli to feel rushed or embarrassed.

"You said you had a nervous breakdown. What was that like?" I asked gently.

"For me it was like watching myself from inside my own head," Calli responded, looking down at his empty coffee cup, pushing it toward Nate, who filled it and passed it back to him. "I was totally disconnected from what I was doing to myself and to my family. As ashamed of it as I am, I see now that I was mentally ill. I've learned how to give myself a break."

A stack of powdered creamer packets rested on the table in front of him, and we all waited patiently as Calli shook one out and dumped it into his coffee. The chunky powder blended uncooperatively into his fresh cup as he stirred it with his finger.

"I'll never forget my dad storming out of the visitation room at the county jail after I got locked up," he told us, taking a sip of his now-milk-colored coffee held in a shaking hand. "He screamed at me and told me how much of a failure I was. As if I didn't feel that already, sitting there in handcuffs in front of my parents.

"After he left, my mom took my hand. She wasn't supposed to touch me, it was against the rules, but none of the guards said anything. They must have guessed it wasn't a good idea to mess with my mom. She looked at me with love—it was the only love I'd seen in weeks—and she said something I didn't know I needed to hear: '*I don't understand, but I'm* here.' We talked a little longer, just as mother and son, and when she left, I knew no matter what came next, that I'd be okay, that I'd made some big mistakes but that I could handle the consequences."

"Your mom said the magic words to you," I told Calli. "Words we all need to hear more often than we might like to admit."

I looked around the room to see if anyone else cared to comment.

"We all look different on the surface, but after hearing these stories and letters it's amazing to me to see that we're each dealing with the same issues," Chet pointed out to the group.

"Right," I told him. "We're each dealing with similar issues, but in our own way. So to borrow a phrase from Calli's mom, we don't have to understand one another in order to be there for one another."

We wrapped up the session with a little more chitchat about ketchup packets and other contraband. Mr. Craig joked that he was saving up the ketchup so he could make a Bloody Mary, and we all laughed.

On the car ride home, I thought about the men and how they had yet again defied my expectations. The words they hadn't used were perhaps even more noteworthy than the ones they had. There was no anger, no finger-pointing or fist-shaking. They were at peace with their decisions and the consequences they bore. They had resisted the urge to heap blame and warnings about toxic people or places. They saw that their lives had taken some bad turns and that they were in a place they never thought they'd end up. Yet they also insisted that it was nobody's fault but their own. Their sense of accountability and self-awareness blew me away, and I was inspired by it, but I also felt a deep sadness that they couldn't see the other factors determining their fates. Their crimes were born out of circumstances often far beyond their control—poverty, mental health, trauma, addiction, and lack of opportunity—yet they were still fighting, still seeking a life that some of them had never actually known.

For most of us, when something goes wrong in our lives, we often look for someone or something to blame. We seek justice for things that are often out of our control. After Afghanistan, when I struggled to find my place personally and professionally, I convinced myself that the reason I wasn't getting hired for positions I'd coveted was because of a bureaucratic system that was rigged and not because I lacked a college degree that most of the positions required. When my drinking became an issue, I made excuses. I had it under control. It wasn't a problem. It just made me more fun. It was only when I started to take responsibility for my life that I started to regain a part of myself that I'd lost.

The letters the men had written to their younger selves were a testament to what they were currently doing right rather than what had gone wrong. Despite the way their lives had turned out, they were able to find the good in the bad choices they'd made. It was something that took me years to figure out in my own life.

Getting to know the men in my writing group, it was clear to me that many of them were victims before they ever victimized anybody else. They'd never had the chance to process trauma from their early lives, and it manifested in harmful behaviors and characteristics. Now that they had the time, however, they were doing the work to understand just where they'd gone wrong and find the things, even in prison, that they had to be grateful for.

They were an example to me of the power of total accountability, taking a good look at yourself, and being completely honest about where you'd gone wrong. The purpose wasn't to flog yourself with self-blame but instead to identify the things in your life that you might have taken for granted.

CHAPTER 17

Love in All the Right Places

October is one of our favorite months to be home in Maine. The summer tourist traffic has long since died down, but the days can still be sunny and mild, even if the nights are much cooler. Nora and I spend our mornings sipping coffee and answering emails from our "home office," which on warmer days is just our laptops at a picnic table in our backyard. Fred alternates from sun to shade and from chasing critters to sleeping peacefully. Ruby tosses her favorite mini tennis ball at our feet for us to throw again and again until she, too, takes a nap in the sun.

In October of 2019, I knew that soon enough we would be leaving again for another round of speaking engagements. We loved our life, and we were proud of all the work we'd put into creating it. We'd gone from a handful of small book events to being invited to share our story with entire communities and major organizations in the corporate and nonprofit worlds. There was just one thing missing. We'd never talked about getting married before. Even though we both knew we'd found our soul mates in each other, we never felt the urge to formalize it. But it was important to me to demonstrate just how dedicated I was to Nora. She'd already done that for me. She'd moved from Boston to D.C., started a new life in a new city, only to uproot again a year later so we could move to Maine and I could focus on writing. Since then we'd established a livelihood together, against the odds and, in some cases, good common sense.

It was time to pop the question.

With the guys' help, I'd coordinated and developed a plan to propose to Nora in early November. The men of the writing group were eager to brainstorm with me and to hear about how everything was coming together.

"Make sure and rehearse what you want to say," Mr. Craig warned me one day from his wheelchair. "Or it'll fly right out of your head when the time comes!"

It was reassuring to have people I could confide in, safe in the knowledge that they wouldn't reveal my plans. For weeks I talked it through with them, going over the details and the challenges of sneaking around to get the ring and communicate with Nora's family.

I'd seen the ring I wanted to get her a year earlier, a simple but elegant piece with a hunk of Maine-mined tourmaline as its main stone. It was green and blue and caught light like a diamond while also standing out in its own way. Just like the girl who would be wearing it. Throughout September and October I coordinated with Nora's entire family, her best friends, and a few of her cousins to come to Maine for a surprise engagement party. Coded texts flew back and forth between us, and I made secretive phone calls when I was out in the truck or whenever Nora left the house.

My plan was to take Nora to the beach, ask her to marry me, then come back to the house where all her friends and family would be waiting. When I'd told Tim and Kay, our neighbors, about my proposal plan, they generously offered to allow Nora's family to stay in their guesthouse. It was above and beyond the call of neighborly duty, and I'll forever be grateful to them for that. In the coming weeks, I squirreled away party supplies and food in their guesthouse so everything would be ready for the engagement party.

The date was set. I just needed the weather to be on my side.

On the day of the proposal, the weather gods did their part: It was a perfect sunny day on the coast of Maine. Just cool enough to enjoy an outdoor fire but warm enough not to need a big coat and gloves. I suggested to Nora that we head over to nearby Kettle Cove, a popular local beach with rocky bluffs and a big U-shaped sandy cove. It was just down the road from the little cottage we were renting. I figured we could always come back to Kettle Cove to reminisce about the day we got engaged, even when we moved on to someplace else. I did my best not to rush Nora. The guys had reminded me that if I were too eager to get out of the house, she might become suspicious. Then she'd pick up on other changes in my behavior, and the whole plan could unravel. I did my best to put on my spy hat and act cool.

Meanwhile Nora's oldest sister, Ariel, was my quarterback, wrangling her entire family in the parking lot of a nearby coffeehouse, all the while waiting for the greenlight text from me that we were out of the house. That meant they could swarm the place and start setting everything up for the party.

Just after 11:00 A.M., Nora and I were on our way out of the house, driving up the narrow dirt road that leads to the nearest hardball road. That dirt track had never felt longer. What if an anxious or misinformed family member jumped the gun and headed toward the house, leaving us face-to-face and my plan up in smoke? Thankfully, Nora and I got to the end of the road without meeting anyone. As we turned to head toward the park, I sent a prewritten text to Ariel with a thumbs-up emoji and "GO GO GO" in all caps. Her first task would be to park all the cars in our neighbors' driveway. If Nora spotted any of their cars when we returned from the beach, she'd catch on that all her friends and family were waiting for her, and the second surprise of the day would be ruined. After everyone was safely parked, Ariel was going to lead them into our neighbors' guesthouse.

From there it would be the job of the Five Uncle Club to swing into action and get the party started. The Five Uncle Club, or FUC, is an elite and exclusive organization made up of myself and the other partners of the five Parkington sisters. We're a tight-knit group, and we take a lot of pride in our duties as uncles during family gatherings, duties that include but are not limited to pizza runs, always having a Frisbee or something to throw close by, and maintaining a constant stream of good tunes and chill vibes. I knew once the uncles were on the scene that the party was in the right hands. I needed them to start a fire in our outdoor fire pit, ice down the drinks, and shell the lobsters I'd had steamed at Luke's Lobster, our favorite local lobster shack, that morning when Nora thought I was helping a neighbor chop wood.

Nora and I arrived at Kettle Cove and unloaded the dogs. It was a perfectly clear day, ideal for a walk along the bold coast of Maine. The parking lot was crowded, but the park is big enough for everyone to spread out, so as we walked onto the beach, we felt like we were the only ones around, except for one person in a hooded jacket going slowly, looking for sea glass. We made our way toward the water, Nora and Ruby walking just in front of Fred and me. Without warning I handed her Fred's leash. "Here, can you hold this for me real quick?" I said passing the leash off to her before she could answer.

"Ya, what's up?" she said without turning around.

"Oh, well, there's just something I wanted to do. . . ." I said with a tone in my voice that I'd never heard before. My heart was racing, but I was steady. Thanks to Mr. Craig's advice, I knew what I wanted to say and how I wanted to say it.

"What?" she said turning around, seeing me down on one knee, my hat in the sand, and my eyes focused on hers. "Honora Kathryn Parkington, I am so proud of who we are as a couple and what we've built together. I love who I am when

I'm with you, and I can't imagine going another day without proving to you that for the rest of my life you are the only one for me. Will you be my wife? Will you marry me?"

I stayed on one knee, holding the ring in my left hand and holding her up with my right as I felt her body sink when she realized what was happening. She reached her arms down to pull me up to her, and for a while we just hugged. I showed her the ring, but she wasn't looking at it. She was staring back at me with a look I'll never forget.

"Yes. Of course. I love you."

Fred and Ruby sat together in the sand, looking up at us, waiting for us to collect ourselves. Nora had dropped their leashes, but they weren't going anywhere.

For a moment we just held each other without saying anything else. Nora's knees were still a little shaky, and I let the moment wash over us for as long as I could. After a little while, I signaled to the person in the hooded jacket to head toward us. As she got closer, Nora received her second surprise of the day. It was her best friend from Cape Cod, Jenny. They'd met at the bus stop in the third grade and had been inseparable ever since. Jenny, her husband, Joe, and their two-year-old little boy had driven up from the Cape the night before. I'd wanted her on the beach to photograph the moment for us and to help us celebrate over the weekend.

"Is that my best friend?!" Nora said just as she recovered from my proposal. The two friends hugged, and Nora started to rattle off how excited she was and how she had no idea.

"Okay, okay, we have all weekend to talk about it," Jenny said, wanting to give us some space. "I'm gonna go get the boys, and I'll meet you guys at your place, okay?"

Nora, the dogs, and I walked over to the dry sand and sat

down to process what had just happened. The ring I put on her finger could have been made of string for all she cared. What mattered most to both of us was that our love was solidified through total commitment to each other.

After an hour or so sitting in the sand with the dogs, we headed to the truck. As far as Nora was concerned, we had to get back to the house to tidy it up for Jenny and her family. The short ride home gave me a chance to glance quickly at my phone. I'd gotten a text from Ariel that simply read "The fire is lit," to which I responded with a heart emoji and a thumbs-up.

As we pulled in to our driveway, I prepared Nora for her final surprise of the day. Just before we made the right turn that led to our house, I said, "I have another surprise for you—well, actually a bunch of them . . ." and as our truck came over the rise in our driveway, she saw them. All four of her sisters, her two brothers, sisters-in-law, her mom and dad, cousins, friends, and all their kids standing in a big group at the end of our driveway, the ocean at their backs.

"My entire family! It's everyone! They're here for us?!" she said, in shock for the third time in just a few hours. She was frozen, staring at the most important people in her life, all gathered at our home on the water. Fred and Ruby barked and howled, excited at the sight of so many visitors.

"When I called them, I didn't have to ask. They all said they'd be here before I could even explain what I wanted to do," I said with tears in my eyes. It was the best gift I could think to give her.

We spent the next two nights cooking outside on the grill, laughing around the fire, and celebrating the love Nora and I share. It was simple and perfect.

The men of the writing group had been among the first to

know of my secret plan. I couldn't wait to head back up and tell them that I'd pulled it off without a hitch.

It was November 6, 2019, and I was planning on putting a full day in at the prison. In a few days, Nora, Fred, Ruby, and I would be leaving for a quick speaking tour. I wanted to spend as much time as I could with the guys and dogs of Maine State Prison before we left.

In the parking lot, I got out of the truck and walked through the big metal doors as usual. I was excited to see the guys and share the good news about my engagement to Nora. On the walk in with Fournier, however, I received some sobering news. Typically, on the walk from the lobby to the Veterans' Pod, I would ask Fournier questions about the dogs and the guys and he would get me up to speed. This time I didn't even have to ask him a question.

"LJ was taken to the vet last week for a physical and X-rays," Fournier explained, referring to Nate's puppy and the star student in the training class. "It was just a standard checkup, but they found something that isn't good."

It turned out that LJ had a degenerative condition in his hips that meant he would have chronic problems. Nothing that would be life-threatening if treated properly, but it meant that he could no longer be a part of the program.

"America's VetDogs can't responsibly place LJ with a veteran knowing that he's going to be physically limited in the duties he can handle," Fournier explained. It wouldn't be fair to LJ or the veteran.

"He's such a good dog, and Nate has done an incredible job with him," Fournier went on, the disappointment clear on his face. "Paula says he's one of the best dogs she's ever seen from any program. They're going to have their head veterinarian check the X-rays in case there's anything else that can be done, but it's not looking good."

"How is Nate doing?" I asked as we continued down The Mile.

"He's upset," Mike said with a helpless shrug. "Understand-ably, he's grown really close to LJ, and it shows in how far the dog has come in his training. Typically dogs that fail out of the program get adopted by donors to America's VetDogs. Appar-ently there's a long waitlist."

"Ah, man, that doesn't sound right," I said, desperately trying to think of an upside. I understood the protocol and the reasons LJ couldn't continue in the program, but he was too special a pup to just go to whoever happened to be next on a list.

"To make matters worse, I just lost Shea, my dog of fifteen years, last week," Mike told me, the pain in his voice clear as a bell.

"Ah, man. I didn't know that. I'm so sorry," I said, looking over at my friend. He'd talked about Shea all the time and had mentioned before that she was getting close to the end of her days.

"She had a great run. I loved that dog with all my heart, and I'll always miss her," he said matter-of-factly, looking down at his feet.

We walked into the puppy classroom, where Nate and LJ were sitting together in the corner. Nate was on the floor with LJ between his knees, the dog's big paw resting on a Nylabone as he slept. LJ was already over fifty pounds and still growing. I thought about how dedicated Nate had been in his training and how instant the bond was between him and LJ. It had been a privilege to watch the two of them work together each week.

The training class began as normal, with the men demonstrat-ing the things they'd been working on since last week. Despite

LJ's news, Nate and his pup showed off their latest skills. LJ was now able to walk across the wooden teeter-totter on command, Nate leading him gently with the leash up one side until it tipped, making the usual loud *bonk!* before turning him around and walking up the other side to the same effect. The entire time LJ looked up at Nate to make sure he was doing it right. Their bond was obvious, and Nate was weeks ahead of his fellow trainers because of his deep dedication to LJ. He treated LJ as if he were his own dog, because he knew that is what would make him the best dog he could be for the veteran who would end up with him.

After LJ's demonstration, which included some off-leash work that was far above the expectations for his age, Paula offered a hint of hope.

"You've done an incredible job so far, Nate," she said. "I know it might not look good for LJ in the program, but our head veterinarian still needs to review his X-rays, so don't give up hope just yet. We'll know more by the end of the week. He still needs you."

"Thank you, Paula," Nate said with a smile. "He loves to learn, and I love to teach him. I won't stop until the day he leaves, whenever that happens to be."

The rest of the puppies went through their demonstrations with the men. Sayville, inspired by LJ, attempted to walk up the ramp and down the other side, but as it began to tip, she hopped off, looking up at Cory as if to say, *Sorry, that thing is freaky.* Even so, it was a big improvement from the week before when she tried to bite the ramp instead of walking over it. Webber could make it over the ramp but only after a few attempts and with a lot of extra motivation in the form of treats.

The puppies' off-leash work was improving as well. Sayville and Cory were clearly a unit now. She looked to him anytime there was a distraction and before doing just about anything.

This attentiveness was forming the basis for all the skills that she needed to learn in order to graduate. Overall, Paula was happy with the pups' progress, and she heaped praise on the men for their hard work and dedication. For Cory and Charlie, this was a huge boost in their confidence. They were both first-time primary trainers and, like first-time parents, seemed to be constantly questioning if they were getting it right. Luckily, they had the encouragement and guidance of Kidd, the seasoned professional and patient mentor. Despite pledging to not get too involved so as to spare his heart, Kidd had taken every opportunity to assist the new trainers whenever they needed him.

After my break I returned to meet with the writing group.

Before I could spring the good news on them, however, Calli spoke up. "So did she say yes or did she come to her senses?"

"Ya, we've got a bet going in here. The odds were not in your favor," Kidd added. It was the kind of ribbing I was hoping they would give me.

"She said yes, but I'm still pinching myself to make sure it really happened," I said with a smile.

"Ah, man! Congratulations!" the guys all said.

"I wish we had something better to toast with in here than this oily coffee," Chet said.

"You guys were the ones I wanted to celebrate with the most. You were the first to know about my plan, which went off without a hitch," I announced proudly.

I told the guys how surprised Nora was and how her family and the FUCs had helped orchestrate my vision. It felt great to share some good news with them. I wanted the guys to see that they'd been a part of the day, even if they couldn't be there.

CHAPTER 18

Strength and Vulnerability

We returned from our brief speaking tour, and I quickly fell back into my old routine: bumping up the coast in our truck, Fred at my side, listening to the new Sturgill Simpson album for the thirtieth time, and taking in the Maine coast.

As we got closer to the prison, I heard Fred start to stir in the backseat. He peeped out the window, no doubt recognizing the area by the familiar mom-and-pop seafood stands along the way, boarded up for the winter. The truck slowed to make our first turn in more than fifty miles off Route 1, and Fred began to stubbornly paw at the window button on his door, his nails scratching on the plastic until the window slid down. It felt good to let in a little icy Maine air, and I cracked my window, too, while turning the heat up a bit. It was still just about a mile to the prison entrance, and we both needed a little wake-up call after our long drive up.

I pulled in to the parking lot and found our spot in the farthest space available, always preferring to park far from the entrance so I could use the walk in to stretch my legs and give Fred a chance to do the same.

The lot was unusually full for a Wednesday afternoon, and I noticed that many of the cars had government license plates. I made a mental note to ask what was going on.

Fred was at the end of his leash looking back at me impatiently as if to say, *Hurry up, I wanna see my friends!* It was how he always behaved when we arrived at Maine State; he loved the place.

Palmer was waiting for me in the lobby, and Fred gave him a big howl and a squeal while I signed the volunteers logbook. Then we took our familiar route in, heading through the metal detector. Palmer filled me in on the reason for the unusual number of visitors in the parking lot: A new program was just beginning at the prison. Starting today certain men would be prescribed Suboxone, a drug used in the initial phase of medically assisted treatment for opioid addiction.

"The program has been in the works for years, and it's supposed to be incredibly successful," Palmer said with a hint of skepticism in his voice.

"You sound a little unsure about it," I said.

"I think the program will work great. I'm just not sure how we expect people to stick to it when they're out. I worry they'll just get back on drugs once they're out of the system and have access to them." What I'd initially detected as skepticism in his voice now sounded more like concern. I looked forward to hearing the guys' perspective on it once we made it to the pod and I had a warm cup of prison coffee in me.

We headed down The Mile toward the Veterans' Pod, the cold wind swirling around the prison yard sending a chill up my back. Fred was on the end of his leash, leading the way, sniffing the air, and peeing on piles of snow that lined The Mile, marking his territory so the other dogs of Maine State Prison would know he'd been there. A group of inmates en route to the gym held the doors open for us, and Fred thanked them with a grin and a wag of his tail as he confidently pranced into the facility.

"Someone had their vitamins today," one of the men joked, looking down at Fred, who was looking right back up at him.

"He's just excited to be here," I replied with a smile as we made our way past the tinted glass of the guard's office just inside the door of the minimum-security wing. Fred didn't even register how unusual it was for anyone to be excited to be inside a prison. His joy somehow brightened the darkness around him, and it was contagious.

We arrived at the Veterans' Pod and entered our classroom, where the guys were waiting. Fred happily bounced into the room, going from guy to guy saying hi and getting some enthusiastic rubs from his prison friends. Seated around the table were Kidd, Nate, Chet, Marcus, Calli, and Mr. Craig.

Marcus had two cups of coffee waiting for me in my spot.

"I know you drink that first one wicked fast, bud, so I got you a refill ready to go," he said, his Maine accent shining through in all its glory.

The guys were buzzing a little bit. They explained that due to the new drugs being distributed today, there was a shortage of staff, so they'd been locked in their cells and they were happy to be out.

I listened to the men make their usual complaints about the guards for a few more minutes. Yet again, these men weren't asking for better food, more TV channels, or improved living conditions for themselves. The main thing they always complained about were the issues they faced with the dog program, issues that affected the training of the dogs.

I decided to point this out to them.

"Did you ever notice that your most consistent complaint is always something to do with obstacles you face in the dog program?" I asked. "I think a lot of people would be surprised that your number-one issue is on behalf of the dogs and that your concerns are reflective of the work you're doing. What does that say about you guys and your priorities?"

There was a slight pause as the men thought about the question.

"I'd say we're a bunch of entitled assholes who just want what's best for our dogs," said Nate in his typically dry and sarcastic tone.

"Like any dog owner would, right!?" I echoed with a smile as the room seemed to take a deep breath.

The week before, I'd given the guys the subject of "vulnerability and strength" to write about and prepare thoughts on. I was interested in how their attitudes to vulnerability had changed throughout their lives. But it was also a very personal choice. My relationship with vulnerability had evolved in recent years, especially since I'd met Nora, but until my sessions with the guys I hadn't ever verbalized it to anyone. My proposal to her was more than an inevitable check in the box. It was about making myself vulnerable to her and declaring my total commitment to our future. Through their stories and their examples, the guys had helped me to understand that when you open yourself to a situation or another person, no matter how scary it feels at the time, the benefits are always worth the risks.

"Just by participating in the dog program, you're making yourselves more vulnerable," I told them, leading us toward the topic for the week, "but the choice you've made requires a lot of strength. So they go hand in hand."

There was a brief pause as the guys gnawed on that thought, and then Kidd piped up with something from his notes.

"Extreme growth comes from an ability to be vulnerable."

"Looks like you've got some more thoughts on this subject, Kidd," I said.

Usually Kidd read from his notebook or a printout. But today he put away any notes he had.

"In the past I was afraid of being vulnerable, and that was a mistake," he told the group. "When I was young, I didn't want to let my dad down. Before he died, I told him I was going to join the army, and I'll never forget the pride in his eyes. But I failed. Big time. Not at the soldier part, at the life part.

"After my wife took my son, leaving me in Texas, I was nineteen years old and alone in a new world. Instead of seeing the opportunities that lay ahead of me, I acted out of fear. I pushed people away through drugs and alcohol. I didn't want them to see my vulnerabilities. I left the army and surrounded myself with the wrong crowd. It felt right at the time, but my insecurities were disguising the real issue I was having. I was afraid of facing my own fears, and by hiding from them I gave them power.

"I convinced myself that there was something wrong with me. That I wasn't worthy of healthy relationships or that if I did open myself up to someone, I'd be betrayed again. It became less of a fear of failure, I guess, at that point. I knew I'd failed. It became a fear of vulnerability. I became an expert in excuses. It fueled my addiction and kept its boot on my chest for years.

"What I see now is that even when we fail, there is always a path to redemption. It's never easy, but I saw when I made myself vulnerable to God, my fears made sense. They were still there, but I could put them in my pocket. They weren't in the driver's seat anymore. That's what I mean when I say there is opportunity in fear. It often represents a weakness, something we can deal with if we choose to. The alternative is to ignore it, but I've seen in my life how that just allows it room to grow and influence decisions. Does that make sense?"

Kidd looked around the room. The guys all nodded knowingly.

"Little by little I started to do the opposite of what my mind was telling me to do," he explained. "When someone would punk me out in the dayroom, instead of fighting them or reacting negatively, I'd disengage, remove myself from the situation.

Soon I started to see that most of the fights I was getting into weren't worth it. I was a lot happier when I wasn't playing into the bullshit that goes on around here."

Kidd went on to explain that once he resolved to examine himself and the decisions he'd made in his life, he was forced to understand that the mess he'd created wasn't irreversible. If he wanted to do the work, he could create the changes.

"You dropped your guard," said Chet, who up until this point had been quietly listening while drawing an outline of the state of Maine with colored pencils on a folded piece of construction paper. The artwork he did was sold in the prison store in town as greeting cards. "When I got here, I could finally let my guard down. It wasn't easy at first, but coming home to Maine put me at ease. I didn't need to prove anything to anyone here. Then I met the guys in this group who were on their way up, making changes to themselves that defied everything about what I'd seen in the feds, and it inspired me to chase that feeling. I noticed that ever since I dropped my guard, I've gotten to know a lot of people that I never would have associated with otherwise. I'm better for it."

He put down his pencil and looked around at the group.

"It's an interesting problem we face as men," I told Chet and the others. "Especially for anyone who has served in the military. We're conditioned to put our needs in the backseat. If you're hurt, rub dirt on it, if you're tired, suck it up. These are useful characteristics in competition or warfare, but what about when it's over? There's no amount of Motrin you can take and water you can drink to cure anxiety or process mental trauma."

"Ya, no amount of oxy either," Chet said with a shrug and a smile.

The group all chuckled a little bit and let out a collective sigh. This was not an easy subject for any of us, but they were diving into it head-on.

"Mr. Craig, what was it like for you coming up in the world? What messages did you get?" I asked the eighty-year-old man, nodding in his wheelchair.

"Well, I don't know," he answered. "I didn't get a lot of messages. I just knew how to get through the day. My dad was at his worst when he was sober, so I just did whatever I had to do to keep him drunk. If he started beating on me, then I knew he needed a drink. One time we were on a train—I was taking him to Philadelphia to see a boxing match. He woke up from a nap and slugged me right in the jaw, knocked one of my molars out. He didn't know it was me. I just went to the bar car and got him a few beers, and he went back to sleep."

"That must have given you a lot of anxiety growing up, never knowing if your dad was going to start hitting you?" I asked.

"Well, as I got older I started working for myself," Mr. Craig continued, deflecting my question. "I started my own lawn-care business when I was thirteen years old, and by the time I was sixteen, I had three people working for me. I even cut Joe Biden's grass. Best part about that was I got to help my mom out. She didn't have much, and I bought her a new fridge when hers broke, and when I got my own truck, I'd take her to New York City for shows on the weekends. She loved those trips."

I decided not to press him anymore. I didn't need him to admit outright that even he had his own vulnerabilities. He'd shown the group in his own poetic way how he'd dealt with the challenges and fears he'd faced. He was a living example of the old-school "suck it up and be a man" approach, and he had the emotional and physical scars to prove it.

For the rest of us, we all had to think about how much of this way of dealing with our feelings we were willing to endure. It certainly had its place in the military and in prison. In the military you can't have an effective unit if everyone is constantly expressing his or her own fears and vulnerabilities. And you're asking for a world of hurt if you walk around a prison with your heart on your sleeve. The exception for the guys were the programs they'd gotten involved with, like dog training and this writing program, which offered them safe spaces to let their guard down in a natural way—to simply exist.

"What about you, man?" Nate said, with a sincerity that made me sit up a bit. "You come in here every week, you talk to us about your life. That takes a lot of vulnerability, that takes a lot of strength, and it's pretty amazing to us."

"Thank you for the compliment, Nate," I responded, "but I think it's obvious that I get more out of my time with you guys than you do. It's like Chet said. He was inspired by the people he observed in here who were making changes to themselves that were beyond the norms of prison life. When I came in here the first time, I saw that, and I wanted to be a part of it. You inspired me. I hope you can take this lesson away from our session today: When you're in a situation where you think you're being vulnerable and you feel insecure about that, you're actually exhibiting strength, integrity, and independence, and those things are attractive and inspirational to others. It's one of the many lessons that little dog who's sleeping under the table has taught me over the years. Just like the dogs you guys in here work with, Fred was an example of how strength and vulnerability go hand in hand. He wagged his tail at me when he had every reason to do the opposite. He made himself vulnerable, and it has certainly worked out for him.

"The problem is that the moment you start to make changes to yourself for the better, people from your old life start lashing out," I observed. "You're probably already dealing with that in here, right?"

"Ya, absolutely," Chet replied. "It is part of the struggle. I get the comments all the time: *'Chet's gone soft, Chet is a cop lover,'* stuff like that. In the past it would have worked, I would have gone back to my old ways, but I've been clean long enough to see the demons in comments like that. It's a trap, and it hurts my family more than it hurts me."

"Right, it's a trap," Nate agreed. "Just like a lot of what we're told as boys is a trap, the idea that 'being a man' is somehow related to our ability to suffer in silence. It just sets us up for failure down the road."

Everyone in the room seemed to have seen the fault in the version of manhood we were sold as young people. It was a one-dimensional approach that ultimately robbed us of options.

"It's just a matter of understanding that the rules of manhood don't always work in your favor," Chet pointed out. "All the games are rigged in that casino."

"I like that," Calli said, giving Chet a fist bump.

"Ya, that is a really great way to sum up our time today," I said, looking at the clock for the first time in three hours.

We'd all learned something about ourselves during these weeks together, and I was starting to see that I had even more in common with the guys than I'd thought. Our current circumstances aside, we were all men doing our best to find our place in the world without relying on a definition of manhood we'd been sold. A definition that had almost killed us.

I felt compelled to squeeze meaning out of every minute of my time with the men. I'd be leaving again soon to go on the road, and I wanted to go out on a high note with the group. I'd also begun the earliest drafts of this book and was starting to talk with the men about how it was coming along. But I realized I hadn't asked them a very important question yet. . . .

"If there is one thing you want people to know about you and your life in here in my book, what would it be?" I asked.

Marcus poured me one more paper cup of my favorite brew.

There was a collective silence around the table as the men thought about my question.

"I don't care about anyone else. I just want my little girl to see the value in me," said Chet with tears beginning to form in his eyes. "That I'm no clown-vic."

"Clown-vic" was one of my favorite terms I'd added to my vocabulary since spending time with the guys. It was Chet's word for convicts that act up just to get what they need from the staff, regardless of how it affects the rest of the population.

"You want your daughter to know you weren't wasting your time in here?" I asked gently.

"Ya, I mean, I did in the beginning, when I was in the feds, but I've really changed, and I hope she can see that," he replied with a self-affirming nod. "Spending time with you guys and Fishman every week has really shown me a lot about myself."

"I guess we're the ones that need to give ourselves a second chance before anyone else can," Kidd said, looking at Chet and the rest of the guys proudly.

The other men echoed in different ways what Chet and Kidd had so eloquently shared in their responses. Then we spent the last few minutes of our time together laughing and joking about the prison food, including Mr. Craig's theory about how the chicken was actually little pieces of plastic dipped in flour and fried in motor oil.

As we chatted, I realized that for the first time none of the guys had shared anything in writing. They all seemed to have collectively thought about our topic over the week and arranged their thoughts in their minds. To me it demonstrated a cohesion within the group that I could have never anticipated. We were our own think tank.

"How do we summarize today, guys? What's our takeaway?"

I asked as Calli collected the paper cups from around the table to toss out.

"I think it's important for us to realize that we're evolving as individuals faster than the system we're living in," Nate said as he rubbed Fred's ears. Fred had been quietly working his way around the table, taking turns sleeping with his head on everyone's feet.

"That is a great way to look at it," I said, as I gathered my notebook, hat, and Fred's leash. "Give yourselves a little bit of a break in here. You can't expect the system to accommodate your growth when it's still operating under the assumption that you're all demented criminal geniuses."

"As much as I'd like to be a genius of any kind, I don't think any of us were ever criminal geniuses. Otherwise we wouldn't be in here," Nate said with a smile.

"Ya, we'd be in the White House!" Mr. Craig jabbed as he backed his wheelchair away from the table, drawing a loud "Ohhhhh!" from the guys. Mr. Craig had a way of dropping bombs like that on the group in between naps.

"Okay, thanks for saving that one for the end," I said, shaking everyone's hand as we exited the classroom. It was just before four o'clock, and the guys would be heading to dinner soon.

Fred and I left the facility, escorted by a member of the guard force. Palmer and Michael Fournier were busy in meetings and training.

Outside, the wind had died down a bit, but the temperature was dropping fast. Fred's breath bellowed out like smoke from his long nose as he exhaled the fresh Maine air.

We got to our truck, and I sat for a moment while it warmed up.

"If it was all over today, buddy, I'd be proud of what we've done together," I said, looking back at Fred who was settling in for our two-hour drive home.

I found myself saying this to Fred more and more over the past couple of years. Each time I looked at my dog, I was reminded of where his life began, and then in a rush of joy I'd also recall how far we'd come together. From a dusty battlefield in Sangin to our rusty old Land Cruiser, from living the college life to living the way life should be in our new home state. Fred had connected me with who I was before the marines and shown me that when I'm true to myself, everything else falls into place. He was the reason I'd come to Maine State Prison. He'd opened the door for me to be able to share something of myself with the guys here and learn a lot about who I am in the process. My bond with Fred had gone beyond the normal expectations of man and dog, something the guys of Maine State Prison understood well. Since our first days together, Fred had been an example to me of the strength required to be vulnerable. It's always easier to make excuses and react with anger when things don't go our way. But when we accept the challenge of vulnerability, we open our hearts to love, and nothing is stronger than that.

CHAPTER 19

LJ's Second Chance

It had been nearly two months since my last visit to Maine State Prison. For Nora, the dogs, and me, it felt like we'd packed a year's worth of events into those intervening weeks. We'd traveled to Colorado, Wyoming, Nebraska, and Washington, D.C. In Colorado I served as a groomsman in the wedding of our friends Joe and Amy. Joe and I had served in Sangin together. He'd somehow survived a Taliban bullet to his helmet on one of our first days there. Some of his only memories from the days after his injury are of a certain little white dog that would come check on him from time to time, the same dog that happily pranced around the dance floor at the Cherry Creek Marriott, where the wedding was being held, wearing only a bow tie and a smile.

After the wedding we headed north for a speaking event in the coal-mining town of Gillette, Wyoming. We spent a night with community members sharing our story and learning about their town. As I watched the room fill up to capacity, I looked down at my watch and noticed the date. It was November 21. Tomorrow would be the nine-year anniversary of Fred's arrival in the States from Afghanistan. Looking around the room in the Gillette library, at all the people who'd shown up to hear our story, I felt my heart begin to swell. In the moment it felt like a dream, as if in an instant I'd wake up and the memory of Fred and our journey together would fade away over coffee. Looking down at Fred, who had made himself comfortable on the foot of a retired marine in the front row, and over at Nora, who was happily chatting with a mother and her young son, Ruby at her side, I knew I hadn't imagined it all, and more important, none of it had been an accident.

I began my talk by referencing the date.

"Tomorrow is Fred's nine-year anniversary of coming to America. I can't think of a more suitable place or better people for us to celebrate with. Thank you for welcoming us to your community. . . ."

In attendance that night was the entire Gillette Wild junior hockey team. They wore their jerseys and fluffed out their hockey hair with pride. Afterward their coach invited Fred and me to drop the first puck in their game against a team from Cody the next night, an invitation I happily accepted. So on the ninth anniversary of Fred's journey from Afghanistan reaching its end, he took part in the opening ceremonies of a youth hockey game in Gillette, Wyoming. He had proved once again how far the wag of a tail could take him.

Nora and I fell in love with Gillette and spent an extra night in the town, exploring eastern Wyoming during the day and driving through the holiday light display in town at night. Eventually we said our good-byes, promising to return again. We were heading to one of our favorite places in the world, Jackson Hole, where we planned to spend Thanksgiving in a quaint cabin. As we rolled into the little town nestled in a high valley beneath the Grand Tetons, the four of us were all smiles. We put the windows down and let the cool mountain air pass through the truck, and as if on cue it began to snow. We checked in to our cabin and spent the next three days watching the mountain fill up with powdery snow. I spent the mornings writing before we'd venture out on the day's adventure. On Thanksgiving Day we drove into the elk preserve just outside Jackson Hole and watched a family of moose frolic through a snowy field, laughing as a bighorn ram stopped traffic with its intense glare and menacing strut. We both missed having Thanksgiving at home with family, but there was something special about spending it on the road in a place like Jackson. It reminded me of being deployed during the holiday season. It was never something I got too upset about; it felt good to be working and serving during a season when we celebrate giving and receiving. Every holiday season since leaving the marines, I usually find myself getting anxious and frustrated. But not this year. Nora and the dogs were my new unit, and we were out in the field doing what we loved. It felt right.

Thinking of the guys back at Maine State and how they were spending another holiday in prison made any road blues we were suffering fade away. Our ability to move around the country freely was never something I wanted to take for granted. I knew that my friends were staring at the same walls and the same faces they'd been looking at for years. As the landscape unfolded before my eyes, state by beautiful state, I tried to remind myself how much I had to be grateful for.

The dogs, exhausted from a day of exploring, happily let us slip out so Nora and I could have Thanksgiving dinner at the famous Silver Dollar Bar & Grill in the Wort Hotel. We found a spot at the bar between a group of snowboard instructors and a man in a cowboy hat with a mustache that looked like it could order its own drink. We got ourselves a round and headed over to the Thanksgiving buffet. At one point in the night, while we were still sitting at the bar eating our food, I received a text. I stopped stuffing my face long enough to glance down and see it was from Michael Fournier.

"Hey, man, just wanted to let you know, LJ is officially out of the program. . . ." he wrote. As fast as I could, I looked back up again without finishing reading the text, wishing I'd never seen it in the first place. It was the news I'd hoped would never come. I didn't want to let it ruin our night, but I couldn't help noticing that nothing on my plate tasted as good as it had a minute before. I thought about Nate and the guys saying good-bye to LJ. It was something they'd known they'd eventually have to do, but now they had to do it in a way that robbed them of the joy of a job well done. It would be a very sad holiday season for Nate and the rest of the guys in the dog program.

We finished our dinner and boxed up a bunch of turkey and sweet potatoes for the dogs before bundling up for the walk back to our cabin along the quiet snowy streets of Jackson. As I put on my coat, I glanced at my phone again and noticed another text from Michael Fournier. It was a picture, so I swiped the screen to have a look. Wait a minute. It was a picture of LJ's big head resting on Fournier's knee with a warm fire glowing in the background. I looked back at the first text. The part I hadn't looked at read ". . . but he's officially our new family dog!!"

It was a Thanksgiving miracle. I held up my phone so Nora could see.

"I knew LJ's story wasn't over yet!" she said.

I sent a quick text back to Fournier simply saying, "He's home now. Nice work, buddy."

While it wasn't how anyone had seen LJ's time at Maine State Prison coming to an end, it felt beautifully, unexpectedly right, the way it was supposed to be. I couldn't wait to get back to Maine and hear more about how LJ was adjusting to his new life as a family dog.

Our next stop was back in Denver, where I served as the keynote speaker at a holiday party for a financial company. Then a quick stop in Nebraska to meet up with Dustin, another RECON marine who had arranged for a mini reunion in his hometown. We spent three days camping, hunting, and reconnecting with each other. Dustin had started his own nonprofit called Out Beside You, a clever play on the RECON marines' motto, "Never Above You, Always Beside You." Then it was on to my hometown, Washington, D.C., where Nora and I hosted another blowout Schmalls Fest. This was our annual fund-raiser concert in honor of Justin Schmalstieg, my friend and fellow marine who was killed while protecting our patrol from an IED in Sangin. My band, the 50 Year Storm, went above and beyond, adding new songs to our setlist and filling the venue with twice as many people as we'd had the previous year. Justin's family came down from Pittsburgh in full force, dominating the dance floor and sharing stories about Justin over shots of whiskey. It was the perfect way to end our six weeks on the road.

Back in Maine we spent a quiet Christmas with Fred and Ruby. Our families understood that we were a little weary of traveling and didn't give us too much guilt over missing another holiday with them. I was anxious to get back to the guys at Maine State Prison, but a flu bug and holiday staff shortages kept me from seeing them until just after the New Year.

On January 3, I finally drove up to spend the day at the prison, excited to get caught up on the remaining puppies' progress and reconnect with the guys. I'd have to make the most of my time with them before we were back on the road for another tour that would take us to Las Vegas, Arizona, and New Mexico. Fred pulled at the end of his leash as we walked through the parking lot. He was excited to see all his friends after weeks away. What he didn't know was that one of his favorite prison buddies was waiting for him in the lobby. As we came through the front door, Fred saw LJ and Fournier standing together, LJ patiently sitting at his new owner's side, looking up anxiously as he caught sight of his funny little Afghan friend. The pair had bonded on the days when I'd bring Fred in for the writing group. Fred would always wait patiently for LJ in the dayroom, and the two of them would put on a show for the guys, wrestling and playing on the smooth concrete floor. Fournier gave LJ the go-ahead to say hello and the dogs happily greeted each other, two special dogs with unlikely stories and happy endings.

Fournier had brought LJ in to work with him for the day, a practice he hoped to continue to benefit him and the men of the Veterans' Pod. He loved LJ, but he wanted to make sure the guys, especially Nate, had regular visits with him. He was their dog, too. We let Fred and LJ get caught up, laughing as Fred demonstrated his signature butt-swipe maneuver that always confused his opponents as he swung his rear end around, raising it up to smack the usually taller dog in the snout. Then it was time to head in to see the men. On our walk Fournier caught me up on life with LJ.

"I didn't realize how much I needed a dog until I lost Shea," he explained as we waited for the big metal slider door to open. "She was just so consistent that I kind of took her presence for granted. We'd been through a lot together in her fifteen years, and when it was all over, she left a big hole."

"Ya, man, as much as you think you're prepared for that loss, I'm sure it's a lot different when that day finally comes," I sympathized, looking down at Fred and LJ as they walked side by side down The Mile.

"There isn't much you can do," Fournier said, shaking his head. "But I'm proud to know that I gave Shea everything she needed and she gave me so much more. As painful as it is to say, I'm grateful for the timing of her passing. Because if she hadn't left us when she did, we wouldn't have LJ. I wouldn't have been able to bring him into my home—it wouldn't have been fair to Shea. So in a way she set me up for this next chapter with LJ."

The sad and beautiful words were clearly heavy in his throat.

"These dogs always find a way to teach us something," I pointed out as we entered the housing unit.

"They sure do," Fournier replied as he led LJ into the Veterans' Pod, his first home.

We spent the next hour letting LJ romp around with his puppy buddies Webber, Sayville, and Fred. It was a good exercise in discipline and recall for the two pups who were still in training. Fred didn't need to play by their rules, and it was clear he knew it. His low growls and high-pitched yips always seemed to startle his Labrador friends, who no doubt had never heard a dog make noises quite like those. Even so, their first instinct was to look up at their handlers, regardless of how hard Fred tried to get them to play. It was a true testament to the bond they shared with their trainers. Even LJ, who'd been out of the program for a few weeks, hadn't forgotten to ask for permission before responding to Fred's relentless pleas for attention. For a while Fournier, Nate, Cory, and Calli all just stood around in a circle and watched the happy dogs take turns trying to dominate one another.

Eventually our puppy circus ran out of gas. Webber and Sayville were flopped down on the floor with their heads resting on their handlers' feet. LJ lay on his side panting while Nate rubbed his belly and massaged his big paws. Fred, seemingly a little disappointed that his pals had lost interest in him, looked around the pod for something else to do. Suddenly he spotted someone he recognized coming down the staircase on the other side of the wide-open common area. It was Chet. Still on his leash, Fred pulled and howled in frustration at me for not letting him go and get at Chet, who had stopped to have a quick conversation on his way across the dayroom.

Eventually Fred's urgent barks and intense glare reached their target.

"Is he yelling at me?" Chet asked, equal parts shocked and honored to have been summoned by Fred. He quickly excused himself from his conversation and made his way toward us.

As Chet came within a few feet of us, I let go of Fred's leash, and my stubbornly positive four-legged buddy trotted toward his large tattooed friend just as he does when he sees a member of his family. I realized that for Fred, Chet and the rest of the guys at Maine State Prison *were* a part of his family. Chet knelt down and rubbed Fred's ears and scratched his head—Fred never let anyone touch his head whom he didn't trust and love. Chet grabbed his leash as he stood up and walked Fred the rest of the way across the dayroom to me and the other guys, who were starting to file into our classroom. Fred was at his side, the two of them with matching smiles.

"Well, that just made my year," said Chet as he extended the other end of Fred's leash to me.

"Nah, you're stuck with him for today, buddy," I said, patting Chet on the back as we turned and walked into the classroom.

"You guys mind if we join you today? LJ doesn't want to leave the pod yet," Fournier said, looking down at his still-sleeping dog.

"Ya, absolutely, but just because you have LJ with you," Nate said with a smile.

We joined the men—Kidd, Calli, Marcus, and Del—who were already at their seats, coffee in their cups and notebooks in front of them.

CHAPTER 20

A Whole New World

June 17, 2020

"So what do you guys think of what's going on out here in the world?" I ask my group of friends inside Maine State Prison, waiting a few seconds for my question to filter through the air waves. Although most of the world is now intimately familiar with Zoom, this is my first time hosting a call using the video-conferencing service. It's been more than four months since I saw the guys at our February writing session. In that time the world has changed beyond recognition.

My last visit to the prison was just before we left for another round of speaking events in Florida and South Carolina—and right around the time the new coronavirus, or COVID-19, was bringing our country to a grinding halt. On March 10, during our event at a university in Florence, South Carolina, students sat apart from one another in the auditorium and we were restricted from shaking hands with those we met. The seriousness of the virus was just starting to sink in. The day after the event, Nora and I drove fifteen hours straight home to Maine, stopping only for gas and bathroom breaks. We didn't plan on leaving home again anytime soon.

A few days after we got back, I emailed Michael Fournier at Maine State to see how everyone was doing. His reply back was grim but hopeful:

We're ok, only essential people in and out of the prison right now.
No cases yet.

It was clear I wasn't going to be able to visit the guys for a while, but that was okay with me. Their safety was paramount, and I didn't want to be the one to inadvertently bring a virus into the prison environment. I would never be able to forgive myself.

In the meantime I had a book to finish. After our events in March, we'd cleared our calendar so I could focus on writing. Between work on my chapters and reviewing notes from my sessions with the guys, I managed to stay constructive during the lockdown. I was grateful that working from home had already become routine for Nora and me over the last few years when we weren't on the road.

When I wasn't writing, I was following the news. In the coming days and weeks, we watched helplessly as the virus moved through towns and cities, taking advantage of deep flaws in our health-care system. The total number of deaths went up and up with terrifying speed, from three thousand in March to fifty-five thousand in April to a hundred thousand in May. Americans from every demographic were being affected, with the most economically disadvantaged communities, particularly Black and brown ones, disproportionately so. Prisons became hot zones as the virus worked its way from bunk to bunk and cell to cell.

I kept checking in with Fournier at the prison.

"So far so good," he told me.

Thanks to the quick actions of Commissioner Randy Liberty and the Maine State Prison staff, the prison was still in the clear.

Meanwhile, in addition to the toll taken by the virus, racial tensions and divisions within our country reached a boiling point. On March 13, a twenty-six-year-old woman named Breonna Taylor, an emergency medical technician in Louisville,

Kentucky, was sleeping in her bed when she was shot eight times. Her killers were members of the Louisville Metro Police Department, who used a no-knock warrant to invade her home looking for drugs that were not there. Just a few weeks before Breonna was killed, a twenty-five-year-old man named Ahmaud Arbery was shot in cold blood by armed vigilantes in Glynn County, Georgia, while he was out jogging. On May 5, footage of that video was released to a national outcry. Then, on May 25, a forty-six-year-old man named George Floyd was killed when a Minneapolis police officer pushed his knee into Floyd's neck to pin the restrained man to the ground for eight minutes and forty six seconds while he begged for his life, pleading with the cops to let him up and let him breathe. A teenage girl captured the events on her phone, a video that went on to be viewed millions of times online around the world.

All three of these deaths were violent, tragic, and completely unnecessary losses of life. Their commonalities, however, did not stop there. All the victims were Black people killed by white men who were either police or former police and who were not immediately charged for their crimes. The cops who stormed Breonna Taylor's apartment fired indiscriminately, over twenty times, after her boyfriend defended himself with a licensed firearm against what he thought were thieves. Ahmaud Arbery's killers were a father-and-son team, the father a retired cop. George Floyd's killer was a seasoned law-enforcement officer with over nineteen years on the Minneapolis police force.

Floyd's death gave new momentum to the Black Lives Matter movement within our country, emboldening the call for justice for the victims of this type of brutality and for police reform in our communities. Mass protests took place across the nation throughout the months of May and June, polarizing family and friends and, much like the coronavirus, exposing deep flaws within the foundation of our nation. People from all walks of life were waking up to a fundamental truth: that our country's original sin of slavery isn't buried in the past. Instead its ripple effect is felt at every level of our society to this day.

As these seismic events in our nation unfolded, I couldn't help but imagine what the guys of Maine State must be thinking. I knew from our sessions how perceptive and insightful they were, not only about themselves but about national and international events. I also wondered how they must be doing. They had limited programs to distract them anymore. Fournier had told me that the dogs had been taken away to their weekend puppy handlers and staff members of America's VetDogs. All visitation was shut down, including those from yoga, music, or writing teachers. And the guys were confined to their separate pods, unable to move around the different parts of the prison.

Whatever the warden and staff were doing was working, because by mid-June there were still zero reported cases of the virus within the prison walls, a minor miracle. The tally elsewhere in the country was a lot less impressive. Despite states across the country issuing stay-at-home orders, more than 125,000 Americans had died in less than four months, and the five largest clusters of COVID-19 in the country were within prisons.

On June 15, I decided to email Fournier to ask him if there was any way I could have a Zoom session with the guys. I missed them and wanted to know how they were doing—and what they were thinking. Fournier got back to me the next day.

"How about we set up a Zoom meeting tomorrow?" he asked.

The next thing I know, I'm sitting at my laptop, with the guys of the Purposeful Tails Writing Group—Chet, Marcus, Kidd, Calli, Del, Nate, and even a new member, Sean, Kidd's roommate—all seated around the camera like executives on a conference call.

I can see that Fournier has gathered them in our regular classroom. After months apart, seeing their faces sends a wave of emotions through me. Although I had spent weeks reflecting on our time together while writing this book, I have missed my friends more than I'd realized.

"It's great to see you guys!" I exclaim.

The guys all cheer and wave into the camera.

"How we doing, guys?" I ask.

"Well, we're stuck in our pod. We've got no dogs and no visitors," Kidd says from his normal seat at the head of the table. "It sucks for us, but it's better than the alternative. We've got a lot of elderly and a lot of immunocompromised guys, too, so the virus would really have a field day if it got in here."

"Speaking of the elderly, where is Mr. Craig?" I ask.

He's the only one of the regulars I don't see around the table.

"He's gone!" Calli says, filling me in. "They shipped him up to the old folks' home in Charleston. He's doin' great up there, says he gets to order Chinese once a week, and the food is much better. Glad they got him out before we all got locked in. His snoring would have driven me crazy by now."

The facility in Charleston, Maine, is a minimum-security prison where the men have more freedom and opportunity to work outside and begin their transition into the world. It also holds the state's elderly prisoners who need medical care and more accommodations. I was happy for Mr. Craig that he was seeing out his days in a place where he could be a bit more comfortable.

But Mr. Craig isn't the only one about to get shipped out to a minimum-security facility.

"Ya, a bunch of us all got cleared for minimum custody, just before the virus hit, so we're supposed to be outta here, too, but we have no idea when," Kidd says.

I knew that Kidd, Marcus, Sean, Calli, and Chet were all

getting closer to the end of their sentences and would be eligible to transfer to minimum custody soon. In a little less than four years, they'd be out of prison, and their second chance at life— and all the challenges that came with it—would lie before them. While that might not seem like a short amount of time to most of us, when you've done more than ten years in prison, anything less than four is a breeze.

"Ah, man! That is great," I tell the guys. "At least you know you're cleared. Just a matter of time now, I guess. Who all made it?"

"Me, Marcus, Sean, and Calli," Kidd replies. "I wanna go up to Charleston. It's further away, but that's what I want. I want to focus on myself and not get distracted by old habits. It's gonna be a whole new world for us, man. We've all been in here for around ten years. In minimum, our windows open, and we can work outside and move around without so many walls."

He is describing the place as if he were heading to an all-inclusive resort in the Caribbean.

"I hear you can smell the exhaust fumes from the road," says Sean dreamily.

"Ah, man, I'm so pumped for you guys," I reply.

I think about how many changes have taken place since they'd entered the system. They'd watched their children grow up through pictures and weekend visits under guard supervision, and they'd lost years with family and friends that they'd never get back. On top of that, the world they'd left behind has been replaced by a more digital and divisive one. People communicate through text and social media more than when they left. Will they feel isolated and cut off? Will the pain from lost time with family and friends be too much to handle and drive them to the comfort of their old habits? Just thinking about it gives me anxiety, so I can't imagine how they will feel.

Then my thoughts turn to Chet. I'd assumed he was also due to transition to minimum security soon.

"Mine is hanging in the balance," Chet says, as if reading my mind. He's sitting behind Kidd, his long hair hanging down past his shoulders.

"What's going on, Chet? Are they all backed up from staff shortages because of the virus?" I ask.

There is a big laugh in the room shared by everyone, and I realize I've missed something.

"Ya, it's something like that," Chet says once the laughter dies down.

"Oh, no, what did you do?" I ask, crossing my arms.

"I got some new stuff," is all he says.

"He's trying out to be a hockey player when he gets out," Marcus chimes in, triggering more laughter from the guys.

I laugh along with them, but I can't help but feel sad and disappointed for Chet. He'd come so far during our time, and I'd really hoped his days of using his fists to solve his problems were behind him. I don't press for too much information, but it seems like being locked in the pod with the same guys for months had gotten to him, and he'd let someone get under his skin. I feel sorry for whoever it was.

"Hey, I saw you on the news!" Chet says, happily changing the subject. He explains that he'd been watching the local news one night and was surprised to see me standing outside a supermarket next to my Land Cruiser. It was in mid-March when the virus was really starting to affect the country, and we'd just returned from our latest round of speaking engagements. I'd gone out to try to get some food and supplies to stock our empty fridge and cupboards. In the parking lot, I'd been stopped by a reporter who wanted to get my reaction to the first cases showing up in Maine.

"I don't even remember what I said!" I tell them with a laugh. "I was just glad my local grocery store hadn't run out of frozen pizza and toilet paper."

Just then Fred, who's been napping in his favorite chair, shakes his head and hops down from his seat. Clearly he's had enough of not being in the conversation. He lets out a frustrated bark and a loud whine as he prances toward me. The men all hear him and start calling to him.

"Hey, Fred! We want Fred! Where is that boy?! Get him some stilts!" they all call.

Fred lets out another loud howl in response.

I scoop him up and put him in my lap, his paws resting on the table in front of my laptop so he can see his pals.

"Ah! He's such a good-lookin' dog, man!" Marcus says.

For a while the guys heap praise and love on Fred as he soaks it all in.

"He misses you guys," I say, rubbing the fur around Fred's neck. "He's doin' great, he's got a new girlfriend the next house over. Her name is Osa, and she's got long legs and a pretty white coat. They go romping in the ocean together every day."

"Oh, wow, glad to hear someone is getting some love these days!" Kidd responds.

"Ya, Fred, you earned it, buddy. She better treat you right," Marcus says, and we all laugh.

I put Fred down, and he settles back into his favorite spot.

I decide to switch up the conversation and ask the guys their opinion about what's happening in America right now, with police brutality in the news yet again. Only a few days before our call, on June 12, Rayshard Brooks, a twenty-seven-year-old unarmed Black man, fell asleep in his car in Atlanta, Georgia, blocking a restaurant drive-through. After arriving on the scene, the cops Breathalyzed Brooks and found him over the limit. They got into a tussle, and Brooks ran away. He was shot in the back twice and died later in hospital.

I want to know what the guys think about the passionate outcry for racial justice and police reform taking place across the country in the form of protests in every city, town, and even in rural areas.

"Defund the police . . . AND PRISONS!" Chet shouts from the back, cupping his hands around his mouth.

The guys all laugh but settle down quickly.

"It's hard for us to relate to a lot of this, actually," Kidd says. "I didn't meet anyone Black until I joined the army. We all knew the cops in my hometown. They bought tires off my dad, or they went to our church—they were members of our community. If you were really bad, they'd drive you home, not to the police station. Anytime I got caught drunk-driving or partying somewhere, they'd just break it up and drive all the kids home, or at least follow us until we made it back safe. It makes it more difficult to connect to the whole situation going on in other communities, because to be fair, it hasn't been my experience. But that doesn't mean it isn't something affecting Black communities across the country. All you need to do is switch on the news to see that."

"Yeah," I agree. "We all need to look at our lives as white men and think about how different they'd be if we were Black. I've taken an inventory of the times I've interacted with the police—there were multiple occasions in my life where my skin color definitely gave me the benefit of the doubt."

I tell the men about the time I was on the road with my friend Josh in the summer of 2015, in Clarksdale, Mississippi, when we were stopped by cops while pulling out of a McDonald's. The cops were wearing camouflage pants and body armor and all had M4 rifles pointed at us. At the time I remember thinking that they had more optics and fancy doodads bolted on them than I'd had in Afghanistan. I wasn't even sure they were police at first.

One of them approached the Land Cruiser with his M4 pointed at me. "KEEP YOUR HANDS WHERE I CAN SEE THEM, NO MOVEMENTS!" he demanded loudly. A second officer with an M4 approached from behind the Land Cruiser, the flashlight on the end of his rifle illuminating the inside.

"We got a report of someone causing trouble at the drive-through in a blue SUV," the cop told me from behind his rifle.

"If you're looking for the Hamburglar, I think he went that way," Josh said, pointing with his head, shooting me a quick wink.

The officers quickly realized that we weren't guilty of anything other than wanting some junk food, and they were gone before we even had time to process what had just happened.

"At the time we were able to shrug the night off as a strange experience," I tell the guys of the writing group. "Looking back now, I'm pretty confident that if Josh and I had been Black, those cops would have had us out of the car and on our faces, especially after Josh made his crack about the Hamburglar. . . ."

There's a quiet moment as the guys consider their response.

"It's not like we're interacting any more with the police now that we're in here," Kidd points out. "But it's the same attitude with the guards, the same sense of total authority that they have, and it can get out of hand, fast. Ninety-nine percent of the time when a guard is overstepping or just being a hard-ass about something, we just suck it up and walk away. But then there's the one kid that's just had enough, and we've all been there. And you put up a fight. When that happens, the guard doesn't know what to do, and he goes straight for the mace—he escalates it. That's what happened with the guy this week in Georgia. He bucked up, and the cop didn't know how to handle it."

Kidd is referencing the recent Brooks shooting at the hands of police officers.

"The cop shot him in the back because he wasn't in control," Kidd observes, shaking his head. "But he didn't need to be in control. He didn't even need to be there! It's a tragic example of what we see in here every day, a concept of authority that isn't realistic, and when someone challenges it, it creates a totally excessive, emotional reaction."

"We're in here, man, they caught us, it's all over. There just isn't any reason for them to continue to kick us while we're down," Nate says.

"Too often with the staff in here there is no delineation. Whether you're someone who's trying to fly under the radar or if you're a troublemaker, they treat us all the same way," Kidd adds. "Certain guards talk to us like we're constantly doing something wrong. If we talked to them that way, we'd get cuffed and dragged out, so why can they talk to us that way?"

"Ya, I get that," says Marcus, speaking with the authority of the only Black man in the room. "It's all about power to them. I used to get mad at the guards, but now I just laugh, especially since I made minimum. But when they come in my room and tell me I can't cut another man's hair, talking all tough like he just caught us red-handed, I have to laugh, because it's silly and small. But for people on the street interacting with cops—those cops got guns, it can get deadly really quick. I honestly don't know how I'm going to function on the outside. Getting minimum is great, but I'm terrified of the outside. It's got nothing to do with being Black and everything to do with my addiction and my time in prison. It's just fucked me up beyond recognition."

Marcus's words hit me hard. I've never seen him so defeated. For a minute the room is silent and the gravity of the obstacles ahead of each of the men is more apparent to me than it's ever been. Kidd looks over and acknowledges his friend's pain, telling him that what he's been through carries trauma. We talk some more about the news, all agreeing that there's going to have to be some kind of change, that American law enforcement can't continue on its current path.

I decide it's time to ask the guys what else they've been doing since I last saw them.

"I've lost twenty-five pounds since the lockdown started," says Del, speaking up for the first time from his spot next to Marcus. "I'm crushing workouts with these guys every day, and it's helped my mind just as much as my body. It has put me in a better place, and I'm proud to say I've started talking with my daughter for the first time since I've been here."

"That's what I'm talkin' about Del!" I tell him. "Hell ya, man!"

"Ya, I mean she only knows me in here," he says. "But I still want her to know me and know that she has a daddy that loves her."

"And he's fit, too!" says Marcus, grabbing Del's arm and making him flex. This causes all the guys to flex their biceps into the camera with big smiles on their faces. I even join in, and for a moment we're just a bunch of boys goofing off for one another.

"For real, Del, I'm really glad to hear that, man. Nice work," I say.

"I've been video-calling with my daughter, but she's a teenager now and she mostly just checks her hair in the camera," Nate says with a laugh and a shake of his head. "I told her to do her hair before she calls next time so we can actually talk. She's just at that age."

As usual the men are most proud of their children, and whenever our conversations turn to them, they take on a hopeful and proud tone. Kidd talks about his plans to have a home for his son, a place he can always count on.

"That is something I want to provide for him his entire life," he says. "I can never make up for the time we lost when I was in here. All I can do is be the best dad I can be once I'm out."

"Another positive thing that's happened recently is we got our certificates from the Department of Labor for dog training—me, Kidd, Sean, and Calli," Nate says, pushing his glasses up his nose.

"Oh, that is awesome! Well done, guys. You certainly earned that," I say.

"Ya, I guess in a way this lockdown stuff has made me really appreciate the work I get to do with the dogs," Nate goes on. "I miss my newest one, Zale. He's gonna go nuts when we finally get him back in here. This place is a lot different without the dogs."

"Ya, I bet. What do you miss most about having them around?" I ask.

"I think it's mostly the work," Nate says proudly. "Zale makes me smile, and our connection is amazing, but when we're training and working on new behaviors, that's when I feel like I'm at my best."

"That's pretty great, man," I say. "The other day I was thinking about the dog program and our little writing group, and I think the most compelling thing about both these programs is that their success falls completely on your shoulders. If you guys took advantage of the opportunities you have with the dogs to violate rules or if you just didn't take the training seriously, the program would fall apart. Same for our writing program. I came up with a loose syllabus with some ideas and a framework, but you guys made it work. You came in every week and poured your hearts out. When these programs succeed, it's thanks to you."

"Craig, you've gotta understand something," says Chet, sitting forward in his chair and looking right into the camera. "I've got about twenty years locked up behind one door or another, and the two biggest things that have made a difference to me have been you and Jon Fishman, my drum teacher. You're both volunteers. You don't know the impact a volunteer can have on your life until it's your life. So we all thank you for that."

"Thank you, Chet," I say, taking a sip of coffee while I try to get control of my emotions. "That means a lot to me. If I say much more, I'll lose it, but please know that this is just the beginning, I'm just getting started."

"We appreciate the time and attention at an individual level more than you know," he says, sitting back in his chair.

Speaking of time, ours together has flown by. Palmer and Fournier come in to tell us that another group needs the classroom, so we need to wrap it up. The men collect their things and start to stand up. Leaving the room, they shout various good-byes at me:

"We love you, Craig!"

"Thank you, man!"

"Go take Fred for a walk for us!"

"We'll see you soon!"

Sitting at my computer, I hold back tears as I watch them leave, waving at my computer and smiling. The men of Maine State Prison are tattooed on my heart. Their pain, triumphs, concerns, and ambitions are mine, too. I'm connected to the men in my group. They are my friends. I am proud to have them in my life. Just because we lock people up, that doesn't mean they're not our problem anymore. They're still Americans, they're still humans, and they're not going anywhere. As I close out the meeting and shut my laptop, I realize that I'll likely never see my group of friends all in the same place and in person again. But just as in my journey with Fred, I have gotten more than I could have imagined by opening myself up to them. It may be over, but it was worth it.

What I hope is clear from this book and the stories in it is that the people who are spending time or have spent time in the justice system have the potential to be our greatest assets. Right now we treat them like surplus livestock, pushed off from one department to the next, without taking into account their real individual needs. Imagine what would happen if we listened to the needs of the people we've locked up, finding ways to remove obstacles for them rather than creating them? Change would happen at every level.

If we want to break the cycle of poverty and crime within our society, we need to first abandon our emphasis on policing and punishment. We need more people in law enforcement who focus on public safety and service, who embody the motto "Protect and Serve," people who approach situations looking for ways to de-escalate and defuse rather than intimidate and confuse. We need prison wardens and staff like the ones at Maine State, who see potential in their inmates and nurture that. We need everyday Americans to shift their perspective on what it means to be a returning citizen, employers who are able to see beyond someone's past and provide a second chance to people who truly deserve it.

My time with the men of Maine State Prison will always be precious to me. The lessons I've learned because of them have shaped how I will live the rest of my life.

Listening to the guys and their stories, I've come to have a deeper appreciation of the role that luck has played in my life. I've worked hard, and I'm proud of my accomplishments. But I've also been lucky: lucky to have been let off in the past, lucky to have found Fred, lucky to be born in a place like Burke.

My whole life I'd been running away from the suburban D.C. bubble where I grew up. I resented it. But the men of Maine State Prison helped me to realize that the bubble I'd tried to escape from had actually formed a kind of invisible barrier around me all along, protecting me, allowing me to make mistakes that would've landed other people who came from less comfortable backgrounds either in prison or an early grave. Growing up, I didn't have to worry about food, shelter, abuse, or neglect like they did, and I've benefited greatly from that. These benefits aren't something I earned; they came with my skin tone and the zip code of the family I was born into—blessings that are not extended to everyone in our country. My relative affluence, my education, my stable family background, my *privilege* have been the source of so many of my opportunities and my security. I see that now. These days I'm finding purpose in my privilege—it's become my motivation to help others who didn't have the same breaks I did. People just like me who simply weren't as lucky.

The men of Maine State Prison have helped me to stay connected to an important side of myself, too, a side that in many ways defies society's expectations of how a combat veteran, a U.S. Marine is supposed to behave. In prison every day can be a literal battle. The men are constantly testing one another, watching for weaknesses and potential leverage. A story about your past can be used against you, revealing to a friend that you find joy in something can turn it into a way for others to manipulate you. It is an environment that requires constant vigilance, not just for protection from physical harm but more frequently from the mental traps that lie around every corner. The men of the writing program, however, found a passport out of that environment. They came to our sessions with open hearts and insights to match, and their hard-won vulnerability has motivated and inspired me.

I see the world differently than I did before. I no longer feel obligated to fulfill other people's expectations of me. I understand that the battles I faced in Afghanistan do not have to define who I am here at home. That the only conflicts I have left to fight are the ones I choose, the ones that I determine are worthy of my effort and attention. When I first came home, it felt like the war was all around me, that every day was a fight to prove to other people that I was okay. To admit anything else would be to admit defeat. Vulnerability was weakness, compassion was a luxury. Not anymore. I've learned that the true measure of a man is how often he can ask for help, demonstrate vulnerability—and show love. Because love requires strength.

I've also learned the value of listening. These days I'm beginning to believe that all that's required to remedy the disparity and discord in our great nation is for us to listen to those who have the courage to ask for help. Because when we listen to each other, we become invested in one another.

Author's Note

A few weeks after my first Zoom with the men, Calli, Kidd, Sean, and Marcus were all transported to the minimum-custody facility just down the road from Maine State Prison. Once they were settled in, Fournier set up another Zoom call for us and we caught up. It was great to see them in a new environment. They had a lot to talk about between their new accommodations, which have windows and doors that open without locks, and their new jobs with less supervision. They were starting to feel like free men again and it was a beautiful thing to see.

In the late summer, I resumed weekly meetings with the men of the Veterans' Pod. Fournier was back at the prison regularly and shared with me that many of the men had been asking when the group would start again. He put another sign-up sheet on the guards' desk and it immediately filled up. There were some familiar names: Chet, Nate, and Del. But the rest of the group were all newcomers.

During our first meeting, Chet sat in the back patiently letting the new guys introduce themselves and share a little about what they hoped to get out of the group. When it came to Chet's turn to share, he happily exclaimed, "This place is just a bus station to me now; I'm waiting on my ride to Charleston." He'd officially been cleared for transfer to minimum custody. Any day now he'd be bused up to the state's most northern correctional facility. He'd be back in the region of Maine where he'd begun his life, preparing to start it over again.

For the new participants of the writing program, their first assignment was to share a story of a dog and how it had impacted their lives. For me, it is a story that continues to this day.

Acknowledgments

Eve Claxton—Collaborator & Writing Coach: Your guidance, patience, and heart made this book possible. Thank you for caring as much about the men and the dogs as I do.

Chad Luibl—Literary Agent at Janklow & Nesbit Associates: Your contributions to the literary world will have a positive impact on our present and future generations. I am proud to be among the incredible authors and storytellers you represent.

Honora Parkington—My Partner in Life, Love & Work: I am who I am because of you. You give me confidence, courage, and, most important, the love I need to carry on. We are just getting started.

Rachel Kahan—Editor at William Morrow: Thank you for your dedication to this book and for encouraging me to challenge myself as a writer. I am proud to work with you and look forward to what is next.

Alivia Lopez—William Morrow: Thank you for all your hard work on our behalf. We are fortunate to have you on Team Fred.

Danielle Kolodkin—HarperCollins Speakers Bureau: You are responsible for thousands of people across this country hearing our stories in person. We would not be able to do what we do without you. From the bottom of our hearts, we thank you.

Eliza Rosenberry—HarperCollins: Thank you for always sharing our enthusiasm and passion. We love working with you and we're proud to have you on Team Fred.

Jessica Lyons—HarperCollins: Thank you for making us a priority and for helping us navigate the world of publicity. You are a valuable member of Team Fred.

Kaitlin Harri—HarperCollins: Thank you for helping us share our story with the world. We love having you on Team Fred.

Randy Liberty: Thank you for granting me access to Maine State Prison. You did not have to trust me, but I am glad you did. You did not have to create a Veterans' Pod, but I am glad you did. You did not have to bring in puppies from America's VetDogs, but I am glad you did. You don't have to do a lot of the things you do as a law-enforcement leader, but we are all glad that you do.

Michael Fournier: The work you do in Maine State Prison has a positive impact that transcends its walls. Thank you for your friendship and honesty. Fred and I are looking forward to many Maine adventures with you, LJ, and our families.

Jason Palmer: Your hard work and dedication to the men of Maine State Prison is an example to us all of how we can serve out of uniform. Thank you for making Fred and me feel welcome at Maine State Prison. Semper Fidelis.

Kidd: You are a talented speaker, writer, and dog trainer. Thank you for always making fun of me the appropriate amount. Your unflinching commitment to self-betterment is an inspiration to us all. I am proud to call you a friend.

Nate: Thank you for keeping the group honest and for always being prepared to talk about the difficult stuff. I am proud to call you a friend.

Chet: You are a gifted poet and a true artist with a lot to offer the world. Thank you for sharing a little bit of your talent with me. I am proud to call you a friend.

Mr. Craig: Thank you for listening and for always being prepared with a dirty joke or an inspirational story. They were often the same thing. I am proud to call you a friend.

Calli: Thank you for your hard work on behalf of the dog

program, book club, and Veterans' Pod. You kept our group focused and I am proud to call you a friend.

Del: Thank you for diving headfirst into our group. I know it was not easy but I am glad you showed up. I am proud to call you a friend.

Marcus: Thank you for your honesty and humor. You are a light to all those around you and I am proud to call you a friend.

Sean: Thank you for your contributions to the group and for your hard work on behalf of veterans and their families. I am proud to call you a friend.

Harry & Gary: Your devotion to your friends and family is an example of pure love and loyalty. We are eternally grateful for your support of our story, your fatherly guidance, and motherly guilt.

Matt: Thank you for your understanding and flexibility. You are a gifted trainer, and the dog program is lucky to have you. I am proud to call you a friend.

America's VetDogs: Thank you for providing veterans with dogs that allow them to enjoy a lifestyle they fought to protect. Thank you for allowing this veteran to document the process and share it with the world.

Paula & Rebecca: You allowed me to be a fly on the wall without ever making me feel like a pest. Thank you for answering my questions, no matter how silly they were. Most of all, thank you for your hard work and dedication to our nation's veterans.

Prince: Thank you for sharing your story with me and for making the trip to Maine State Prison with Chess.

Staff & Guard Force at Maine State Prison: Your jobs are not easy. You serve on the front lines of a fight that our society often ignores. Your duties are thankless, selfless, and endless. Despite this, you maintain a positive and progressive environment for the men in your charge. Thank you for going above and beyond and for always making Fred and me feel welcome.

Our Fred Family Across the Globe: Thank you for making us a part of your life. Your support of our story is inspiring and humbling. We look forward to continuing to share our adventures in stubborn positivity with you.